Trust and Ethics in Finance
Innovative ideas from the Robin Cosgrove Prize

Trust and Ethics in Finance
Innovative ideas from the Robin Cosgrove Prize

Editors

Carol Cosgrove-Sacks / Paul H. Dembinski

Globethics.net Global 6

Globethics.net Global
Series editor: Christoph Stückelberger. Founder and Executive Director of Globethics.net and Professor of Ethics, University of Basel/Switzerland

Globethics.net Global No. 6 (Formerly Globethics.net Series)

Carol Cosgrove-Sacks / Paul H. Dembinski (eds.)
Trust and Ethics in Finance: Innovative ideas from the Robin Cosgrove Prize
ISBN 978-2-940428-40-3 (online)
ISBN 978-2-940428-41-0 (print)

Cover Design: Juan-Pablo Cisneros
Editorial support: Páraic Réamonn, Sibilla La Spina

Globethics.net Head Office
150 route de Ferney
1211 Geneva 2, Switzerland
Website: *www.globethics.net*
Contact: *infoweb@globethics.net*

Availability: This book can be downloaded from the Globethics.net library, www.globethics.net, for free. Print copies can be ordered from Globethics.net, infoweb@globethics.net, for CHF/USD 13 (South) or 25 (North), plus postage

CONTENTS

"Trust is the lifeline of finance – building trust is essential"

Professor Tamar Frankel, Boston University School of Law[1]

[1] From the Emilio Fontela Lecture, meeting on Ethics, Finance and Responsibility, Observatoire de la Finance and the Award of the Ethics in Finance Robin Cosgrove Prize 2011, Geneva

REMEMBERING ROBIN

Robin Cosgrove graduated from Oxford University in 1996 with an MA in Japanese and Economics. He joined Barclays (BZW) on their Japanese Equities Desk, moving to Japan and later to Dresdner Kleinwort Benson Securities. Subsequently he joined UBS Warburg, moving to Morgan Stanley Japanese Equities, with clients including Gartmore, Penta, Moore Capital, Lotus, Wharton, Barings and Fidelity. In 2004 he moved back to London to become the manager of the RAB Capital Japan Fund. He travelled widely in emerging markets and planned to create a foundation to assist young finance professionals to obtain international awareness and training to help them develop a commitment to ethical financial practices that he believed was essential for them to attract sustainable investment and secure economic development. He was uncompromising in his demands for himself and for his friends and colleagues and believed passionately that sustainable success could come only through high standards of integrity. Sadly he died before his plans could come to fruition.

PREFACE

John Plender

Has the business community lost the ethical plot? Over the past two decades successive boom and bust cycles have thrown up extraordinary examples of ethical failure. First, the dot.com era in the US produced scandals at Enron, WorldCom, Tyco International, Qwest, HealthSouth and sundry others. Andersen, one of the big five global audit firms, disintegrated when the US Department of Justice investigated its audit failures at Enron.

In the first decade of the new millennium Europe saw fraud at Parmalat, where the US and European investment banks turned out to have connived in concealing the Italian dairy company's dire financial plight. Royal Dutch Shell, once regarded as a beacon of ethical solidity, was found to have cooked the books by inflating its production reserves. Volkswagen was beset by charges of bribery and corruption, while Siemens ran into trouble with the US Foreign Corrupt Practices Act.

Then in the protracted financial crisis that began in 2007 the behaviour of US banks in the sub-prime mortgage market was shown to have been outrageously rapacious towards borrowers, while retail banking in Europe was marred by a succession of mis-selling scandals – the financial world's pet euphemism for rip-offs. Fraud charges have been brought against senior executives of Fannie Mae and Freddie Mac, the big US semi-official mortgage institutions. Goldman Sachs, the world's pre-eminent investment bank, has been exposed by a departing senior executive in an article in the New York Times as being hell-bent on fleecing its clients, which Goldman bankers referred to as muppets. It had earlier paid $550m to settle a case brought by the Securities and Exchange Commission for misleading investors without admitting or denying wrongdoing.

In China the falsification of company accounts has turned into an epidemic, leaving auditors unable to form an opinion. The Japanese company Olympus provided one more example of concealment of losses. All of this took place against the background of top executives' pay spiralling to unprecedented levels regardless of corporate performance. In banking the bonuses continued even after the banks were the recipients of the greatest bail-out in financial history. Finance was at the epicentre of ethical failure.

It has to be acknowledged, then, that the environment into which the Robin Cosgrove prize for innovative ideas in finance was launched was more than a little challenging. How can this be rationalised? Some argue that these ethical aberrations were simply a reflection of the business cycle. When times are good and share prices soar, ethical standards tend to drop as people become greedy and succumb to temptation. When companies fail in the bad times and fraud is exposed, moral standards are re-emphasised. Yet there is surely more to it than that.

I would argue that there has been a secular decline in ethical standards. In part this stems from the change from a world of heavily regulated and cartelised markets, in which managers enjoyed paternalistic power with relatively little accountability, to one of liberalised markets in which greater emphasis is placed on shareholder value. Chief executives are now in a capital-market pressure cooker, with fund managers and analysts becoming ever more vocal in their demands for value. Their definition of value is narrowly financial. Together with the requirement for quarterly reporting, this has bred a hitting-the-numbers culture, with attendant temptations for executives to cook the books to meet capital market demands.

This spur to short-termism has been compounded by the growth of performance-related or equity-type incentives, whether in the form of conventional bonuses or stock option rewards. The metrics used to calculate these performance-related rewards are mainly such crude yardsticks as total shareholder return and earnings per share, usually measured over absurdly short time periods. The accounting numbers in the calculation are, to a degree, manipulable. The result is that incentive structures are at odds with the requirements of decent ethics. When that is the case, it is inevitable that ethics will sometimes become the casualty.

The problem of short-termism has been compounded in finance by the growing opacity and complexity of markets, notably the over-the-counter markets in derivatives and structured products. Also by the ascendancy of traders over corporate financiers and commercial bankers in the banking hierarchy. A transactional culture now prevails. On the trading floors, many regard themselves as hired guns, borrowing the capital of the bank to support their individualistic pursuit of personal profit. Loyalty to the organisation is minimal. The culture of the trading floor owes more to the animal kingdom than to the fiduciary ethos that used to be seen as central to the workings of finance.

Equally problematic are the assumptions of economics and of modern finance theory, which put heavy emphasis on the behaviour of "rational" agents who seek to maximise their own welfare through opportunistic behaviour. The pursuit of material wealth is assumed to be the justification for individual and group behaviour. For anyone lacking much of a moral conscience this amounts to an implicit ethical – or rather, unethical – agenda, given that acting other than opportunistically is perceived as irrational.

Much of the response to the scandals referred to earlier has been in the form of increased regulation. An ethics industry has grown up, with myriad ethics courses appearing in business schools and countless consultants devising ethics codes for large corporations. People at the top of the corporation have thus outsourced ethics. An internal market has thus developed to shift moral responsibility around the organisation. All of this has spawned a culture of compliance and done nothing to prevent a plethora of corporate scandals and ethical lapses. Few are convinced by the statements of ethical principles produced by large corporations, still less by investment banks. So what can be done to address the ethical deficit in business and finance?

The progenitors of the Robin Cosgrove prize rightly perceived a need to raise consciousness about the advantages of an ethical culture in finance. And one of the themes that emerge repeatedly throughout the essays in this book is the economic and social value of trust, whether in economies, markets or corporations. Trust is particularly important in financial markets. This becomes obvious if a comparison is made between financial and retail activity. With food, drink and clothes, consumers are quick to detect poor quality and will take their custom elsewhere. In contrast, many retail financial decisions are infrequent. People often make a decision on their pension only when they join the pension scheme and when they are preparing to leave it. By the time you discover you have made a mistake with a pension, a mortgage or car loan, it may be too late to do much about it. This makes it harder for the financial markets to identify rogues than in other industries. It is a sad fact that financial institutions that engage in widespread mis-selling rarely go out of business. They may be fined by the regulatory authorities. But senior management often regards the fines, which anyway fall on shareholders rather than managers, as an operating cost of the business.

This has bred a serious loss of confidence among the public about banking and finance. Against the background of excessive boardroom pay, the legitimacy of wealth creation and of the Western forms of capitalism is increasingly questioned. That underlines the importance of the Robin Cosgrove prize agenda. And the good new is that the environment for that agenda is not uniformly hostile. Many business people now recognise that companies and financial institutions operate in the social system and that their activities have social consequences. They also grasp that in running a business most decisions cannot be taken on the basis of a pure economic calculus and that simply complying with the law is not enough.

I would argue that ethics provide a complement to the internal constitution of the company that sets out the objects and rules for the conduct of the company's business. Likewise that the contract between management and shareholders is necessarily incomplete: shareholders cannot be expected to sanction each and every decision taken by operational management. In fact, most shareholders – and not just ethical investment funds – would wish management to avoid making the maximum possible profit if, for example, this entailed abuses of human rights. To give just one illustration, how many pension scheme beneficiaries would be happy to profit from financing the building of a pipeline in Myanmar with forced labour? There are occasions when management has to make its best judgement of shareholders' views and allow ethics to trump a narrow profit-maximising course of action.

A reading of the essays that follow encourages the view that trust in business and finance is vital. It creates social capital that facilitates co-operative behaviour both in society and in organisations. Bad behaviour erodes trust and forces people to place heavier reliance on the law and regulation. And the more transactions have to be governed by contract, the more cumbersome and expensive business and finance become, as everything has to be negotiated, agreed, litigated and enforced. Such legalism, as a substitute for trust, gives rise to what economists call transaction costs. At a social level, according to the American thinker Francis Fukuyama, a lack of trust imposes a kind of tax on all forms of economic activity. At the corporate level, I would add, trust is an informal, low-cost substitute for cumbersome internal controls within the company and external regulation without. In an ethical culture everyone knows they can do the right thing decisively and with confidence. The business will tend to attract high calibre people of principle. Relations with customers and the general public will be enhanced.

The recent protests against capitalism and inequality in New York, London and elsewhere have underlined the public dissatisfaction with the response to the financial crisis. We have learned from experience that it is not possible to regulate people into good behaviour. In that sense, the Robin Cosgrove essays are an alternative agenda. If they help persuade their readers that trust matters and that the workplace is not morally neutral territory where it is acceptable to shed personal morality as they walk through the company's doors, they will have achieved something of real value.

INTRODUCTION

THE EVOLUTION AND GLOBAL ROLE OF THE ROBIN COSGROVE PRIZE, 2006-2013

Carol Cosgrove-Sacks

Financial innovation and the prize

Innovative ideas are the lifeblood of the financial sector. They have fuelled the exceptional growth of the financial sector during the last twenty years. Financial innovation generated an extraordinary variety of new financial products – exchange trade funds (ETFs), credit default swap transactions (CDSs), collateralised debt obligations (CDOs) to name but a few – that have driven rapid acceleration in the value of financial markets and generated vast profits for both financial enterprises and for individual investors. During this same period, the Grameen Bank, generally regarded as the originator of microfinance innovations at the service of the poor, became an independent bank in 1983 and since then there has been a worldwide proliferation of financial enterprises and not-for-profit organisations that have focused on innovative ways of placing finance at the service of goals other than profit. The fact that the finance bubble burst in 2008 engendering widespread collapse in financial markets and an ensuing economic crisis in many countries does not mean that innovation in finance of itself is good or bad – so much depends on the way it is managed and on the codes of behaviour that guide individuals and the organisations within which they work.

The values that guide finance professionals and the core role played by trust in the modern finance industry have proved to be dominant themes of the best papers submitted for the Ethics in Finance Robin

Cosgrove Prize since it was launched in 2006. Inviting young people to submit innovative ideas to advance ethical approaches to the world of finance in all its many manifestations has stimulated a global debate on the role of ethics and integrity in finance. It is important to note that that the prize was first launched before the topic of ethics in finance became fashionable. It is not a reactive exercise to the current crisis. The aim is to prompt a shift in thinking throughout the world of finance – the fresh ideas submitted for the prize have global relevance. Since launching, the prize awards celebrate outstanding young people thinking and writing about ethics in finance.

Many of the authors of the papers submitted would agree with Adair Turner, chairman of the UK Financial Services Authority (FSA), who recently argued that the global financial regulatory system in total has failed to address fundamental problems.[1] Since the launch of the Robin Cosgrove Prize, what is known as Basel III has been agreed, requiring that the core part of the capital reserves of banks should consist mainly of common shares of the bank and its retained earnings. These requirements have been reflected in the EU's Capital Requirement Directive, with more emphasis on risk assessment systems. It is noteworthy that the best papers submitted for the prize in 2007 remain highly relevant, addressing issues like these and indicating that the problems are far from solved in the interim.

The evolution of the prize

Why did we launch the Robin Cosgrove Prize? Robin loved life as a young investment banker working in Tokyo and London. He was passionate about success and about integrity. He believed that banks and the finance sector in general bring benefits to people and to commerce.

[1] Turner, Adair, "Shrinking the City", in: *Prospect*, London, January 2012, p.42.

He travelled widely throughout the world. His experiences convinced him that the finance sector should serve the common good as well as making profits. He was concerned that complicated financial products would blur ethical and practical considerations.

For him, trust was the essence of good banking. But he feared that many young finance professionals were losing touch with the fundamentals. He hoped to promote better understanding of the critical importance of trust, ethics and personal and corporate integrity in all aspects of finance. Sadly, at much too young an age, he lost his life in an accident on Mont Blanc.

The mission of the prize is to stimulate innovative ideas for promoting ethics and integrity in the finance sector. The prize reaches out to young people familiar with banking, finance and investment, with special attention to emerging markets, to attract innovative ideas. The aim is to strengthen the sustainability of ethics in banking and finance and to reinforce its implementation throughout the world.

Based at l'Observatoire de la Finance in Geneva, Switzerland, and with substantial support from finance sector enterprises in London and Madrid, the prize has evolved into a globally relevant tool to encourage young people under 35 to reflect on trust, integrity and ethics in finance. The prize website – *www.robincosgroveprize.org* – has reached thousands of readers and generally features in the top ten results for searches on the internet for "ethics in finance".

From the start, the prize was intended to be comprehensive in its coverage of finance, interpreting it in the widest possible terms to include financial markets, financial services, financial management, finance theory, market regulation, due diligence, reputational risk, insider trading, derivative contracts, hedge funds, mutual and pension funds, insurance, socially responsible investing, microfinance, micro-credit and solidarity financing, risk management accounting and compliance.

Similarly, no specific definitions were proposed for ethics, leaving it to the young people competing for the prize to define from their individual perspectives how they saw such concepts as accountability, responsibility, integrity, trust, and a wide variety of approaches to what have sometimes been interpreted as ethical and occasionally moral or religious codes for behaviour.

The first global competition was launched in Geneva in 2006, financed by Robin's family and friends and by RAB Capital of London, inviting papers written in English or French with innovative ideas for ethics in finance. Prizes were awarded in 2007. An essential foundation for the success of the competition was the creation of an international jury [see Appendix I] comprising respected academics and practitioners from across the world with a wide variety of professional experience, some of whom had known Robin.

The second global competition and the first regional Ibero-American competition (supported by MAPFRE of Madrid) were launched in 2008, with the awards in 2009. English and French continued as the languages for the global prize, while papers written in Portuguese or Spanish were invited for the regional prize. A second jury was of necessity created, with respected academics and professionals able to judge the entries in the relevant languages for the Ibero-American prize [see Appendix II].

In 2010, the third global competition was launched in London (at Barclays Bank global headquarters) and the second Ibero-American competition was launched in Madrid and in Buenos Aires, Argentina (sponsored by MAPFRE), and the awards were given at a ceremony hosted by the State of Geneva, Switzerland, in November 2011.

The fourth global competition and the third regional Ibero-American competition will be launched in June 2012, and the award ceremony is foreseen for the third quarter of 2013. (As of writing, the precise locations of the launches and the dates have yet to be confirmed).

Throughout the period since the prize was established, the juries have agreed that the central theme – Innovative Ideas for Ethics in Finance – remains highly relevant. The numbers of candidates for the prizes have risen steadily. The very best papers from the regional prize have been translated into English or French for subsequent evaluation by the international Jury, and the final seven or eight best papers approved for publication in the journal of L'Observatoire de la Finance, *Finance & the Common Good/Bien Commun.*

The diversity of submissions in terms of topics and of the authors' nationality and their professional roles has varied very widely. Consistently since 2006, some 40 per cent of candidates have been female.

In 2011, the global prize, with papers submitted either in English or in French, attracted interest from candidates from the following 48 countries: Albania, Argentina, Australia, Austria, Bangladesh, Belgium, Benin, Brazil, Cambodia, Cameroon, Canada, Chad, China, Columbia, Czech Republic, Denmark, France, Germany, Greece, Guatemala, Iceland, India, Ireland, Italy, Kenya, Lithuania, Macedonia, Madagascar, Malaysia, Morocco, New Zealand, Niger, Nigeria, Pakistan, Peru, Philippines, Poland, Romania, Senegal, Singapore, South Africa, Spain, Sri Lanka, Switzerland, United Kingdom, Unites States of America, Vietnam and Zimbabwe.

The Ibero-American prize, with papers submitted either in Portuguese or Spanish, attracted interest in 2011 from candidates in Argentina, Bolivia, Brazil, Colombia, Dominican Republic, Haiti, Mexico, Panama, Peru, Uruguay, Venezuela, and from Portugal and Spain.

About this book

The twenty-three best papers submitted for the various competitions for the Robin Cosgrove Prize between 2006 and 2011 offer a fresh and stimulating range of perspectives on why ethics is considered to be important both in terms of personal conduct of finance professionals and the operation of financial markets and institutions. Robust ethical standards are critically important for the success of the finance sector. Doing the right thing because it is the right thing to do may seem simple, but in complex financial transactions, all too often considerations of ethics and integrity may be squeezed. Ethics and integrity are the two pillars of trust – and without trust, no financial organisation can command confidence.

By publishing the collected best papers submitted for the prize to date, the book aims to

- advance the vision of ethics in finance
- stimulate a global debate among young people regarding ethical standards in finance
- promote the prize as an agent for change, going beyond compliance to promoting real value.

Of the twenty-three papers selected for publication by the prize juries over the course of the prize to date, seven are from 2006-7, eight from 2008-9 and eight from 2010-11. They came from twenty-five authors – two papers had combined authorship. The authors came from a wide variety of countries: Argentina, Australia, Brazil, Canada, Denmark, Egypt, France, Germany, Ghana, India, Kenya, Madagascar, Mexico, Pakistan, Poland, Singapore, Spain, United Kingdom, Uruguay, the USA, and Zimbabwe. They really are from all six continents!

The book is organised in four parts. *Part I* introduces the Robin Cosgrove Prize and its global reach to young finance professionals across the world. The current introduction explains the origins and evolution of the prize and the contents of the book. The second, by Professor Paul H. Dembinski of the University of Fribourg and l'Observatoire de la Finance of Geneva, reflects on the debate regarding ethics in finance and the current financial and economic crisis in Europe. The third, exploring the synergies between the prize and Globethics.net, is written by Dr Christoph Stückelberger, its founder and Executive Director.

Part II has the general title Ethics in Finance – Beyond Compliance. Here, the papers presented for the prize are organised as distinct chapters. These nine chapters examine systemic issues. In many of these papers, trust is a core theme. Many of the young authors would agree with Beth Krasna, Director of the *Thinking Ethics* project, who wrote "Perhaps the most important future challenge… is the breakdown of trust-trust in organisations, trust between organisations and the individuals within them, trust in sources of information, and trust in political and financial institutions".[2] Trust and the value systems guiding finance professionals were a major trend of the papers that won the prize in 2007, 2009 and 2011.

1. *Ethics: A Diet for Highly Leveraged Financial Markets* is by Jakub Kuriata, winner of the global prize in 2011. He is Polish and a Credit Risk Analyst at BNP Paribas, London.
2. *Ethical Cash Management? A Possible Solution* is by Leire San-Jose, winner of the regional Ibero-American prize in 2009. She is Spanish and Assistant-Professor and Research Fellow in Ethics in Finance, University of the Basque Country, Bilbao, Spain.
3. *Ethics and Order in the Disorderly World of Finance* is by Elise Pellerin and Marie Casimiro, joint winners of the global prize in 2009. They are French: Elise is an Ethics Analyst working in Paris, and Marie is the Ethics Officer, CNP Assurances, Paris.
4. *Ethics or Bust: Beyond Compliance and Good Marketing* is by Clare Payne, winner of the global prize in 2007. An Australian, she was at the time Assistant Director of the Integrity Office of Macquarie Bank, Australia, and has gone on to be a Consulting Fellow on Ethics in Banking and Finance at the St James Ethics Centre, Sydney, Australia.

[2] Krasna, Beth, *Thinking Ethics: How Ethical Values and Standards are Changing*, Philias Foundation, London: Profile Books, 2005, p. 126.

5. *Ethics: The Key to Credibility* is by Felippe Araujo, who won 2nd prize in the Ibero-American competition in 2009. A Brazilian, he was a finance professional working in Tokyo and is currently at Nomura Bank in Brasilia, Brazil.
6. *Emotions, Personal Ethics and Professional Life: The Lost Link* is by Meredith Benton, who won 2nd prize in the global competition in 2009. An American, she was a student at INSEAD and is currently Senior Director of Partnerships, AMTRACK.
7. *The Financial Sector and the Behaviour of People: What to Do?* is by Carlos Eduardo Estapé Viana, *ex aequo* winner of the 2nd prize in the regional Ibero-American competition in 2011. An Uruguayan, he is a Public Accountant in Montevideo.
8. *Decision: The Space between the Code of Ethics and Ethical Behaviour* is by Carmen Lucia Carmona Paredes, *ex aequo* winner of the 2nd prize in the regional Ibero-American competiton in 2011. A Mexican, she is working as a finance sector consultant in London.
9. *Ethics: An Essential Prerequisite of the Financial System* by David Sifah was specially commended in the global competition in 2009. A Ghanaian, he works as a Retail Banker at Barclays Bank, Accra.

Part III entitled Ethics in Finance-Standards and Values collects the papers that focused more clearly on factors affecting the behaviour of finance professionals. The challenges of making finance more ethical are well analysed by Paul H. Dembinski, Director of the Observatoire de la Finance and co-president of the prize jury. An "approach to the issue of financial ethics – or rather ethics in finance – [that] involves finding methods and regulations that will make financial transactions more 'ethical'"[3] fails to deliver changes in behaviour. The authors and topics in Part III are diverse, facilitating a fresh appraisal by these young people of the guiding principles that in their views have most relevance.

---

[3] Dembinski, Paul H., *Finance: Servant or Deceiver?* London: Palgrave/Macmillan, 2009, p.159.

10. *Social Impact Ratings: How to Make Responsible Investment Appealing* is by Jonathan M. Wisebrod, *ex aequo* winner 2007 of the global prize in 2007. A Canadian, he is a Director of Villari Asset Management, Singapore.
11. *The Reconciliation of Finance and Ethics: Integrating the Interior and Exterior Dimensions of Reality* is by Faly Ranaivoson, who won 2nd prize in the global competition in 2011. He is from Madagascar and works as a Research Consultant in the finance sector in Geneva.
12. *Financial Derivatives and Responsibility – How to Deal Ethically with Financial Risk* is by Simone Heinemann, who won the 3rd prize in the global competition in 2011. A German, she is developing a PhD dissertation at the Ruhr University Bochum on financial derivatives and the ethical problems arising from systemic risk.
13. *Internationalism, Institutions and Individuals: Systemic Changes for a Systemic Ethical Crisis* is by Geoffrey See, *ex aequo* winner of the global prize in 2009. A Singaporean, he is a University Fellow at Yale University, USA, and Executive Director, Choson Exchange, China.
14. *Accountability and the Second Line of Defence* by Immaculate Dadiso Motsi-Omoijiada was well-evaluated in the global competition in 2011. She is Zimbabwean and is studying for her PhD at HEI, Geneva.
15. *Redefining Capitalism: An Ethical Rating and its Contribution to Development* by Jaime Pozuelo-Monfort was well-evaluated in the global competition in 2007. He is Spanish, currently studying for a Masters in Law at Georgetown University, Washington, DC, and a regular contributor to the Huffington Post.
16. *When Small Companies Dabble in Disinformation* by Saif Ullah was also well-evaluated in the global competition in 2007. A Pakistani, he was at the time a PhD student in the University of Alberta, Canada.

Part IV brings together papers with the theme Ethics in Finance – Solidarity and Sustainability. The authors view ethics in finance in the context primarily of solidarity, micro-finance and micro-credit, social responsibility and sustainable environmental investment practices. Awareness of ethics in finance frequently seems to start from considerations of corporate social responsibility and socially responsible investment, as well as concerns for environmentally sustainable projects. There is a vast range of SRI funds and schemes. There is a broad-based concern to include social and environmental risks in credit risk assessment systems.[4] Whilst advancing awareness of the relevance of non-financial goals for the common good, the chapters here demonstrate also the need to go beyond these approaches and link them directly to ethics as a framework for behaviour.

17. *Solidarity Finance and the Democratisation of Money* is by Nicolás Meyer, winner of the regional prize in 2011. An Argentinian, he is Director of Nuestras Huellas, a not-for-profit organisation in Tigre, Buenos Aires.
18. *Ethics vs. Finance? An Analysis of the Origins, Problems And Future Perspectives of this Relationship* is by Bruno Federico Fernández, *ex aequo* winner of 3rd prize in the global competition and of 2nd prize in the regional Ibero-American competition in 2011. He is an Argentinian economist, working in the Central Office of Public Funds in the Economic Ministry, Tucumán State, Argentina.
19. *In Search of Honesty and Altruism* by Raina Abdul Rahim Mousa was specially commended in the global competition in 2007 and awarded a special prize from Raiffeisen Bank, Geneva. She is Egyptian and at the time was a PhD student in the department of accounting and finance, Birmingham Business School, University of Birmingham, UK.

---

[4] Pentzlin, Daniel (ed.), *Seven Steps to make Banks Sustainable in 2011*, Berlin: BankTrack, Friends of the Earth Europe, *et al.*, 2011, p. 8

20. *Microfinance: Getting Money to the Poor or Making Money out of the Poor?* by Joy Mueni Maina Kiiru was well-evaluated for the 2007 global Ethics in Finance Robin Cosgrove Prize. She is Kenyan and at the time was an Assistant Lecturer at the School of Economics, University of Nairobi.
21. *The South and Carbon Dioxide: Every Cloud has a Silver Lining*, written jointly by Jem Bendell and Inderpreet Chawla, was well-evaluated in the global competition in 2007. Jem, who is British, is Director of Lifeworth Consulting, Geneva, Switzerland. Inderpreet, who is Indian, is a Project Manager with the United Nations Environment Programme Finance Initiative in India.
22. *Investing as if People and Planet Mattered* by Pernille Jessen was well-evaluated in the global competition in 2009. She is Danish and works as a post-doctoral Researcher, Institute of Economy, Aarhus University.
23. *Virtuous Enterprises: The Place of Christian Ethics* by Jan Thomas Otte was well-evaluated in the global competition in 2009. He is German and works as a financial journalist in Germany.

Conclusion

Trust and Ethics in Finance brings together the fresh and innovative observations of the best candidates in the first three series of the Robin Cosgrove Prize. The chapters provide interesting insights into how ethical behaviour may be encouraged and how this represents positive benefits not just for the individual but for the overall good of enterprises and of society. Business managers and human resource development professionals in the finance sector can profit from these insights, understanding the motivations for young people working with them to make a difference and to do well by doing good.

The innovative ideas contributed by the prize winners have broad relevance for the finance sector across the world. The themes addressed in 2007 still have a freshness that has stood the test of time and the problems identified in the various chapters continue to confront the finance sector. New rules and tougher regulation coming from the Basel III agreement, for example, may strengthen the macro-management of finance but are unlikely to solve the ongoing systemic crisis unless more innovative and more ethical approaches become the norm.

In mid-2012, planning the launch of new global and regional competitions in the Ethics in Finance Robin Cosgrove Prize, one may reflect on the extraordinary talent revealed in these chapters. The commitment of young finance professionals and advanced students to look beyond compliance and to consider best practice for promoting trust, integrity and ethics in their work demonstrates vibrant concern across the world for these fundamental themes.

ETHICS AND THE ECONOMY: A TENSE RELATIONSHIP

Paul H. Dembinski[1]

There are those who would claim that the main reason for the financial crisis, and its impact on the economy, is failure to act ethically. In other words, all we need to do is put ethics back into the economy, make capitalism more moral, and hey presto, the world will be restored to health and insulated forever from economic crisis and upheaval. Yet once we move beyond this widespread piece of wishful thinking and start trying to define what ethics in the economy actually means, the consensus melts away.

The economy: An elusive notion

Before discussing the relationship between ethics and the economy, we must first look at the many different definitions of "economics" and "the economy".

These terms have their etymological roots in the ancient Greek word *oikos*, which can be translated as "household". Thus, in the writings of Aristotle, *oikonomia* means the organisation, the "law" – and by extension the wise management – of the household. It is thus an activity that takes place in an enclosed space where, under the watchful eye of the head of the household (the classic *pater* – or *mater* – *familias*), people

---

[1] The author is grateful to Roland Burrus, Etienne Perrot and Domingo Suranyes for their comments on preliminary versions of this text.

work together to produce goods that they directly or indirectly consume. Hence there is no direct analogy with the present, for a Greek household is not the same thing as a business or a modern national economy. Today's businesses produce to sell their products in a market. In the ancient Greek world, on the other hand, the wise manager sought to keep his household independent and self-sufficient; trade with the outside world was at most a stopgap measure, to be avoided if at all possible. Management of resources was merely one aspect of the authority of the *pater familias*, who assigned tasks and functions to members of the household. This is quite different from present-day economies, made up of independent players that are free to make their own choices. Some writers, such as Pierre Calame, use the term *oeconomy* to refer to the whole planet, viewing the pursuit of organisation and wise management in terms of global governance.[2]

The role of the economy within society is so extensive – and hence obvious – that few writers see any need to define it. Those that do are divided into three main groups. According to the first group, the followers of Paul Samuelson (author of the seminal reference work *Economics: an Introductory Analysis*, 1948), the economy is concerned with how three kinds of decisions are made: decisions about production (how to produce?), consumption (what to produce?) and distribution (for whom to produce?). For others, like Lionel Robbins (*An Essay on the Nature and Significance of Economic Science*, 1932), the economy (like management) is concerned with all the knowledge and practices that ensure optimum use of limited resources in order to satisfy a maximum of needs, which by definition are unlimited. Finally, for anthropologists such as Maurice Godelier (*Rationality and Irrationality in Economics*, 1972, first published in French as *Rationalité et irrationalité en économie*), the economy stands for all of society's relationships with its mate-

[2] Calame, Pierre, *Essay on Oeconomy*; originally published in French as *Essai sur l'oeconomie*, Paris: Editions Charles Léopold Mayer, 2009.

rial environment, particularly those that help satisfy its material needs. For anthropologists, and thinkers who see social relations as an organic whole, the economy is therefore embedded in, or indeed inextricably fused with, society.[3]

This variety of definitions raises a question that, although crucial, is nowadays seldom asked: to what extent is the economy a separate entity? In the eighteenth century, with the work of Adam Smith (part of the intellectual legacy of the Reformation), the economy came to be acknowledged as a specific, autonomous area of human life. Ever since then it has been a separate feature of Western society (especially the English-speaking countries), divided off from both politics (the free market!) and morality. Given that self-interest and reason are seen as the triggers for economic activity, it could be said that arithmetic has made conscience redundant and has hence to some extent taken the place of morality, perhaps even ethics.

The debate on the technical as well as ethical independence of the economy is by no means over – nor, of course, is the debate on the role of ethics within it. Three theories can be mentioned at this point: those of Luhmann, Walzer and Dembinski. According to Niklas Luhmann, a German sociologist and philosopher who died in 1998 and whose works belong to the functionalist school, social systems evolve towards higher levels of complexity by spontaneously developing specialised ad-hoc subsystems. These respond to new challenges, applying their own specific logic and rules of operation. As Luhmann saw it, contemporary society is a set of functionally specialised subsystems, including the economic and financial subsystems. The heteronomy of the specific logics of the various subsystems that coexist within a wider overall system is not a problem, said Luhmann, for each is confined to its own area and hence does not threaten the coherence of the whole, which is maintained

---

[3] Servet, Jean-Michel, *Le grand renversement: de la crise au renouveau solidaire*, Paris: Desclée de Brouwer, 2010 and – the classic work of its kind – Polanyi, Karl, *The Great Transformation*, New York: Rinehart, 1944.

by complementarity of functions.[4] The system thus has an innate tendency towards optimisation that prevents clashes – and potential violence – between the various logics. It is kept in stable equilibrium by a mysterious, and perhaps naïve, law of functional complementarity.

Michael Walzer's work on spheres of justice analyses society as a set of spheres of activity, each governed by a different principle of justice. To Walzer, like Luhmann, coherence between the various principles is not a crucial issue, for each sphere is largely independent in determining how it produces justice. However, Walzer focuses on the importance of politics, whose job it is to ensure that the various logics do not clash, and hence that the spheres remain (peacefully) separate.[5]

Paul H. Dembinski's analysis of social systems revolves around the notion that each system's survival depends on maintaining a minimum degree of coherence between the various logics operating within it. This is achieved when a given principle of organisation (or logic) succeeds in dominating all the components or spheres in the system.

However, in any social system – even one that is seemingly in equilibrium – there are clashes between rival principles of organisation that constantly challenge the dominant one. Thus, says Dembinski, one can never be sure that the system will remain coherent or stable.

The past half-century has seen the rapid rise, and nowadays the virtual hegemony, of the efficiency ethos. This allows every player to pursue the desired results by whatever means seem most efficient, however exploitative they may be. In daily life, the principles of organisation derived from today's efficiency ethos inspire and justify individual behaviour, which shapes institutions and the associated rationalisations, which in turn confirm the original principles. This process yields a theory of

---

[4] Ossipow, William "Deux pistes pour penser les relations entre éthique et finance", in: *Finance & the Common Good/Bien Commun*, No. 36, 2010, 125-35.

[5] Walzer, Michael, *Spheres of Justice: A Defense of Pluralism and Equality*, New York: Basic Books, 1984.

systemic transformation in which present-day financialisation is merely one episode.[6]

The debate on the structure of contemporary social systems, and the economy's place within them, illuminates and explains the wide range of differing views on the relationship between ethics and the economy. For those who see the various spheres or subsystems as separate, each one has its own specific ethics. Accordingly, once the validity or usefulness to society of a given subsystem is accepted, the only ethical issue for the players within it is how to make it work smoothly. Ethics is thus endogenous to each subsystem or sphere. That is why so many authors refer to the ethics *of* business. The sole criterion of what is good and what is bad is whether or not it helps the system to function properly. In this view of ethics, any system that works is ethical.

Those who see the social system as a coherent whole governed by a single dominant logic reject this. To them, ethics is exogenous to the various subsystems. There are two versions of this theory. The first is a Marxist view in which each social system (or, as Marx put it, social formation) develops its own specific ethics whose purpose is to keep the system going. Ethics is thus endogenous to each social formation, but not to the subsystems or spheres within it. One can thus speak of the ethics of capitalism. The other view, found mainly but not only among religious believers, is that the source of ethics lies outside all social systems and organisations, which are simply frameworks within which people constantly pursue a good life. People are therefore called upon to express this transcendence in their actions. Rather than the ethics *of* business, this group of thinkers focuses on ethics *in* business. A scarcely perceptible semantic difference thus conceals an irreconcilable difference in views on the origins and purpose of ethics.

---

[6] Dembinski, Paul H., *Finance: Servant or Deceiver?* Basingstoke and New York: Palgrave Macmillan, 2009; first published in French as *Finance servante ou finance trompeuse?* Paris: Desclée de Brouwer, 2008.

As Duncan Foley has stated, even if the contrast between these two views remains important in the world of ideas, the functionalist approach is in practice totally dominant in the twenty-first century. In a recent work called *Adam's Fallacy: a Guide to Economic Theology*,[7] Foley points out, with only slight overstatement, that the division of society into two ethically distinct spheres began with Adam Smith. One is the economy, which has a positive impact on society because it is governed by the pursuit of self-interest that typifies *homo oeconomicus* (in which the pursuit of self-interest is guided by objective laws to a socially beneficent outcome); the other is the rest of society, particularly the private sphere, where the pursuit of selfish interests must be reconciled with other goals (in which the pursuit of self-interest is morally problematic and has to be weighed against other ends). Foley says that today's world is still largely ruled by this ethical duality, not to say schizophrenia, which continues to distract it when making both individual and collective choices.

According to Paul Ricoeur's famous definition, ethics means aiming to live "a good life with and for others in just institutions".[8] Ethics is thus a stance that people adopt in all circumstances of life, whether in political, economic or interpersonal relations, and whether in the public or the strictly private realm. Ricoeur's definition leaves no room for the schizophrenia inherited from the Enlightenment and further reinforced by positivism – every act, without exception, involves the same pursuit of a good life. Anthropologically speaking, these two views of ethics – which for simplicity's sake we will call Smith's view and Ricoeur's view – are thus totally incompatible. This brings us back to the aforementioned contrast between ethics *of* business (which is endogenous to

---

[7] Cambridge MA: Belknap Press (Harvard University Press), 2006, 260.

[8] Ricoeur, Paul, *Oneself as Another*, Chicago: University of Chicago Press, 1992; originally published in French as *Soi-même comme un autre*, Paris: Le Seuil, 1990 (quotation from page 202).

the context) and ethics *in* business (which is exogenous to it, and transcends it).

To survive in the post-Smithian world, people thus need (at least) two separate ethics: one for the economy, and the other for everything else. Luhmann's ideas, which posit a multiplicity of specialised subsystems and logics, are thus merely extensions of the dichotomy introduced by Smith. It follows that only those capable of changing the logic of their behaviour according to the context – people with multiple, interchangeable ethics – can survive in such a highly specialised environment. In contrast, those incapable of making such adjustments will be unfit to survive. The difference between Smith's and Ricoeur's views thus implies a fundamental difference in outlook, between people with more than one ethical face and those with a single, coherent system of values – a difference that pervades the current debate on ethics and the economy.

Four areas of conflict

In the second part of the article, the two aforementioned ethical options will be used to shed light on four key topics and point out their differing, not to say conflicting, implications.

Remuneration

From the point of view of the ethics *of* business, the issue is not so much the actual level of remuneration as the way in which it is determined. Smoothly functioning markets are supposedly all that is needed to ensure true prices. As long as market forces have been given free rein, their verdict is implicitly just (in the moral sense), for it helps increase economic efficiency and hence every player's welfare. However, this does not convince the advocates of ethics *in* business, who move beyond mere procedure to question the justness of the level of remuneration, particularly in terms of commutative justice. Debates on the just price, which go back well beyond the Enlightenment, are part of a continuing effort to identify the level at which prices or remunerations may be deemed unjust or unjustified, either as such or because of their impact on social cohesion.

The nature of businesses

The modern business (joint-stock company) is a fairly recent legal entity. It is a place where capital and labour can work together to create added value, to which they are ultimately entitled. Is it an instrument used by owners of capital to maximise their return on investment, or a community of stakeholders with a common purpose? The answer to this question is crucial when deciding whether the management of modern businesses should focus on shareholder value (which means outright exploitation) or acknowledgement of the partners' wish for a just distribution of effort, risk and reward. Here again, those who advocate ethics *of* business will go for economic efficiency, whereas just distribution of the fruits of joint effort will be the criterion adopted by those who reject ethical schizophrenia.

Philanthropy has a good press these days. Captains of industry who distribute fortunes built up in the course of a lifetime are much admired. However, a seldom-asked question is which of the two approaches to business management enabled them to build up their fortunes in the first place – exploitation, or partnership with stakeholders.

Conflicts of interest

Conflicts of interest at the forefront of the economic (and sometimes political) stage have an insidious, latent impact on individuals and institutions that find themselves torn between clashing loyalties, motivations or interests. Such situations mainly arise (though not always) when there is considerable asymmetry of information, or understanding, between the parties involved in a transaction. In societies where two thirds of national income comes from services and is generated by the manipulation of information, if not knowledge, there is a constant need for experts or proxies. Whether they be bankers, lawyers, car mechanics, accountants or physicians, experts tend to prescribe things – especially their own services. Conflicts of motivation between their clients' wishes and concern for their own turnover are as old as the professions that are most at risk. That is why traditional professional associations drew up such strict codes of ethics and closely scrutinised the characters of new recruits before admitting them to their ranks. There is no equivalent in the managerial and financial professions that now account for most economic activity. Is that because these professions are not liable to conflicts of interest – or because, on the contrary, such conflicts are a key source of income? Those who advocate strict ethics *of* business see conflicts of interest as something that can only be eradicated by competition, smoothly running markets and circulation of information – in other words, the problem is technical rather than ethical. But those who, like Ricoeur, believe that all human behaviour follows the same principles do not agree. As they see it, the situations of conflicts of interest cannot be eradicated, but they can be controlled. This means that the players most at risk must be made aware of their ethical responsibility to act in their patients' or clients' best interests – a responsibility they must assume even, and perhaps most of all, when they feel tempted by the markets.

Ricoeur's definition of ethics covers both *the individual and the social dimension* of every act. Thus aiming to foster just institutions is as much part of the pursuit of ethics as aiming to live a good life. In this sense, any action marginally helps either to validate and consolidate, or else to destabilise and reorient, the institutions within which it takes place. Thus each act is meant to improve the justness of institutions, which are imperfect because by definition they are not good.

Those who advocate the ethics *of* business are less concerned about improving the institutional context. To them, the institutional framework is merely the legal context for the rules that must be followed if the market is to function smoothly. However, this is a formal requirement – the market will function if everyone follows the same rules – rather than a substantial requirement that the rules must be intrinsically just.

Beyond schizophrenia

The coexistence of two irreconcilable ethical cultures – and the resulting schizophrenia – is very deeply rooted in Western economic and managerial practice and theory. Since it is deemed normal, and hence natural, it is accepted as a fact of life and arouses little protest. Yet it is fundamentally unhealthy, for two reasons. First, it traps many economic players in an ethical inconsistency that they find very hard to break free from by their own efforts, from within. Second, it is a source of division that may yet lead to a confrontation between the fragmented individuals who have embraced the legacy and ethical fatalism of *homo oeconomicus* and the integrated ones who reject this.

Today's crisis is replete with scandal, in the profound sense of the term, and the public has repeatedly waxed indignant not just at some people's behaviour, but also at the excuses provided for it. Current calls for more ethics and a more moral capitalism may also reflect a wish that the economy should once more be governed by the standards that apply to other aspects of society and individual life. The crisis could thus provide an opportunity to end the exemption from ethics that the economy has enjoyed for upwards of two centuries. However, if this revolution is to take place, we must take a fresh look not only at economic practice, but also – and perhaps above all – at the body of supposedly scientific literature that has served to justify this exemption.

In 1948, in a booklet in France's famous popularising *Que sais-je?* series, François Perroux warned that capitalism is incomplete, held together by a sense of ethics that is external to it: "For varying lengths of time, an earlier, uncapitalist mentality sustains the frameworks within which the capitalist economy operates; yet the latter's very expansion and success… undermine the traditional institutions and mental structures without which there can be no social order. Capitalism erodes and corrupts, devouring the vital juices whose rise it cannot control".

From Leo XIII to Benedict XVI, via Calvin and his modern-day followers, Christians have always claimed that the freedom of the market is invaluable as long as politics protects the economy and the financial sector from their self-corruption and they are firmly controlled by a set of shared moral values that transcend the economy. It is above all from without (through ethics and politics) rather than from within that capitalism can be made more moral. Perroux was well aware of what was at stake when he wrote: "If [the degeneration of capitalism] is to be detected and controlled in time, political leaders will need to be unusually clear-headed in diagnosing it and exceptionally vigorous in treating it".

At the end of this brief discussion, the question of whether capitalism can be made more moral comes to the fore once again. Four years after the crisis first erupted, most of the remedies that are now prescribed are either purely technical (such as equity ratios, regulation of over-the-counter trading and capping of remunerations) or else deontological (more codes of conduct, greater compliance by financial institutions, control of conflicts of interest and so on). Even if some of these measures are ethically inspired, they are still clearly based on the ethics *of* business approach. Their obvious limitations can be summed up by a question that was asked in ancient Rome and remains unanswered to this day: *Quis custodiet ipsos custodes*? (Who will watch the watchmen?)

Ethics *in* business offers a path that, however steep and arduous, may solve this problem by explicitly resorting to action beyond the realm of purely economic practice and theory. But this will depend on a willingness – political and otherwise – to confine the efficiency ethos to strictly economic activities.

CREDO + CREDIBILITY = CREDIT

Christoph Stückelberger

Globetics.net is honoured and proud to publish this stimulating collection of articles of the Robin Cosgrove prize on Ethics in Finance. Economic ethics (or business ethics) is a key theme for our global ethics network in the global online library and its special collections, in the network with its global Directory of Business Ethics Experts, in international research workgroups such as on a new global currency regime, and in our Global Ethics Forums on the value of values in business. Ethics of financial markets is a key topic within economic ethics since capital markets are the fuel of economies and whole societies.

Financial ethics,[1] or better ethics in finance, is one of the most important challenges in overcoming the current economic crises. It is at the same time a problem that is as old as money itself. Lending capital has led, and leads again and again, to an increase in the gap between poor and rich. This two thousand years experience led to the interdiction of interest and with Calvin in the Reformation to a very careful, socially responsible way of limiting and strongly regulating financial markets and interest rates.[2] The magic powerful attraction of money that makes us greedy and leads to speculation, overspending and indebtedness is equally old. All world religions in their holy scriptures warn against

---

[1] See McCosh, Andrew M., *Financial Ethics*, Dordrecht: Kluwer Academic Publishers, 1999.

[2] See Stückelberger, Christoph, "No Interest from the Poor. Calvin's Economic and Banking Ethics", in: Stückelberger, Christoph/ Bernhardt, Reinhold (eds.), *Calvin Global. How Faith Influences Societies*, Globethics.net Series No. 3, Geneva 2009.

greed as the taproot of injustice, oppression, exploitation, corruption, mistrust, conflict and war. They all show ways to overcome greed and find ways of sharing, trust, fairness and mutual benefit in trade and economic interactions.

Each generation therefore has to develop spiritual strength and find voluntary rules and legally binding regulations to transform money from a malediction to a benediction, from an addiction to a liberating service.

Ethics in finance covers all financial activities: banking ethics,[3] stock market ethics, insurance ethics, ethics of gambling, debt management, microfinance, speculation, black markets, money laundering, etc. Even though the vital importance of the financial markets is recognised, the number of publications on ethics in finance is very limited compared to the huge number on bioethics, medical ethics or homosexuality. This is one reason the Robin Coscrove prize is so important and innovative: because it stimulates and supports this redirection of financial markets.

The financial crisis was and is also a crisis of trust in the banking system, in leading banking professionals, in political control mechanisms and in the rationality of consumers and investors. Trust is a basic condition of economic transactions. Economy in a market or a plan system cannot work without trust on all levels. And what builds trust? Not opportunism, not selfishness, not short-termism, not personal or institutionalised greed, but long-term planning and strategies, faithfulness to values and convictions are the ground for trust. Credo (the belief, the convictions, the ethical values of a person, group or institution) leads to credibility. And credibility leads to credit-relations between creditor and debtor where – built on trust and control – credit is given and taken for responsible investments and economic development. Therefore, the simple formula for trust and ethics in finance is:

Credo+Credibility=Credit.

---

[3] Thielemann, Ulrich/ Ulrich, Peter: *Brennpunkt Bankenethik*, Bern: Verlag Haupt, 2003.

PART I

BEYOND COMPLIANCE

1

ETHICS: A DIET FOR HIGHLY LEVERAGED FINANCIAL MARKETS

Jakub Kuriata

> "Men often, from infirmity of character, make their election for the nearer good, though they know it to be the less valuable."
>
> - JS Mill, Utilitarianism

In the recent few years the emphasis in the discussions relating to ethics and finance has been a natural consequence of the high-leveraged investment and the excessive risk taking by banks, which were among the causes of the financial crisis of 2007 – 2009. The prevailing sentiment was that the financial system was on the verge of collapse and the subsequent efforts of central banks, financial regulators, governments and other market participants have been focused on designing a new framework to increase the stability of financial markets. As Lehman pointed out in 1988, the mechanisms of financial intermediation create "the majority of interesting philosophical questions about corporate capitalism" largely because financial institutions accumulate and manage particularly large funds and require the participation of increasingly sophisticated intermediaries. Against this backdrop, it is not surprising that among the vast array of topics in financial ethics, the most urgent issue to be addressed is the ethical dimension of the recent failure of financial markets and to what extent ethical theories might be pertinent in designing the financial markets of tomorrow.

Preliminary remarks

One of the main caveats in the discussion about the failures of contemporary finance is that participants speak different languages. Nielsen (2010) highlights that many modern economists "separated the study of economics, evolutionary forms of capitalism, and structurally related ethical issues, such as 'monopolistic practices' from ethical judgements about those issues". It became a rule rather than an exception to present economic models in the form of elegant mathematical equations without mentioning ethical dilemmas, even on the list of omitted topics. At the same time, as Haakonsen (2002) put it, in a brilliantly concise formula, "modern moral philosophy is primarily the hunt for a universally normative doctrine". For an economist not overly acquainted with the history of ideas, the question "what is ethical finance?" is far from being trivial. On what grounds can we base the ethical judgement of financial markets? Shall we adopt a deontological or teleological perspective? Can we overlook that the perception of finance has varied across the centuries largely due to the amalgamation of social practices and religious views?

A useful formula to overpass this conundrum is to begin with underlying assumptions that will be simple enough and acceptable for the largest possible audience. Two essential elements of Aristotelian virtuous ethics seem to carry a noteworthy common denominator: happiness or human flourishing (eudaemonia), as the ultimate goal (telos) of human actions, and the definition of happiness according to certain virtues. It is worth highlighting that Aristotle considered that virtues need to be exercised. In this respect, virtues can be compared to skills: one cannot acquire them only by following a class or reading books. To become a skilful car driver one must drive a car on the streets.

Although not completely free of legitimate criticism,[1] this dual perspective of telos/virtues will guide us through the rest of the text.

Another question that needs to be addressed is the nature of the contemporary financial sector. According to Biais, Rochet and Woolley (2009), technological change and inflow of resources and skilled workforce, together with market liberalisation, enabled creation of new techniques (securitisation) and new strategies (hedge funds, private equity funds), which deeply transformed the industry. Nielsen (2010) advocates the idea that high leverage is a major characteristic of today's financial landscape. In addition, one must think about the pace of globalisation of the financial sector, which matches, if not outperforms, the pace of trade globalisation. It has certainly contributed to the spread of risk across the world; but while previously, the consensus was that this process would help manage the risks and losses, it appeared that globalisation was the nexus that transformed local financial turbulences into a global one.

I find it appropriate to elaborate on the groundwork of ethics in finance because we believe that too often the public tend to deal with problems as they surface, i.e. by focusing on the scandals related to fraud and deceit without paying too much attention to the increasingly complex nature of financial markets and their role throughout history.

In the remainder of the paper, I argue that the only realistic approach to judge the financial markets is teleological: financial markets contribute to the positives of life when their functions perform correctly and efficiently. Purely deontological ethics have never been applied into finance. We live in a world of regulations and compliance. I therefore outline a simple framework aiming at improving the functioning of financial markets by fostering financial markets' stability. At the same time, simply complying with regulations is not sufficient to develop virtuous

---

[1] According to Schopenhauer, *The Basis of Morality*, "It is Kant's great service to moral science that he purified it of all eudaemonism". The attempt made by the ancients to prove that virtue equals happiness, "was like having two figures which never coincide with each other, no matter how they may be placed".

behaviour. I will argue that all market participants should engage in a dual process of education (due to high rates of financial illiteracy in the society) and dialogue over the division of the financial industry in contributions to the common good. I am aware that this analysis shall apply mainly to developed countries even though some conclusions may be relevant for emerging countries as well.

Incentives versus moral motivation

The famous answer of James Tobin is that economics, in one word, is about incentives. Relatively early, economists developed the idea of homo economicus and tried to understand what forces drive his behaviour and motivate his choices relating to work, consumption, and leisure. In the vast majority of economic models it is assumed that individuals are self-interested and they behave as if they were maximising a certain utility function under existing constraints. This echoes a simplified version of utilitarian ethics, as advanced by JS Mill. There are, of course, models aiming at understanding altruistic behaviour, models stressing imperfect information of the economic agents and a plethora of other deviations from the homo economicus ideal-type. There have been even attempts to include Kantian ethics into formal economic reasoning but without too much impact[2]. However in general, economic models ignore the question of moral motivations behind agents' decisions.

The following moral motivations according to three major schools of thinking about ethics; Aristotelian theory of virtue, Kantian deontology and utilitarianism of John Stuart Mill, were investigated by Colle and Werhane (2008). They found that Aristotle and especially Kant asserted that the moral motivation must unavoidably stem from intrinsic motiva-

---

[2] Laffont (1975) established a utility function in which individuals maximise their utility according to the Kantian principles ("act as if you wished that your actions become a universal law"). White (2004) argues that *homo economicus* can follow imperfect duties but firstly, he does not attempt to model it and secondly he substantially weakens Kantian ethical theory.

tions of each individual. On the other hand, Mill asserts two options, the individual is motivated by the need to satisfy external requirements or it abides to internal motivations; he undoubtedly assigns moral superiority to the latter. Aristotle, Kant and Mill agree also on the fact that human life has an aim (although they differ when it comes to defining this aim), which implies that a human being must use reason in order to be capable to understand this ultimate goal.

Moral motivations in the ethical system are the equivalent of incentives in economics and in both cases one must assume that individuals are endowed with some form of reason. If we try to apply this to financial markets, one should immediately see that we face here an intellectual conundrum. How can a balance be met between authorities implementing a system of surveillance and punishment in order to obtain ethical behaviour from the market participants with the need for an intrinsic moral motivation behind human acts?

Clearly, compliance with rules and regulations is not enough to establish whether an act is ethical or not. In particular, within the Kantian perspective this is not only insufficient but is insignificant as to whether we abide by the existing law or not. Kant would argue that a merchant (or a banker) that applies a fair and equal treatment to all its clients because he knows that this will achieve optimum behaviour and being unlawful would be harmful for his business does not act morally. Only good will can be discerned as good, without restrictions. We believe we do not risk too much by stating that contemporary finance authorities would never rely solely on the faith that financiers will follow Kant's categorical, imperative or Aristotelian virtuous ethics.

Today, no one seriously questions the idea that markets are imperfect and need corrections in certain areas or circumstances. Many people are calling for more and/or better incentives for the market participants. In reality, various institutions are in charge of regulating and controlling financial markets[3]. By multiplying the restrictions and increasing supervisory bodies we are hindering the development of virtuous character but in contrast we admit that potentially better supervision may bring us closer to the objective, which is better functioning of the financial market. This approach could be classified as teleological since it favours the assessment of the behaviour with reference to its goals. However, what remains to be determined is by which categories exactly should we judge financial markets? This requires a short enquiry into the roots and history of the financial industry.

Teleological approach – how to judge financial markets?

It should never be forgotten that according to conventional economics the role of financial markets is to allocate available resources to their most productive use. Another role, less emphasised but equally important, is to redistribute and allocate risks from those who have risk-aversion to those who can manage risks. But the extent to which it was understood is questionable. Many people claim that human misery and degradation are caused by financial institutions and not by lack thereof. The church's ban on charging interest beyond the principal value of a loan (usury) is symptomatic of some prejudices about finance. Interestingly, the condemnation of excessive interest fostered by Dominican and Franciscan friars in the thirteenth century began with a period of sharp rise in interest rates, due to increasing money supply. The latter was a direct consequence of the discovery of new silver mines in Germany (Mews and Abraham, 2007). Eventually the ban was never rigorously applied because of many exceptions being approved. Investment in partnerships and early forms of joint ventures and profit sharing were not forbidden. Neither was charging penalties for late repayments of the

---

[3] Still, many people are frightened by globalising financial markets – mainly because, as Paul Krugman once put it, "it epitomizes what they dislike about markets in general: the fact that nobody is in charge".

principal. St. Thomas Aquinas had already a vague understanding of credit risk when he accepted that there might be limited legitimate compensation for potential loss to capital incurred by the lender (Mews and Abraham, 2007). But the idea that, for example, a lender might charge the borrower because of the opportunity cost[4] of not investing in a partnership, in land or in commerce proved to be too controversial for the majority of thirteenth century theologians (Munro 2002). The consequences were devastating especially for the poor, who were obliged to turn to small, unofficial lenders, loan sharks in today's terminology, who were charging exorbitant interest (perhaps a risk premium for living under the constant threat of God's punishment).

It emerges from this brief description that critics of usury could hardly accept the existence of specialised financial intermediaries while they were favouring investments in business projects and profit sharing. More generally, the hostility towards financiers across the centuries of our history was rooted, as shown by Ferguson (2009), "in the idea that those who make their living from lending money are somewhat parasitical on the 'real' economic activities of agriculture and manufacturing." Ferguson's financial history of the world offers a compelling description of how the invention of banks contributed to the cultural and economic flourishing of Northern Italy in the late Middle-Ages, how the invention of the stock exchange and central banking fostered the rise in trade and military power of the British Empire and how in general, countries that are now among the richest in the Western world, were those that developed banking, insurance and corporate finance systems relatively early. Certainly, it would be simplistic to assume a linear relation between the pace of financial innovation and development, however, the vast majority of academic economists agree that there is a statistically significant and positive correlation between the development of the financial sys-

[4] *Interesse* – which was a root of the word "interest" and was derived from Latin by jurists in Bologna.

tem and the pace of economic growth (for an excellent review see Levine 1997).

We tend to forget all of this during the periods of financial turbulence when we paradoxically think that finance is a source of instability rather than stability and innovative financial products are weapons of massive destruction. There are some easy explanations of this phenomenon. The financial crisis of 2007-2008 caused massive job losses and deterioration of the quality of life for many people. But what we also know is that financial markets have always known booms and busts, as did emerging economies on all continents. Crises, defaults and recessions occur on a regular basis, as showed in the influential book by Reinhart and Rogoff. Banks, monetary institutions and governments tend to believe that due to better-informed policies, enhanced management tools, technical progress and many other factors, they will be able to avoid past mistakes. Crises, caused by a burst of the asset bubble, are likely to repeat themselves in the future because, as highlighted by Robert J Shiller, who wrote extensively on asset bubble formation, they are impossible to predict with accuracy.

Besides, economic difficulties are also due to other factors, among which I would mention one: the unprecedented pace of growth of populations and economies. As showed by Jeffrey Sachs in his recent article "Need Versus Greed", the world's output grew from USD 10 trillion in 1960 to USD 70 trillion today. It helped many people come out of poverty. As a consequence, the planet's resources and commodities (being the most striking example) are being depleted at an alarming rate. Sachs claims that in the last few years, the greed, not only of bankers, but also of the Western countries, which consume a very large fraction of the world's resources to maintain very high standards of living, is the main culprit. What is the role of financial markets in this? Financiers alone cannot address all the development issues that the humanity is facing. Yet they can assure more economic stability and they should increase their awareness of the ethical challenges in the globalised, highly leveraged world. Ultimately, this is what they should be accountable for.

Diet for financial markets

Using our Aristotelian dual telos/virtues framework, a diet for financial markets should involve four building blocks:

Debate
Incentives
Education
Targeting

Adequate incentive structures and proper targeting of products are designed to curb excessive risk taking and therefore achieve the goal of better stability of the financial markets. At the same time, we believe that debate and education (of all market participants) are necessary in order to develop virtuous behaviour among the market's participants. Two things need to be highlighted before going into details: firstly, I prefer evolution to revolution and we are of the opinion that financial markets need a therapy after the shock of the sub-prime crisis rather than a shock therapy. Secondly, many of these prescriptions are already being discussed and even implemented by the authorities (in particular with respect to incentives) and in those cases our proposals are intended to cherry-pick the key areas and to suggest further improvements that are deemed necessary.

Incentives

I begin with the discussion of a few necessary improvements of the regulatory framework. This section might cover a vast array of topics that we are unable to enumerate in this restrictive format. We would like to focus on some incentives pertaining to main structural issues identified earlier: very high leverage and excessive risk taking.

Set of recommendations, now known as Basel III, represent a step in the right direction, in particular in the areas of liquidity requirements. However, with regard to capital adequacy regulation, the recommendations stand halfway; they fail to address a number of critical issues that contributed to the recent crisis.

Firstly, the development of credit derivatives was used by banks to effectively transfer credit risk to third parties and allowed them to reduce their capital requirements. In the paper for the BIS conference, Duffie (2008) argues that banks transferring credit risk have less incentive to monitor the creditworthiness of the borrower. It makes it possible to maintain larger portions of illiquid and/or very risky assets. The result of these practices was to raise "the total amount of credit risk in the financial system to inefficient levels". Secondly, risk calibration neglects the systemic risks to which financial institutions are exposed. The domino effects of the failure of a major bank in the market were well documented during the recent crisis. Thirdly, our measures of credit and market risk are imperfect despite evidenced improvements and being stated as fact rather than criticism. The measuring of risks stemming was inadequate, for example, from correlations of credit risks in mortgage-backed securities. Two latter arguments are advanced in a very interesting paper by Hellwig (2010). Given the above, there are legitimate doubts that new capital requirements will effectively reduce the leverage.

The solution to this would be introducing non-calibrated, crude measures of leverage in addition to current capital adequacy measures. Although Basel III initiates leverage ratios from 2013 (as an experiment), they seem to be far too prudent. A careful assessment of the economic impact of such measures must be performed first, but equity/asset ratios of 8-10% would be much more efficient in preventing bank insolvencies and costly bailouts.

One has to bear in mind that large and complex regulations, such as Basel III, certainly have an economic impact on financial intermediation and play a key role in the development of the economy (see the study of Basel III prepared for BIS). Reducing lending capacity of banks and/or making costs for lending higher will most probably translate into an economic slow down. Critics of Basel III, like Hellwig, argue that reducing leverage, restricting moral hazards and lowering systemic risks in the financial system, will result in lower risk premiums being asked by equity investors. Thus, in fact, the increase of the cost of lending will be much smaller and the benefits in terms of system stability will be significant. This trade-off, if there is one, must be a matter of political choice.

Apart from capital regulations, the attention of the public was on the compensation levels of executives and more generally senior financiers across all sectors of the industry. The argument usually goes that it is unfair for bankers to receive large fractions of the profits when the economy is doing well but the costs of bailing out financial institution has to be borne by taxpayers (which by the way amplifies the moral hazard problem). The concern with executive pay is legitimate yet the issue that needs to be addressed is whether compensation packages offered to bankers (executives in particular) provide them with an optimum incentive structure from a risk-stability perspective. This is an unorthodox view. Cai, Cherry and Milbourn (2010) explains that from a classical perspective, the calibrating of the executive's pay scheme is "aligning managerial incentives with those of shareholders".

There are few chances for the return of Medici-style family-run banking. The principal-agency problem in the case of the financial industry is amplified by a number of factors such as an increasingly high leverage, deposit protection schemes, explicit or implicit guarantees of the state or access to emergency liquidity windows by the central bank. Kandel (2009) argues that executive pay might be substantially reduced without hampering the proper incentive structure. Some economists, for example, Gehrig, Lutje and Menkhoff (2009) defend the hypothesis that the relation between the size of variable, performance-based remuneration of investment fund managers and their willingness to take risk is insignificant. However, there was a general consensus that remuneration packages encourage more short-term profit maximisation, for example, by increasing leverage, engaging in aggressive trading or loosening control over credit origination standards.

But the key issue is the following – if managers maximise the shareholder's utility, they do not necessarily take into account the interests of depositors, debtors and other stakeholders, not to mention the issues of general market stability. The general audience being authorised to impose on financial institutions the implementation of compensation structures that promote overall system stability is not evident. Financial stability is highly desirable and probably optimal for society as a whole but the means to achieve this goal must be debated.

What public authorities could propose is the introduction of financial stability criteria to calculate the variable part of executives' compensation. It could be recommended (but not imposed!). It is for the banks to establish internally in advance thresholds for leverage, stable funding ratios, overall market/credit risk levels and adjust the compensation accordingly if the objectives are met or not.

Targeting

In order to perform correctly one of the major roles of financial markets, i.e. the redistribution of risks, market participants must distribute products that are adequate to the client's financial literacy (we address the issue of literacy in the subsequent chapter). The application scope of adequate targeting principle is very wide, for example, offering brokerage accounts to retail clients or extending loans denominated in foreign currency to clients having revenues in domestic currency means exposing them to risks they may not necessarily be able to manage. This is another field of financial regulation that has been subject to careful examination, and significant progress has been made. From a European angle, the Markets in Financial Instruments Directive (MiFID) is one of the best examples of this. One of its key objectives is to improve the categorisation of clients according to their ability to understand financial products. Three categories apply; retail clients, professional clients and counterparties.

The last category encompasses other financial institutions. Let us focus on the first two that should be far more risk-adverse. The definition of a professional client is that it must have "the experience, knowledge and expertise to make its own investment decisions and properly assess the risks that it incurs". The remaining clients are retail clients, for whom we assume insufficient knowledge to take informed investment decisions. They enjoy, at least in theory, the highest degree of regulatory protection. However, the alarming failure by banks to assess the credit risks had a direct impact on customers purchasing even basic retail banking products. Was it the fault of retail customers or the banks when in some countries people were massively granted mortgage loans they could not afford (sub-prime)? The question is rhetoric, given the massive asymmetry of knowledge and experience between the banks and the low-income borrowers. Another example is offering clients products with embedded currency risks like loans denominated in foreign currencies to people who cannot hedge the risk (they have no access to the derivatives market).

The same analysis might apply to some extent to professional clients. As a matter of fact, the distinction between professional and retail client is often blurred. Professional clients might be, for example, medium or large corporations who are clients of banks. Those firms are supposed to be managed by financially literate managers who are able to identify and tackle potential risks but the reality is somehow different. In 2008/2009, when the markets were nervously selling assets in the emerging markets, pushing their currencies down, sometimes dramatically, one of the key topics in Poland were currency options. It appeared that Polish companies had entered into currency options with banks without necessarily having any underlying transactions to hedge and bet against apart for the appreciation of the Polish currency. In many cases the purpose of this was purely speculative and it exposed companies to severe losses. The line of defence for banks was that they were dealing with professional clients. Yet in a number of testimonies to the press, both employees of the banks and clients confirmed that companies that purchased the products were not sufficiently aware of the risks they were taking. The line between unethical behaviour and poor business decision is often very thin but in this case the structure of incentives was clearly inadequate. Bank employees had strong incentives to sell because their final salary depended on the volume of products sold, so they were emphasising to clients only the potential gains.

An alternative approach is to amend the structure of incentives in order to promote better targeting of financial products. There are no easy solutions to this problem but financial institutions should be encouraged to take a more conservative approach when assessing the ability of the client to manage risks. From a regulatory perspective, the incentives might come from financial services authorities. A good example was the reaction of the Polish Financial Authority (KNF) to the widespread practice of lending in foreign currencies to retail clients. According to "Recommendation T" banks must perform stress tests of the borrower's ability to service its debt under the scenario of a shift of interest rate and foreign exchange rate depreciation. It also recommends a threshold of debt repayment expenses in relation to monthly net income. Although stress testing is imperfect, implementing these measures is a relatively easy way to improve adequate targeting of financial products.

Debate, education

These two elements are presented together because there are some obvious synergies to be achieved between the two. Debate on the ethical issues in finance should take place within the financial institutions but also in the public realm and involve all types of social actors. One of the latent effects of such a debate will be an increased awareness of ethical issues within society.

Almost all of us are clients of financial institutions and we depend on them to satisfy our basic needs. As echoed by R. Hinde (2007), when the competition mechanisms of the market work correctly, "the ethical demands of the public can affect what the firm does". Naturally, how much the firms are changing their behaviour depends to large extent on how many customers are aware of the ethical issues and whether they decide to take direct action. Some critics would also say that this is inscribing ethical necessity into the logic of market competition. However, I believe that this is a necessary step to develop virtuous behaviour, which in the future will stem more from intrinsic moral incentives rather than regulatory or market constraints.

One of the key constraints is the relatively low financial literacy of the society. Lusardi (2008) made a very convincing case about the current level of illiteracy, highlighting that ignorance of basic financial concepts may be linked to poor savings level (including pension savings), inadequate borrowing decisions and lack of participation in more sophisticated forms of investment. Against this backdrop, taking informed decisions is very difficult. To address this issue I propose the following. Fundamentals of finance and economics should be introduced into high schools at a relatively early stage as a mandatory subject. The objective of this would be to provide all students with a basic knowledge of financial products that they are most likely to come across as adults (savings accounts, mortgage loans, pension plans, insurance etc.).

At the same time financial institutions also should engage in a programme of education for their employees, which should not be limited to basic e-learning programmes with the compliance department. One day of the year should be proclaimed as a Day of Ethics in Finance. The key feature of the Day of Finance would be that it must be prepared in advance. Employees should form working groups and research selected topics in ethics, which should involve the study of classic texts and the analysis of market practices. The results would be presented on the Day of Finance. Other tools could be developed internally by companies, which should be given a flexibility to adapt this exercise to their specific internal characteristics.

Administratively, the Day of Finance could be co-ordinated by central banks or financial authorities; it should not be imposed on financial institutions but rather recommended as good practice. In addition, central banks could put additional pressure on other banks by organising a series of seminars, lessons at schools or advertising campaigns. An integral part of the Day of Ethics should be a round-table debate organised, for example, by national broadcasting companies and well advertised among the public, where different social partners might debate ethical issues. The main objective of the round table would be to promote discussion in an attempt to build a common language with regard to those issues. One of key topics should be the responsibility of the financial industry to promote sustainable economic growth.

Bibliography

Biais, Bruno, *et al*, 2009. "The Lifecycle of the Financial Sector and Other Speculative Industries", IDEI Working Paper, April 2009.

Cai, Jian, *et al.*, 2010. "Compensation and Risk Incentives in Banking and Finance", *Economic Commentary* 2010-13, Federal Reserve Bank of Cleveland.

de Colle, Simone/ Werhane, Patricia H., 2008. "Moral Motivation Across Ethical Theories: What Can We Learn for Designing Corporate Ethics Programmes?" *Journal of Business Ethics 81 (4)*, 2008, 751-764.

Duffie, Darrel, 2008. "Innovations in credit risk transfer: implications for financial stability", *BIS Working Papers* 255, July 2008.

Ferguson, Niall, 2009. *The Ascent of Money. A Financial History of the World*, Penguin, 2009.
Financial Services Authority, Background Information on MiFID, *www.fsa.gov.uk/pages/About/What/International/mifid/index.shtml*
Gehrig, Thomas P. *et al.*, 2009. "Bonus Payments and Fund Managers' Behavior: Transatlantic Evidence", in: *CESifo Economic Studies 55 (3-4)*, 2009, 569–594.
Grosh, Paul/ Vardy, Peter, 1999. *The Puzzle of Ethics,* second edition, London: Fount, 1999.
Hellwig, Martin, 2010. "Capital Regulation after the Crisis: Business as usual?" Max Planck Institute for Research on Collective Goods, Bonn 2010/31.
Hinde, Robert A., 2007. *Bending the Rules*, Oxford University Press, 2007.
Kandel, Eugene, 2009. "In Search of Reasonable Executive Compensation", in: *CESifo Economic Studies 55 (3-4)*, 2009, 405–433.
Kant, Immanuel, 2009. *Fondements de la metaphysique des moeurs,* Paris: Livre de Poche, Les Classiques de la Philosophie, 2009.
Komisja Nadzoru Finansowego, "Rekomendacja T", *www.knf.gov.pl/Images/ Rekomendacja T_tcm75-18474.pdf*
Krugman, Paul, 1997. "We are not the World", *New York Times*, 13 February 1997.
Kraskowski, Leszek, 2009. "Wciskali toksyczne opcje, zarabiali krocie", Dziennik 19 February 2009, *wiadomosci.dziennik.pl/polityka/artykuly/ 139163,wciskali-toksyczne-opcje-zarabiali-krocie.html.*
Lehman, Craig, 1988. "Moral and Conceptual Issues in Investment and Finance: An Overview", in: *Journal of Business Ethics 7*, 1988, 3-8.
Levine, Ross, 1997. "Financial Development and Economic Growth: Views and Agenda," in: *Journal of Economic Literature*, 35(2), 1997, 688-726.
Lusardi, Annamaria, 2008. "Financial literacy: an essential tool for informed consumer choice?" *NBER Working Paper* No. 14084, 2008.
Munro, John, 2001. "The Late-Medieval Origins of the Modern Financial Revolution: Overcoming Impediments from Church and State", *Working Paper No. 2-2001*, Department of Economics, University of Toronto.
Mews, Constant J./ Abraham, Ibrahim, 2007. "Usury and Just Compensation: Religious and Financial Ethics in Historical Perspective", in: *Journal of Business Ethics 72*, 2007, 1-15.
Nielsen, Richard P., 2010. "High-Leverage Finance Capitalism, the Economic Crisis, Structurally Related Ethics Issues and Potential Reforms", in: *Business Ethics Quarterly 20 (2)*, 2010, 299-330.
Sachs, Jeffrey, 2011. "Need Versus Greed", 28 February 2011, *www.project-syndicate.org/commentary/need-versus-greed.*
Schopenhauer, Arthur, 2005. *The Basis of Morality,* second edition, Dover Publications, 2005.
Turner, Adair, 2009. "Rules to keep bankers honest", in: FT Comments and Opinions, 7 December 2009. *www.ft.com/intl/cms/s/0/a56e3630-023d-11e0-aa40-00144feabdc0.html*
White, Mark D., 2004. "Can Homo Economicus Follow Kant's Categorical Imperative", in: *Journal of Socio-Economics 33*, 2004, 89-106.

2

ETHICAL CASH MANAGEMENT? A POSSIBLE SOLUTION

Leire San-Jose

The purpose of cash management is to ensure that companies have the cash they need at the right moment, and at minimum cost. To do this, companies use a range of measures and techniques relating to cash planning, decisions on short-term financing and investment, management of relations with financial bodies and management of financial risks. Other key aspects are monitoring and analysis of receivables and payments management, as well as corporate culture.

By its very nature, this business concept is a complex one, probably because it lies at the heart of corporate management, for its decisions directly or indirectly affect and are affected by (a) all other areas of the company, whether commercial, structural or social, and (b) other companies with which it has relations, and even society and the environment.

Decisions that affect the whole society

Such measures, and above all decisions on cash holdings, thus affect and are affected by groups of stakeholder, yet financial cash-management techniques are based on selfish assumptions and behaviour on the part of companies and their managers and are sustained by distrust of other players. This results in unilateral decisions based on personal goals, which can scarcely generate value for all those involved. In this connection it may be said that financial management, and specifically cash management, include a major ethical component, since unequal conditions, information asymmetry and opportunistic efforts to maximise short-term results may have an adverse financial impact on other economic players or other interest groups.

A twofold problem arises in connection with cash management. On the one hand, as already indicated, cash management affects not only the company's own decisions but also third parties, and ultimately the whole of society. Today's crisis has highlighted the link between companies and banks, since, although the crisis had its origins in a combination of greedy operations involving junk mortgages with a complex system of financial products in the banking sector, the resulting chain reaction has led to the most serious cash problems in history. The scale of this can be deduced from the fact that practically every company now describes its short-term financial position as tricky or indeed disastrous, as witness the large increase in company failures around the world.

At the same time, in order to have an optimum impact on parties' medium- and long-term interests, solutions must be based on mutual trust, and hence on ethics. Yet the need for this ethical basis may come to be challenged by a general opinion – shared by academics and professionals – that this is merely a management problem. But even then it may be argued that there are ethical issues involved, since financial and cash-management strategies are based on selfish approaches. For instance, one of the most important cash-management strategies, advocated in most books and texts on finance and accounting, involves paying suppliers later without damaging relations with them and requiring customers to pay sooner without substantially reducing sales (Gitman *et al.*, 1976). Yet this short-term financial strategy, which is based on companies' cash cycles, does not generate maximum overall value, but a maximum level of own value that cannot be sustained in the long term; still less does it optimise companies' cash holdings.

Create value for all

Up to now, financial experts and operators have focused on studying and proposing techniques and instruments for optimising cash holdings; however, in order to achieve this, at least across the board, the unitary approach must first make way for a comprehensive one in which techniques used create an optimum financial situation for all the stakeholders or companies affected by financial operations. To respond to this problem, we need a change in corporate financial culture, which in our view can only optimise overall cash holdings and generate value for all if financial strategies rest on one basic pillar, namely mutual trust. Situations of illiquidity, insolvency and bankruptcy in which companies find themselves must be analysed not only from the point of view of their own corporate management, but from a broader perspective that takes account of the (essentially adverse) impact on the entire group of stakeholders. Thus, and from the point of view trust among interest groups, it may be considered that improved results – social as well as economic – can be achieved for all those involved if cash-holding techniques are based on the notion of mutual benefit and the common good.

Current cash-management and cash-holding techniques are being developed on the basis of financial theories – pecking order, trade-off or agency theory – that are consistent with the goal of maximising shareholders' interests. They are not, therefore, specifically designed to create value for all stakeholders. Yet our theory may complement rather than conflict with existing cash-holding techniques, for it seeks to create models that maximise value for all the interest groups involved, including shareholders. From the point of view of cash management, this approach relies on the premise that all the interest groups (both internal and external) affect and are affected by short-term financial decisions and hence by liquidity flows.

Cash holdings: The right level

The main purpose of cash management is to ensure that companies have the cash they need at the right moment, the optimum level being the minimum necessary; moreover, studies so far have concluded that companies must main a positive cash level. In this sense it is preferable to hold cash than resort to external finance that costs more because of information asymmetry between companies and outside investors (Myers and Majluf, 1984), problems of agency costs such as underinvestment and asset substitution (Myers, 1977; Jensen and Meckling, 1976) and transaction costs and other financial constraints. Managers must therefore determine optimum cash levels by minimising the cost of obtaining external finance on imperfect capital markets. However, holding cash or its equivalent also raises potential problems. Agency conflicts between shareholders and managers may be reduced if the company has high free cash-flow levels (Jensen, 1986), for managers can put their own interests before those of shareholders. It should also be recognised that excessive conservatism has disadvantages of its own, such as the opportunity cost of holding assets that yield little or no return. Cash holdings create an opportunity cost for the company, for they produce a lower return than that yielded by the company's productive investments; at the same time, the company may incur transaction costs resulting from the purchase or sale of financial assets, and also suffer tax disadvantages.

Are corporate cash-management techniques ethical?

In general, cash transactions between a company and the operators around it should take place under conditions of equality; however, because of power and information asymmetry, agreements are reached under conditions of inequality which are justifiable in terms of contract theory but run counter to the interests of one of the parties. Cash management is based on contract theory (Coase, 1937), in which various parties reach free agreements, under the terms of the law, on the times at which debts arising from various economic transactions will be paid. In theory there should be no ethical problem with this approach, as long as the assumptions of equality and perfect capital markets hold true; in practice, however, inequalities between the parties, such as power and information asymmetry and opportunistic behaviour, as well as market failures and opportunity costs, mean that the agreements reached may not be optimal for one – or indeed either – of the parties.

Nevertheless, interest in ethical cash management is not confined (although this would be sufficient) to a theory of equality in commercial relations or in stakeholders' interests. Thus, and given the role played by cash holdings in cases of insolvency, selfish cash management – as an ethical approach would suggest – may be a key contributing factor to bankruptcy and its various adverse consequences (unpaid bills, dismissals, broken contracts and so on).

In Spain, for example, the current unsustainable short-term cash position has led to mass company closures, doubling the number of unemployed to four million. In the United States 2.6 million jobs were lost in 2008, a figure not seen since 1945. In Britain some 50 businesses close each day, and the situation is no better in Latin America, where unemployment is rocketing and increasingly unmanageable. Specifically, the ILO's Regional Office in Lima has reported that in 2009 the impact of the economic crisis will, for the first time since 2003, raise the average annual unemployment rate to between 7.9% and 8.3%, which means that 2.5 million more people will be out of work. Liquidity problems are increasing in all countries, and this is one of the factors that are causing businesses to close in such alarming numbers.

A more ethical approach

The financial crisis and liquidity problems are connected, which is why the current crisis has highlighted and, disturbingly, helped tone down the worst predictions about opportunistic behaviour when it comes to cash-management strategy. However, and not only at times of recession and economic crisis, consideration may be given to a more ethical approach to cash holdings, one that is based on collaboration between the various players and may (at least in theory) produce the desired optimum level of cash – namely mutual cash management based on trust. Such an approach is justified not only in purely financial terms, for it makes cash management easier, but also in ethical terms, for it benefits all those involved and ultimately contributes to the common good. Financially, collaboration between players would lead to debts being paid at mutually agreed times and would reduce financial risks and transaction costs, allowing players to optimise their economic and financial results; and, socially, it would cushion the adverse impact of monetary imbalances, such as unpaid wages, late payment of suppliers, loss of customers and – ultimately – insolvency.

Mutual cash management based on trust

Relationships between economic players and groups with an interest in the company must be analysed and managed carefully. The financial relationship between a company and the players that interact with it will depend on the nature of the various interest groups; thus the company will have different relationships with its suppliers, its customers, the government, the banks, its employees, its shareholders and the community as a whole. One strategy would be to identify the company's cash operations and then which players are involved, in order to examine their repercussions and so make multilateral decisions that benefit all concerned. Strategic cash operations will be long-term, but the specific decisions will be short-term, because at any given moment we would be talking about cash holdings.

This will require a change of financial culture so that each company's cash holdings are henceforth determined by the interest groups, since these will affect and be affected by the decisions the company makes; but at any given moment our starting point should be the operations rather than the stakeholders, in order to ensure that every decision regarding cash is viable.

A potential conflict

Relationships between the various players involved have been studied in the existing literature on cash holdings. This shows, for example, that there is a relationship between companies' shareholders and their cash holdings. Dittmar et al. (2003) found that, in countries where shareholders' rights are more fully protected, companies' cash holdings are lower, although both variables are related to the level of development of capital markets in the country concerned. Other writers (Pinkowitz et al., 2006; Kalcheva and Lins, 2007) likewise suggest that shareholders look for managers who will reduce cash holdings. Jensen (1986) also points to this potential conflict between shareholders and managers, for an increase in cash holdings will increase managers' power at the expense of that of shareholders. This implies a potential conflict between shareholders and managers over cash holdings, since these may benefit either the former or the latter in the traditional agency dilemma between principals and agents described in agency theory.

Thus, from the point of view of both shareholder theory and stakeholder theory, there may be a clash of interests when it comes to cash holdings. The specific difference is that in the former case (shareholders) we are basically dealing with a problem of governance, whereas in the latter case (stakeholders) we are dealing with a cash-holding problem. Shareholders' rights, agents' possible interests and all the other stakeholders' legitimate rights and interests must also be taken into account.

This conflict matters more than any other cash conflict, for it affects not only cash management but also governance, and so the way in which it is solved may determine how cash conflicts with other stakeholders are solved via the company's financial policies.

However, this should not be the case in a descriptive approach, for financial policies should be aimed at all stakeholders; but, from a legal point of view, the selection and supervision of CEOs clearly rests with shareholders.

One must wonder what real scope they have to exercise those rights (Boatright, 2008), since in many cases real power is in the hands of the company's management.

Pursuing a joint interest

The proposed solution to this conflict, in which clashes of interest and lack of trust between parties lead to increased costs, is collaboration between stakeholders. This will mean pursuing a joint interest that yields greater value for every interest group by lowering transaction costs and reducing risks. It is based on the Mutual Trust Perspective (MTP) proposed by Dees and Cramton (1991): it is unfair to require an individual to take a significant risk or incur a significant cost out of respect for the moral rights of others unless the individual has sufficient reason to trust those others to incur the same risk or cost. This effectively states that "a party will only incur significant costs out of respect for the other party's interests or moral rights if it is satisfied that the other party would make the same sacrifice in the same situation" – an approach based on Kant's categorical imperative, which is often rendered as "do not do unto others as you would not have them do unto you", in other words avoid doing anything that you would not like another economic player or interest group to do to you.

When seeking to establish a mutual cash holding relationship for purposes of cash management, we must take due account of two factors: the expectation that the other party will respond, and the cost. Trust between organisations is not just a decision-making issue; it increases or decreases on the basis of continuing relationships over a period of time. It will therefore be easier if the first step is taken by the party that has more power and fewer costs, or to which a breach of trust would be less costly.

This means that it is easier to establish a mutual cash-holding relationship if this is proposed by the party or stakeholder with more power, provided that the cost of a possible breakdown in this relationship of trust is not too great. Furthermore, if the relationship of trust is to continue over a period of time, the arrangement must have clear benefits for both parties.

The proper balance between interests

A company cannot be conceived of in isolation from its stakeholders, since, aside from the company's virtual existence as a legal entity, in practice it can only be viewed as a web of relationships between its various stakeholders (whether in the broad or narrow sense). The company must therefore take account of the interests of one or more stakeholders. The problem is how to strike a proper balance between their various interests.

This balance is examined from the point of view of corporate ethics, which attempts to determine what that balance should be and how it can be achieved. A number of problems arise here, such as how to justify potential stakeholders' rights, what scope agents really have for arbitration between interest groups' conflicting demands, and relationships with non-stakeholders (i.e. interest groups that do not directly affect or are not directly affected by the company's goals, but may affect or be affected by them indirectly or at some point in the future). In the current crisis, these problems are being looked at carefully.

However, it should be borne in mind that, within companies, most players' direct or indirect interests are monetary in nature. In general, and aside from other psychological and professional components, stakeholders' legitimate interests almost always involve increasing value and earning money.

Up to now, most publications on the subject have explicitly or implicitly focused on management and conflicts over how value is shared out; however, the monetary realisation of value is undoubtedly a key factor in many conflicts between supposedly legitimate interests.

Such conflicts may be either internal or external. Internal conflicts involve stakeholders who are legally and permanently linked to the company, the main groups being shareholders and employees. External conflicts involve those who are linked to the company contractually or operationally, but whose connection with the company is contracted and undetermined, e.g. suppliers, customers, financiers or the government. In all these cases, in theory, the parties may have conflicting interests regarding payment dates – debtors will benefit from late payment and creditors from early payment.

Mutual cash holding

The solution to this conflict may be coercion (a position of strength based on power asymmetry), for example when a shopping centre only pays its suppliers after 90 days, or when the government requires VAT to be paid quarterly. Another solution may be negotiation, for example when stakeholders mutually agree on a payment date. Finally, the solution may be a unilateral concession, for example when a seller finances a customer by only billing him after six months. Whether they involve coercion, negotiation or concession, all such solutions have one feature in common – they solely take account of the stakeholders' own cash management.

The proposal we are making here is that the various stakeholders should also take account of their partner's cash holdings, in order to arrive at a solution that is most beneficial to both. Although this may seem an impossible approach to cash holdings, it is already starting to be introduced in connection with account management using new technologies and joint invoice management between financial institutions and companies, banks' electronic invoices or even factoring and confirming. The extension of such techniques may lead to mutual cash holding, and to a financial culture and financial techniques based on mutual trust, yielding benefits and satisfactory results for all concerned.

The timing of debt payment

Clearly, the timing of debt payment is a fundamental management issue. In fact this is a basic assumption in financial theory, which pays considerable attention to cash management or cash holdings and treats these as key tools in the running of companies. Paradoxically, however, financial ethics has paid little or no attention to the timing of debt payment, which is treated as a purely technical issue. What this means is that selfish corporate behaviour, based on optimisation of one's own cash holdings, is taken for granted.

In a perfect market, in which the strengths of the various stakeholders are in equilibrium, contracts may be expected to produce fair agreements that benefit both parties; in practice, however, the market is imperfect and there is evident information and power asymmetry between the players, so that acceptation of the principle of optimising one's own cash holdings turns selfish behaviour (which exploits asymmetry) into a morally acceptable approach and violates the generally accepted Kantian principle of ethical behaviour between companies.

Even though finance has not developed with ethical behaviour in mind, there is a general consensus that it is unfair for someone to pay a supplier several years after the service has been provided, unless the agreement between the two parties makes the mutual benefits of such an arrangement clear. In itself, such a restriction on delayed payment may imply the existence of ethical criteria of fairness that extend beyond purely contractual requirements. In this connection we may note the Spanish government's decision to restrict delayed payment by major shopping centres.

The approach we propose here goes well beyond the issue of timing of debt payment, or the development of rules, standards and guidelines on how best to manage this in relations between stakeholders. Indeed, in our view, that would mean taking selfish behaviour for granted as a means of interaction, on the assumption that companies, or the various stakeholders, must always seek to maximise their own cash-management interests at the expense of those of their partners. The limits now being imposed are simply designed to ensure that the existing asymmetry does not create unfair situations for the weaker party.

A number of comments need to be made here. On the one hand, negative practices need to be restricted on both ethical and economic grounds; on the other, it would be interesting to know whether the recent recommendations and legal restrictions are in fact motivated by ethical considerations. However, the main contribution of ethics must be to try and change the selfish attitudes on which financial relationships between companies and interest groups have hitherto been based.

We therefore believe it is vital to replace conflict-based selfish approaches with ones that seek to optimise stakeholders' long-term benefits, on the basis of mutual trust. This would not only be more appropriate from an ethical point of view, but would also be more beneficial for stakeholders and for society as a whole. Mutual cash holding by companies or stakeholders with conflicting interests would thus yield greater long-term benefits for stakeholders and society.

A change in attitude is needed

This paper proposes a theoretical mutual cash-holding model based on trust, which is fostered by power asymmetry. Mutual cash holding could produce more beneficial results for all the stakeholders that influence or are influenced by companies.

Existing cash-holding techniques and cash-management models are designed to improve the financial position of the company that applies and introduces them. They thus focus on maximising shareholders' profits and rely on players behaving selfishly. Since no specific account is taken of other stakeholders, value is not generated for all of them. This paper makes clear that cash management is a key factor in the relationship and equilibrium between the various stakeholders and their interests. It is therefore necessary to ensure that cash management satisfies stakeholders' interests, which may conflict in the short term, in such a balanced manner that they converge in the long term. In the long term, mutual cash holding by stakeholders will produce benefits for all of them, by increasing solvency and liquidity, and for society as a whole, by reducing insolvency. It must also be borne in mind that this approach can only succeed if it is introduced by the stronger partner in the relationship.

Its theoretical acceptance will ultimately depend on a change of attitude towards cooperation and the elimination of information asymmetry and of barriers to mutual trust that prevent people from accepting the obvious before even considering how the system might work.

Bibliography

Boatright, J.R., 2008. *Ethics in Finance*, Malden: Blackwell.

Coase, R.H., 1937. "The Nature of the Firm", in: *Economica 4 (16)*, November 1937.

Dees, J.G./ Cramton, P.C., 1991. "Shrewd bargaining on the moral frontier: toward a theory of morality in practice", in: *Business Ethics Quarterly 1 (2).*
Dittmar, A. *et al.*, 2003. "International Corporate Governance and Corporate Cash Holdings", in: *Journal of Financial and Quantitative Analysis 38 (1).*
Gitman, J. *et al.*, 1976. *Principles of Managerial Finance*, New York, Harper and Row, Inc.
Jensen, M.C., 1986. "Agency costs of free cash flow, corporate finance and takeovers", in: *American Economic Review 6.*
Jensen, M.C./ Meckling, W.H., 1976. "Theory of the firm: managerial behaviour, agency costs and ownership structure", in: *Journal of Financial Economics 3 (4).*
Kalcheva, I./ Lins, K.V., 2007. "International Evidence on Cash Holdings and Expected Managerial Agency Problems", in: *Review of Financial Studies 20 (4).*
Myers, S.C., 1977. "Determinants of Corporate Borrowing", in: *Journal of Financial Economics 5 (2).*
Myers, S.C./ Majluf, N.S., 1984. "Corporate financing and investment decisions when firms have information that investors do not have", in: *Journal of Financial Economics 13 (2).*
Pinkowitz, L. *et al.*, 2006. "Do firms in countries with poor protection of investor rights hold more cash?" in: *Journal of Finance 61 (6).*

3

ETHICS AND ORDER IN THE DISORDERLY WORLD OF FINANCE

Elise Pellerin and Marie Casimiro

When prosperity reigns, and the financial markets seem intent on zooming into outer space, the world of Finance happily locks itself away in an ivory tower. But in the sort of crisis period that we are living through now, society feels thoroughly contaminated and claims the right to scrutinise more closely the behaviour of those who control the flow of finance. Declarations, accusations, and legislative activity come thick and fast. And it's then that we are reminded that the circulation of money entails political consequences… and that it ought to follow ethical rules.

Subjected to a media trial, the court of public opinion and accusations from politicians, we suddenly realise that the discourse on ethics emanating from the financial milieu over the past few years has centred on issues such as the carbon balance, renewable energy or recycling concerns that are often far removed from the core issues of business and enterprise – most of all the issues facing companies working in the financial sector! Even though the financial community has finally begun to address matters of social responsibility and sustainable development, it has managed to avoid the really troublesome subjects – first and foremost how to measure its own responsibility… and the ethical demands that result from it.

Ethics or morality?

It is financial market players who are first and foremost confronted with ethical concerns. By players we mean both individuals and the companies that employ them, and beyond these the global structure of the financial world that sets the framework for their behaviour. In order to be able to propose a solution that will foster ethics in finance, we need first of all to decipher this formula and identify what's gone wrong.

Today, the term "ethics" is used loosely in a variety of ways. In common parlance, "ethics" and "ethical" are more or less synonymous with "morals" and "moral" but as a sort of toned-down, softer version of this concept, which might sound altogether too austere, guilt-inducing and Judeo-Christian to some ears. Those who study philosophy know, however, that morals and ethics have nothing to do with each other. Whereas morality lays down a prescriptive system, based on the distinction between what is right and what is wrong, ethics addresses the rules of one's behaviour (ethos) in action. Morality tells you what to do and what to think at any time and under any circumstances. Ethics tries to define what you are able to do starting out from a cocktail of freedoms and constraints.

The domain of ethics is not therefore about distinguishing between Good and Evil, but defining correct and prudent behaviour in a given context – what Aristotle in his *Nicomachean Ethics* (Book II, Chapter 6) called *arêtè*. This Greek word is usually translated as virtue, but not in the sense of the purity of the frightened virgin. It is used to signify the strength of a man who is able to control his passions; that is to say it is not an end in itself, but a means to an end. Ethics, in contrast with morality, does not seek to make Good prevail, or to foster noble sentiments.

It tries to order action in such a way that it is efficient, by means of virtue, which basically means strength.

Ethics: a guide to action

In this sense, ethics is as much about the individual as about society. A well-ordered personal life is a guarantee of happiness, a well-ordered society a guarantee of justice. Ethics has right action – what is orderly – as its objective, not good. The first conclusion from this definition is that ethics is effective, valuable in the true sense of the word. It is productive and adds value. The demands of ethics seem therefore from the outset more likely to prove themselves than those of morality, with which they are often equated. As the famous Liberal maxim has it: we should set more store by a man's self-interest than by his benevolence.

The state of financial intermediation

The second point we wish to underline is that ethics implies a striving towards order. It is never final, never perfect. We might also respond here to Mandeville's thesis – that private vices can generate public benefit. His Fable of the Bees, 1713-1724, recounts the decadence of a swarm of bees. Having been a thriving community based on deceit and vice, the bees condemn their own behaviour and become honest and virtuous. Their society collapses and dies. Mankind is in constant tension between virtuous order and the chaos of passion, and ethics is precisely this search for order.

When we talk about the ethics of finance or financial ethics – which comes down to more or less the same thing – we are not therefore dreaming of finance at the service of good but thinking of well-ordered finance.

Let us just be clear about what we understand by finance. It is the systemic organisation of flows and exchanges of goods and value between people – by definition a means of intermediation between resources and projects. Finance has no moral flag to fly – though the resources used and the projects to be financed may have a moral tinge. Finance does however have to do with ethics, as its goal is to channel resources to projects that in turn will create new resources. If valuable resources are to be channelled into the most promising projects, finance must be well-ordered.

On the other hand, the purpose of ensuring that abundant resources are distributed is not miserly and sterile accumulation in a strong-box. These resources should be a vector for common wealth. That is basically what finance aims to achieve. And the need for ethics is all the greater, given that the purpose of finance is to organise exchanges between individuals, but with a collective goal that is closely related to hedonism – to provide material well-being by encouraging wealth creation.

Basically then, finance has to do with the idea of exchange, of trade, upon which the notion of financial flow is based. Trade takes place when two people driven by two complementary needs agree on the value of an exchange. This presupposes a relationship of trust and recognition of interdependence within a common structure in order to create a world. Our entire human history has depended on such progress.

We have taken the trouble to define our terms here in order to demonstrate that finance does not really require any moralising, i.e. does not need to have rules of moral conduct imposed on it from outside. If we want finance to be ethical, then surely the first requirement is that it should be true to its own vocation as an intermediary of value?

The distortion of ends and means

If finance starts to believe that it is an end in itself and begins to indulge in self-worship, this will undermine its ethics. When it loses sight of the broader horizon, that of common well-being, which financial activity is really all about, and starts to come up with elaborate intellectual arguments that enable it to think of itself as a mechanical process that produces wealth all by itself, then finance becomes detached from the real world and constructs a sort of parallel universe that ends up imploding – before rising re-born from the ashes once more, but that's another story.

One of the causes of this tendency to confuse ends with means probably lies in the vast multiplication of transactions that has turned financial activities in these last few years into a concentrated and centralised – almost industrial – process in which the means of production are the traders' brains and the product is money.

Finance is therefore losing its intermediary status and the virtue we mentioned a moment ago as fundamental in ethics finds itself inverted: from a force in the service of a cause, it is becoming a force looking to find its objective in its own existence, money producing money. Its virtue is then no longer a force for action. No longer aiming to master passions, it glorifies them.

It is the triumph of pride, the *hubris* of which Greek tragedy has much to say, that leads those whom it possesses into excess: ever bigger, ever more complex, more, always more.

Lack of ethics, lack of thought

Might this turning-upside-down of values perhaps be due to a lack of thinking? Intelligence might well be the primary tool in finance, but in the technical field not in terms of consciousness. In the same way that manufacturing industry, driven by competition to unceasingly improve its productivity, gradually harnesses the strength of the worker to that of the machine and ends up making man an adjunct to the machine, the financial mechanics, which have grown way beyond the volume of real trade, begin to get the upper hand over human intelligence, which thus becomes a mere production tool.

The reason we are interested in this whole question of thinking is that what we are trying to do in this paper is to bring finance back within the domain of human responsibility. Now, if you make widespread use of a kind of brainpower that works without thought, without looking at the consequences, without questioning itself at all, this is obviously going to pose a problem as regards responsibility. We have an ethical question relating to the behaviour of financial market players. The kind of brainpower that the financial sector calls for is not required to bring under control the technical processes that have already been developed but to develop them even further, to plunge in and gather together those ultra-fine threads and weave them into an inextricable, delicate, fragile lacework of figures and algorithms. People are expected to apply their intelligence, but not to think. Now, any extreme division of tasks, a characteristic of the industrialisation of processes, where an individual does not see what he's producing, tends to lead him or her to lose all sense of responsibility. And we're already close to that situation in those areas of the financial world where what is produced is something non-material. The individual is then no longer really a stakeholder in terms of conscience; he is a cog in the wheel of an industry in which his intelligence is engaged but not his mind. Just carrying out this kind of job can lead to a divided self, where a sort of disconnect comes about between the intellectual capability that is required of a person and the need s/he feels to think for him/herself. This need is pushed aside, and all too often the person then loses the physical and mental capacity for this type of thinking, since the mind is entirely taken up with extremely demanding short-term concerns, which require permanent attention.

The first step in any initiative to foster ethics in the financial world must, we believe, be of a structural nature. A solution must be found to the status of the individual, who is caught up in a mechanism that makes use of his or her brainpower without calling for any exercise of personal responsibility towards either one's working environment or the common good. In our view, in order to solve this problem, we need to create a new framework, which would attach importance to ethics and make ethics a must in all financial activities.

We also invite you to imagine a sphere of activity where people would simultaneously see themselves as stakeholders in the world of finance and in society, where everyone's interests would be safeguarded and financial ethics guaranteed. This would mean establishing an Order of Finance Professionals. We believe that this is the best way to inculcate a professional ethic. The Order would be responsible for drawing up a charter of professional ethics, monitoring its application and imposing sanctions on any members of the Order who deviated from the rules.

Inclusion of "non-financial" cultures

In practical terms, the Order of Finance Professionals would operate at national level. It would be divided into distinct chambers representing the various segments of the profession: portfolio managers, financial analysts, hedge fund managers, etc. As each segment has its own constraints, objectives and risks, and even sometimes differing interests – for instance, the lending business and portfolio/asset management do not have a great deal in common – each chamber would be organised in a relatively autonomous manner, with its own representatives elected by its own members. On the other hand, in order to avoid excessive lobbying by each individual arm of the profession, the representatives of each of the different chambers would enjoy the right to be informed about the demands being made by the other chambers.

The Order would be governed by a representative council composed of elected representatives of the various professional chambers. This council of specialists could be supplemented by persons with other types of skills: bringing in independents from outside the financial culture might be a second way to guard against lobbying. The idea here would be to co-opt on to the Order's governing body academics that do not have any specific training in the financial field, but are recognised in philosophy studies, sociology, history, law, etc. This diversification of expertise within the Order would encourage the airing of criticisms and points of view that plead for the common good. For example, philosophy experts specialising in the theory of ethics or logical analysis could be of great help in understanding the cognitive systems underlying certain types of behaviour and a professional historian, with his knowledge of the main trends in our history, the various stages of human progress and past crises, might be able to see more clearly what is going on and explain the new upheavals our society is facing.

On the other hand we do not think it would be appropriate to appoint any government representatives to the council; the Order should mark a clear distance from state bodies such as the AMF (France's financial markets regulatory authority) but should of course nevertheless dialogue and cooperate with such bodies.

Procedures for joining the Order

Entry to the financial professions would be regulated in two stages. As a first step the Order would recruit candidates on the basis of a non-financial examination, whose purpose would be to assess their intellectual maturity, their ability to adapt and to reason for themselves. The Order would at this stage verify that each candidate espoused the idea of an ethical basis for finance. This selection method, intentionally non-technical, would serve to open the profession to a diverse range of applicants, both in terms of their academic training and their intellectual profile, thus helping to avoid bias based on a sort of sectarian elitism.

Specific professional training would then be carried out internally, and each recruit would have to pass an examination in order to obtain a licence to practice the profession from the chamber that s/he was applying to join. This is somewhat along the lines of what happens in the legal profession for advocates pleading at the bar and is in the spirit of what the AMF is trying to set up in France. The new system of examining knowledge – targeting the key functions carried out at investment services providers, especially portfolio management companies – was put in place by a decree of 30 January 2009, amending the AMF's general regulation, entering into force on 1 July 2010. To help candidates prepare for this examination, which would cover both technical and ethical matters – to which we shall return – universities would create, in partnership with the Order, appropriate training modules.

Candidates who pass the examination would be accepted into the Order at a highly symbolic ceremony designed to make the recruit aware that he now belonged to a group, with close links between his professional life and the chamber. In fact, following the creation of a professional Order, financiers will no longer be seen by their clients merely as individuals or as employees of such and such a company, but also as members of a professional chamber whose reputation affects that of all its members.

This solidarity phenomenon whose source we have just explained led French stock brokers in the nineteenth century to set up a joint guarantee fund. The Paris Bourse was the scene of an unfortunate speculation on interest rates in the autumn of 1819. In order to avoid a systemic crisis, the Stock Brokers Association took out a loan from a group of bankers. The association set up a joint account to receive the repayments that each broker was expected to make towards reimbursing the loan.[1]

Solidarity and risk sharing

Three years later, when the debts were entirely expunged, the Association debated whether to maintain this guarantee fund. In the interval, experience had demonstrated the advantages of this fund. "It gave the Association a force and power that exerted a positive influence on public

[1] For further details, see Lazuech, Gilles/ Moulévrier, Pascale, *Contributions à une sociologie des conduites économiques,* Paris: L'Harmattan press, 2006.

lending in general" (Lazuech and Moulévrier, 2006). So the Association decided (unanimously, the study underlines) that the joint account would be continued.

One might easily envisage a similar system today: each professional chamber would set up its own guarantee fund. A tax would be levied on every transaction carried out by a member of the chamber and would be paid into the fund. This tax might also be set in proportion to the risk of the transaction. For example, the methods set out in the Basel II accord for calculating regulatory capital might be applied here. The Basel II rules apply to all financial products without exception. The riskier the product, as assessed in accordance with the rules, the more capital the bank is required to hold. The ratio of capital to risk assets must be higher than 8%, i.e. for every hundred euro invested, the bank must have at least eight in its accounts.

This would help to improve balance sheet transparency by the simple fact that every transaction – whether on- or off-balance sheet – would have to be reported to the Order. The information reported to the Order would mention only the volume/value of the transaction, for obvious reasons of competition and confidentiality. In addition, the principle of a variable commission taking account of the balance sheet status of the entity carrying out the transaction could serve to prevent any financial institution from taking excessive risks. Such a system would encourage members to practice efficient self-regulation in order to limit the risk of a financial institution going bankrupt.

Guarantee fund

The primary task of the fund would of course be to finance the Order's expenses, including general administration, human resources, recruitment tests, continuous training, etc. One might also envisage that the Order would help to promote academic research into financial ethics by granting bursaries and supporting conferences.

The fund might also be used in more exceptional circumstances. We are thinking here of the scandals that arise almost every day in the financial news and cast a shadow of doubt over the collective ethics of finance professionals. The fund would insure all transactions – including over-the-counter deals – that today are by no means exempt from counterparty risk, extending the concept of the indemnification tribunal that already exists for organised markets. The fund would step in for the defaulting counterparty, with the primary mission of safeguarding professionals from any actionable misdemeanours committed by their colleagues.

Drafting a code of ethics

Secondly, if one of the members were to be judged liable for his/her clients' financial loss, the Order could, within the limits of its means, contribute to indemnifying the victim. This would, to a degree, help to uphold the honour of the profession. We should be clear that the Order would not take over liability for the actions of the financial professional involved, who would incur professional sanctions from the Order and perhaps, in addition, penal sanctions.

The role of the fund being to intervene if the Order were to fail in its mission of surveillance over the ethical conduct of its members, this would therefore mean that each chamber would draw up a body of rules and would enforce its members' compliance with these rules. The rules would be drafted in such a way that they could be referred to directly when sanctions are imposed. The rules would be based on a formal code of ethics.

The code would be drafted by the financial professionals themselves via the representative process, which we believe would in itself serve to strengthen the effectiveness of these standards. In fact, for the citizens of many Western countries today, the law no longer has the same coercive effect as in the past. For the last few years we have witnessed the development of what the lawyers call soft law. The increasing sources of law, the complexity of the terms in which legal texts are couched and not least the fact that laws, which in the past applied equally to everyone, now very often only apply to a specific category of people – all these factors combine to make the individual feel less bound by the rule of law.

Under these circumstances, our societies are now relying more and more on the notion of contractual relationships between individuals. A rule that has been agreed under a signed contract therefore carries more weight and, strangely enough, now often seems more binding than the law to which it is subject. So if we want the new financial organisation we desire to create to be as efficient as possible, it would be more appropriate to use a means that can convey to the finance professionals this feeling of contractual choice.

Controls and sanctions

This contractual dimension is necessary but still insufficient to ensure that professionals, of whatever ilk, comply with binding standards. A code of ethics drafted by a professional Order that has received government authorisation to apply it would enjoy much wider legal force. This is the model for the code of ethics for the medical profession, for example. Recognised by formal government decree, and enshrined in health and social codes, it forms an integral part of our legal system. For this reason we recommend that the drafting process for the code of ethics for financial professions follow the same logic as the code of medical ethics.

So once the distinct professional chambers have drawn up the code of ethics, the resulting text would be submitted to the authorities, to the Council of State, and finally to the government. Each party would be responsible for checking compliance with regulations and laws already in force, and would have the opportunity to make amendments. Finally the code would be signed off by the Prime Minister and published in the *Journal Officiel* (France's official record of new legislation).

Sanctions imposed by the Order on the basis of the code could go as far as barring a member from exercising his profession or entail measures that would tarnish the reputation of any professionals implicated. Such effective and occasionally severe sanctions can only be imposed by a "legal person" – the Order in this case – that is directly affected by individuals' compliance or non-compliance with the code.

A return to order?

It may seem daring to suggest going back to a form of corporatism to help the financial industry recover its balance, given that corporatism was widely used and developed by totalitarian systems and governments with fascist tendencies not so very long ago – in the twentieth century. And while it may seem easier to set up this kind of model in countries where chambers of stock dealers used to exist once upon a time, it is perhaps these countries that will prove most reluctant to accept reforms perceived as a return to order.

Paradoxically, countries with a more liberal tradition, having greatly suffered from the absence of regulation, might find this solution a persuasive means of both preserving the financial profession and safeguarding the public interest, without any excessive recourse to state intervention. The measures we have put forward are not in the least revolutionary: some have already been proposed and passed into law, while other practical measures have already stood the test of time.

Whatever the fears and apprehensions that arise when the word "corporatism" comes up, we believe that it is possible to impose a form of positive corporatism (to borrow the expression from Professor Gérard Lafay) that would guarantee both the performance and ethical competitiveness of the financial sector – for the greater good of society and of finance professionals as well.

4

ETHICS OR BUST: BEYOND COMPLIANCE AND GOOD MARKETING

Clare Payne

Australia's national dictionary defines ethics as "a system of moral principles, by which human actions and proposals may be judged good or bad, or right or wrong". Other definitions include concepts such as values relating to human conduct, principles of right conduct, rules or standards or a theory of moral values.

Popular understandings of ethics are more likely to include such notions as trust, integrity, honesty, social responsibility and doing the right thing.

Whilst most of us have an understanding of what ethics is, and believe in the importance of ethical conduct in the cooperative functioning of society, difficulty is often met when determining agreed standards of ethical behaviour for the various complex situations in which individuals and organisations find themselves.

It seems that society's ethical goalposts are constantly shifting and this presents particular challenges to the business world and the finance industry.

Laying the foundation for ethical work cultures

Broadly, the finance industry refers to organisations that deal with the management of money. More specifically, this includes banks, investment banks, insurance companies, credit card companies, stock brokerages, private equity and hedge funds.

Measured by earnings, financial services are the largest industry category in the world. The industry represents 26.1% of the market capitalisation of the Standard & Poor's Global 1200. Worldwide profits in the publicly quoted banking sector were approximately $100 billion in 2005. Such statistics highlight the significance of the finance industry to the world economy.[1]

By its very nature – involving money – the finance industry and its economic performance is susceptible to quantifiable analysis and measurement. Historically, the success of the finance industry has been judged by profits. Increasingly however, society is seeking to judge the finance industry's performance and role in society according to broader criteria, such as its social and environmental impact and ethical conduct.

Herein lies the challenge for the finance industry. How does a complex and constantly evolving industry that relies on measurable outcomes to judge performance, satisfy society's ethical expectations of it? This is particularly the case when society – itself resistant to cohesive consensus and susceptible to changing social climates – is incapable of articulating what its ethical expectations are.

---

[1] In 2012 the financial services industry represents 18.4% of the market capitalisation of the Standard & Poor's Global 1200. This is despite the global financial crisis of the late 2000s, which saw a series of corporate collapses including Allco Finance Group and Storm Financial in Australia and Lehman Brothers and Fannie Mae and Freddie Mac in the USA. Again, the response has been largely regulatory with the Dodd-Frank Wall Street Reform and Consumer Protection Act (USA, 2010) and The Bribery Act (UK, 2010). The disparity between CEO and workers' pay has also continued, with the Occupy Movement adopting the "We are the 99%"' slogan in response to evident and unceasing inequality.

What is clear is that the finance industry is currently failing to meet the public's expectations of ethical conduct. This matters, because the finance industry constantly deals in public and private funds and needs the trust and confidence of the public to do so effectively and efficiently. As A. Persaud and J. Plender (2007) state: "If the public is to be persuaded of the legitimacy of wealth creation, trust in business and finance has to be rebuilt and a more robust ethical climate established".

Ethical lapses

Whilst society might find it difficult to define exactly what constitutes ethical behaviour, it seems that ethical lapses are easier to identify.

There has been a range of examples of ethical lapses as the catalyst for significant corporate collapses in the corporate sector since the new millennium, from Enron (US, 2001) to Adelphia (US, 2001), HIH (Australia, 2001), One.Tel (Australia, 2001) WorldCom (US, 2002), Tyco (US, 2002) and Parmalat (Italy, 2003).

Among the ethical lapses experienced by the companies listed above are excessive compensation, misstatements of revenues and operations, improper identification and management of risks, conflicts of interests and fiduciary failure by Board.

The raft of ethical lapses identified as contributing to these and other collapses has served to put corporate behaviour on the public's radar. However, despite such high profile cases as Enron, ethical failures continue to plague the corporate sphere and the finance industry is no exception.

In 2004 there was a $360 million foreign currency trading scandal at National Australia Bank, followed by Marsh and McClennan paying $850 million to settle an investigation into bid-rigging that cheated its policy holders, a $100 million settlement by Merrill Lynch for tainted investment advice favouring large investment banks and Morgan Stanley was fined $2.9 million by NASD for trading violations in 2006.

Regulatory response

In response to these ethical lapses we have seen a proliferation of prescriptive legislation, governance codes and compliance measures.

In the United States the Sarbanes-Oxley Act 2002 (SOX) was implemented as well as comprehensive New York Stock Exchange Listing Rules. In the United Kingdom the *Tyson Report on Recruitment and Development of Non-Executive Directors* (2003) was commissioned and a *Combined Code on Corporate Governance* 2003 established. Australia responded by implementing CLERP 9 Amendments (2004) and various Corporate Governance Codes. Singapore amended its Companies Act (2002) and revised its Corporate Governance Code in 2005.

There is now a commonly held view, within the finance industry, that the SOX is too prescriptive, to the point that it restricts and stifles the way the industry does business. Already organisations are circumventing these legislative restrictions by re-listing and having their equity capital raised in other locations where they can operate under less draconian regulatory regimes.

Others believe that the regulatory reaction has actually served to exacerbate the problem by creating a risk management culture rather than an ethics based culture. Rather than view regulatory measures as a minimum baseline for governance, it is evident that compliance with corporate governance guidelines is actually the ultimate ethical goal for many organisations (CREDO, 2005).

Whilst regulation of the finance industry by formal regulatory mechanisms (self and government) is essential, it is not enough. Legislation cannot address every possibility and every eventuality of human behaviour, especially considering the complexity of modern business and finance. One thing is known, where there is opportunity, money will find a way to finance it.

Financial products are increasingly difficult to understand, especially in new derivative markets where financial institutions trade in instruments such as collateralised debt obligations, credit default swaps, exotic payoff functions and hybrid (multi asset class) securities. These new markets thus pose exceptionally difficult challenges for lawmakers, regulators and gatekeepers such as auditors and rating agencies, who find it hard to keep up with rapid financial innovation.

A comprehensive, constantly developing and responsive regulatory system needs to be one part of corporate governance, with the essential component being a strong ethical foundation. An ethical basis to the operation of finance is not a constraint or limitation on financial agents, but rather the condition that the financial system can exist at all.

The finance industry needs to recognise the shortcomings of legislation and regulation, and acknowledge the complex grey areas where individuals, in both their business and personal lives, have to make difficult decisions that have ethical dimensions.

Persistence of unethical work cultures

Despite an increase in regulation, unethical work cultures persist in the finance industry. Whilst there has been an increase in references to ethical behaviour in company mission statements it is less clear that companies are actually weaving ethical considerations into the day-to-day conduct of their businesses.

The $360 million foreign currency trading losses at the National Australia Bank (NAB) provide a clear example of this lack of correlation between published statements and actual practice. John Stewart, NAB's current Managing Director and CEO admits that "while the National had an agreed set of values, people were not held accountable and values were not reflected in the way people were assessed. Culture change programmes were voluntary and there was a lack of visible and consistent leadership in this area. This led to a focus on achieving short-term profits without regard to the way in which this was done".

Aligning values and culture statements with actual practice is an ethical challenge facing the finance industry. As Australian philosopher Peter Singer (1979) states, "Ethics is not an ideal system which is all very noble but no good in practice. The reverse of this is closer to the truth: an ethical judgment that is no good in practice must suffer from a theoretical defect as well, for the whole point of ethical judgement is to guide practice".

Conflicts of interest

Various real and perceived conflicts of interest continue to present a challenge for the finance industry. Managing these conflicts to the satisfaction of all stakeholders – employees, shareholders, regulators, customers and the public – is an ethical issue for the industry.

There are many situations and relationships within the finance industry where conflicts of interest have arisen and continue to arise. These include:

- Independence of non-executive directors (NEDs). NEDs are appointed to protect shareholders where their interests conflict with those of management. However there has been much reporting on the clubby nature of Boards and corporate governance failures despite "independent" NED positions.
- Shareholders interests versus the interests of clients. A company's obligations to look after their clients' interests can conflict with the short-term interest of shareholders.
- CEO and Board's personal interests versus shareholder interests. Recent proposals for management buyouts have met claims of conflicts of interest.
- Auditors can face conflict of interests through various business relationships, institutional structures and incentives that can be seen to impair their objectivity.

- Analysts face conflicts of interest when balancing financial promotion with their role of providing independent analysis.
- Private equity deals and leveraged buy-outs give rise to conflicts of interest where senior executives typically increase their stake in a company prior to a takeover.
- Many individuals working within the finance industry face personal conflicts of interest on a daily basis, where they find that their employer and/or the finance industry challenge their personal beliefs or moral values.

Executive remuneration

The remuneration packages of finance industry executives, particularly Chief Executive Officers (CEO), have received increased criticism by the public. This potentially raises ethical questions and challenges for the finance industry.

A huge disparity has developed between boardroom remuneration and employee salaries. A recent study shows that 20 years ago, the average CEO of a publicly traded company made 42 times more than the average production worker. The same study shows the average present day CEO makes over 400 times the average employee's income.

Whilst the statistics alone are alarming, there seems little justification for such remuneration packages when there is no compelling evidence that higher executive pay actually leads to better company performance. A study of 3000 companies found that the firms whose directors were the most well connected and that paid their CEOs most lavishly in fact underperformed the market (Surowiecki, 2007).

Not only does the finance industry need to determine what is an equitable allocation between shareholders, executive directors and employees, it also needs to consider ethical issues around various incentive structures and the apparent discretion of compensation committees.

There is also the issue of whether the pay of individuals and results of privately held companies should be reported. Many hedge fund managers argue that their pay should be kept private. They see coverage as sensationalist voyeurism driven by envy and titillation.

Currently there appears to be little alignment between remuneration packages and the sustainability and ethics of a company's performance.

Other ethical challenges

Private equity and hedge funds are private pools of largely unregulated capital. They are removed from the controls of investment banks and often operate according to the lower standard regulatory regimes of the Channel Islands, Spain, Bermuda and Austria.

There are now calls for more transparency and particularly calls for disclosure of positions due to concerns about the risks hedge funds pose, annoyance about their actions and political expediency and lack of information about them.

Globalisation poses difficult ethical challenges for the finance industry. Implementing single ethical codes, value statements or compliance systems across the world invariably encounters problems when various laws and cultural differences are taken into account. It raises the question of whether a common set of company values is really possible for corporations that have operations in multiple jurisdictions.

Corruption remains an ethical challenge facing the finance industry. It continues to affect both developed and undeveloped economies. A pressing problem is the corruption of regulators in developing countries and the subsequent exploitation of weak legal systems. As anti-corruption rules have strengthened, forms of corruption, in developed economies in particular, are becoming increasingly subtle and sophisticated.

The media as convenient scapegoat

The extent of the obligation of the finance industry to consider its social responsibilities and contribute to the societies in which they operate and impact is an ethical issue facing the finance industry.

The *McKinsey Quarterly* survey of 2006 found that the global business community had embraced the idea that it should play a wider role in society. More than four out of five respondents agreed that generating higher returns for investors should be accompanied by broader contributions to the public good, for example by providing good jobs, making philanthropic donations and going beyond legal requirements to minimise pollution and other negative effects of business.

As the finance industry attempts to gain the confidence and trust of the public, the relationship between the industry and the media will present ethical challenges.

With the much-publicised ethical lapses of the last ten years, public scrutiny, particularly by the media, has increased. Consequently the relationship between the finance industry and the media is now strained. More recently the finance industry has claimed that it is presented in a bad light by the media and suffers from overzealous reporting.

A report conducted by KPMG found that Australian Boards are concerned at their inability to reassure the news media, and through it the public, of their concern to promote and safeguard ethical business standards. The report concludes that the media is a convenient scapegoat, but not necessarily a convincing one.

The finance industry will continue to be affected by the influence of the media and this is only likely to increase with projects such as Wikileaks where an uncensorable Wikipedia is being developed for untraceable mass document leaking and analysis.

The persuasive business case for an increased emphasis on ethical considerations in and by the finance industry should be sufficient: ethical lapses can and often do lead to major profit losses and companies can cease to operate as a result. Damage to reputation and confidence loss is hard to measure and difficult to recover from. Scandals such as that of the National Australia Bank invariably taint the whole industry and the corporate sector. It is therefore in the interest of the whole corporate sector that the ethical issues facing the finance industry are addressed.

Whilst ethical codes, value statements, risk management programmes and reputation indexes have become more prevalent, the ethical performance of the finance industry is hard to measure and therefore is likely to continue to trouble and struggle to gain traction in an industry that is accustomed to definite and quantitative rather than qualitative outcomes. There are however structural improvements and educational initiatives that the industry can implement in order to bring about real change to the ethical performance and culture of the finance industry.

Finance industry: Beyond compliance and good marketing

For ethics to catalyse and enliven the finance industry – essentially, for ethics to become a living concept – the industry must move beyond viewing ethics as a matter for compliance and good marketing. Ethical thinking and an ethical way of life need to be woven into corporate culture and thus the day-to-day business of the finance industry.

All initiatives must be endorsed by senior management, including the Board and the CEO, and attendance ought to be compulsory. Responsibility, ownership and communication of any initiatives should reside with Senior Management rather than Human Resources or Compliance.

The finance industry should further consider funding the establishment of an independent Ethics Body to initially have the following responsibilities:

- provide ethics specialists to sit on and advise Boards;
- conduct situational and annual reviews of organisations ethical conduct and make recommendations;

- work with regulators to keep up with developments in the industry;
- facilitate focus groups and evaluation of the way financial institutions do business in new and developing markets; and
- facilitate the sharing of information and experiences between organisations so that organisations can learn from each other rather than managing issues away through clever public relations and payouts.

Ethical conduct should be a key performance indicator along with other standard indicators such as profit generation and business development. It must apply to Board members, CEOs, Senior Management and all staff. Ethical performance should then be linked to salary determination, bonus allocations and other performance incentives that are common to the finance industry.

This proposal will require a complete reorganisation of current incentive structures such as deferred compensation. If unethical behaviour is detected after an individual has left an organisation or division, future payments due to them should not be made without consideration of the individual's role in any unethical or fraudulent business that has been uncovered. Additionally, money already paid to an individual should be retractable following the discovery of unethical or fraudulent business practices.

Extending the accountability of executives beyond their narrowly defined term of employment would serve to curb the practice in the finance industry whereby individuals make vast amounts of money, without regard for the way in which such profits are achieved, and then leave an organisation before unethical or fraudulent practices are discovered or regulatory action is taken.

Rewarding good ethical behaviour

Whilst this proposal will require much legal re-drafting, possible legislative changes to employment laws and financial analysis, it would undoubtedly serve to increase executive's ethical accountability and thus the ethical conduct of the finance industry.

Society is comfortable with imposing financial sanctions, such as fines and operating restrictions upon organisations and individuals for unethical and fraudulent behaviour. Whilst financial punishments for unethical behaviour should be maintained, this system needs to be complimented by a system of rewards. As well as punishing people for poor ethical performance by withholding bonuses or performance pay, organisations should move to a system of financially rewarding good ethical behaviour.

Of course, some will debate the ethics of providing financial incentives for people to behave ethically. Others will consider the difficulty in actually determining and quantifying ethical behaviour as insurmountable.

Ideally, acceptable ethical behaviour would be a natural part of business life and society would not require either a punishment or a reward system. However, the reality is that unethical behaviour has plagued and continues to plague the finance industry, thus proving that relying on the goodwill of individuals alone to recognise and promote right conduct or a system of punishment is not enough. What should drive development in this area is the likely eventuality of increased ethical consideration in business as the finance industry and its participants are unarguably motivated by financial incentives.

Appointment of ethics role models

Organisations should identify and appoint staff to hold the position of Ethics Role Model in addition to their existing business function. Ethics role models should come from all areas of an organisation, particularly profit centres, as well as support areas.

Criteria for selecting ethics role models should be based on their reputation for sound ethical judgement, integrity and trust. These individuals should be encouraged and rewarded by senior management and empowered to play a more active role in the development of an ethical work culture within the organisation.

Ethics role models should be promoted as champions of ethics in the organisation and be available to staff as a point of contact to discuss the ethical dimension of business life. They should also be encouraged to take a proactive, educative role and encourage ethical networks within and outside an organisation. These positions should be considered prestigious and this will only come from Senior Management endorsement and encouragement.

Accountability at the point of innovation and deal-making

The finance industry is complex to the point that regulators, compliance and lawyers do not necessarily understand all, or many, aspects of the transactions and deals that they are subsequently required to sign-off, monitor and regulate.

In order to address this issue the finance industry needs to rethink the structure and responsibilities of their business, compliance and legal teams. Responsibility for the ethical aspect of a deal or innovation must be left to the individuals who understand the deal or innovation.

Rather than, or at least in addition to, deal-makers and innovators seeking sign-off from legal or compliance, legal and compliance teams should require acknowledgement from the innovators and deal-makers that they have considered the ethical dimension of the way they are doing business, including the current impact and the future impact of a deal or product. Additionally, board papers should include a section on ethical implications as well as financial and risk analysis.

The best time for organisations to first impress upon staff that the ethical aspect of business is important to them is at the point of induction.

CEOs and senior management should play an active role in induction programmes by personally attending and detailing how they expect staff to do business, as well as providing examples of what can and has happened when people have behaved inappropriately. It should be clear to inductees what is expected of them and what is acceptable business practice.

The induction process is of particular importance in developing countries and markets.

Tool for engagement and collection

For an organisation to make positive progress in the area of ethics, it must understand its current ethical climate and culture. It is imperative for an organisation to know what its' staff thinks about ethics, how they define it and what they perceive as the ethical challenges facing them and the organisation. Collecting such information and analysing the responses will assist an organisation in designing and implementing effective programmes and strategies.

Factors that individual organisations will need to consider when developing an engagement and collection tool are:

- **Time:** Executives have many competing interests with their main focus being their business role. Training is often viewed as taking them away from their real work. Considering this mindset any collection tool should be designed to be completed in 1 hour or less and executives given a realistic, yet tight, timeframe for completion.
- **Delivery:** Organisations should determine what delivery method best suits them. For a large global organisation an electronic collection tool may be the most effective. Other organisations could consider using simple hardcopy surveys, conducting focus groups or phone surveys. Factors such as organisation size, location and budget will affect the choices in this area.

- **Culture:** any material will need to take into account cultural factors such as language, office location and religious beliefs. The more tailored the programme is, the more engaged the participants will be.
- **Communication:** Ideally a collection and engagement tool would use a variety of mediums including film, voice-overs, text and animation. Most organisations now have staff from at least three generations, all of whom have different methods of processing information. By using a variety of media an organisation has a better chance of reaching more staff.
- **Compulsory**: Completion of the engagement and collection tool should be compulsory for all staff, including senior management, with failure to participate attracting financial consequences.

After an organisation has determined its ethical starting position, the next step is to conduct meaningful workshops based on the content collected from the engagement and collection tool.

Workshops should provide a forum to discuss real ethical dilemmas. Attendees should be given the opportunity to anonymously submit topics or issues for discussion prior to attending. This gives individuals another avenue for raising issues that may be of concern to them and removes the pressure and hesitation of raising such issues in front of peers or superiors.

The process of engagement and collection followed by workshops can be repeated constantly in order to monitor progress and developments and to reach staff throughout their careers and time with an organisation.

As for the CEO and representatives of Senior Management, they should host ethical discussion lunches. Eight to twelve employees should be chosen randomly from across the organisation and invited to attend. This is an opportunity for Senior Management to open themselves to honest discussion and questions on ethical issues.

On a broader level, organisations should seek and internally publish feedback on their business performance including ethical and social performance from clients and industry peers.

Acknowledging and addressing mistakes

While the ideas and strategies already covered are tailored specifically to the finance industry taking into account the nature of the industry and its participants, asking people to focus on their biggest mistake may create discussion among much wider group.

Many ethical lapses and litigious situations started with a simple mistake. Instead of acknowledging and addressing the mistake it was concealed leading to further lies and cover-ups, and ultimately to a complex but avoidable situation.

Hence, the necessity to re-train people to feel comfortable in admitting a mistake rather than attempting to conceal it. By looking at examples of mistakes people have made, we can start the cathartic process of acknowledging that as humans we make mistakes and use the information collected as an educative tool.

Bibliography

CREDO (Centre for Research into Ethics and Decision Making in Organisations), 2005. *A Survey of Ethical Value Practices of the Top 200 ASX Listed Companies*, Fitzroy: Australian Catholic University.

Persaud, A. and Plender, J., 2007. *All you need to know about Ethics and Finance*, London: Longtail Publishing.

Singer, Peter, 1979. *Practical Ethics*, Cambridge: Cambridge University Press.

Surowiecki, J., 2007. "The Financial Page: The Sky-High Club", *The New Yorker*, 22 January.

5

ETHICS: THE KEY TO CREDIBILITY

Felippe Araujo

It is in the very midst of gloom and disappointment that genuine opportunities for success most often come to the fore. Players are forced to sharpen their focus, and chaos puts them more thoroughly to the test. The very feeling that they must redesign the stage rather than abandon it in mid-crisis allows efficient ideas that are capable of exploring hitherto ignored avenues to flourish.

As the world wallows in an economic crisis of historic proportions, the moment has come to take a new look at financial operators' motives and guiding principles. Faced with the evidence that the origins of the present slump lay in financial markets, the press and, to an alarming extent, governments have repeatedly denounced professional practices in the sector. Such a climate of tension merely underlines how important it is to identify the true causes of today's global collapse and take steps to deal with them.

Yet regardless of its origins, the main factor that is now causing stagnation in the financial sector (and related areas of the economy) to persist is the lack of credibility among its players. Potential creditors and debtors are trapped in a web of profound distrust that is preventing such essential mechanisms as the financing of exports and capital goods from operating as they should. Although this distrust is largely due to the fact complex risk-assessment models have been found wanting, it can be allayed, or prevented from recurring, by more effective guarantees of ethical behaviour. The purpose of this paper, then, is to identify the main areas in which financial firms and operators could comply more fully with ethical standards, thereby restoring credibility within the sector and society's faith in financiers.

Ethics: The main problem

Every economy needs financial institutions. Through them, savings are transferred to players who require additional injections of funds in order to invest or to cope with a temporary fall in returns without having to cut spending. Nor should it be forgotten that financial institutions meet society's ever-present need for housing, insurance and shareholder capital.

So, if the financial sector plays a laudable – indeed essential – role, why should financial operators violate ethical standards so often? The most common explanation (Dobbs, 1997) concerns what is known as the agency dilemma. This arises because financial services involve principals delegating the use of their capital to agents. According to the theory of economic rationality, these agents are entirely bent on satisfying their own desire for higher returns, regardless of the consequences. If a particular option offers the agent more opportunity for gain than one that is more profitable for the principal, the agent will be faced with an ethical dilemma.

Pro-principal unethical behaviours

There is a crucial flaw in the agency dilemma, for it underestimates the role of agents' class interests and the importance financial operators attach to long-term gains. If agents fear that unethical choices may have long-term repercussions on their profession's or firm's reputation, or indeed their own, they may rationally decide to defer them. To encourage such moral choices, members of the financial sector have created seals of approval for operators well versed in ethical practices, such as the Chartered Financial Analyst (CFA).

The most serious problems for society as a whole lie in kinds of unethical behaviour that do not normally prevent those directly involved from maximising their gains. Indeed, in the short term, many of them generate extraordinary monetary gains for both agents and principals. I will therefore refer to this as "pro-principal" unethical behaviour.

The use of offshore structures to camouflage deficits yielded outstanding short-term gains for Enron shareholders and executives (Enron shares rose 56% in 1999 and 87% in 2000; in the same two years the firm's Standard & Poor's 500 rating rose 20% and fell 10% respectively). Investors in Bernard Madoff's hedge fund Ascot Partners stated that, before the scam came to light, there were consistent double-digit returns and serious reports of wealth creation (Lenzner, 2008).

Even though such operations do not damage the interests of those directly involved – at least, not in the short term – they do reduce society's faith in the financial sector as well as trust among potential creditors and debtors, for the following reasons:

- they implicitly undermine the authority of social conventions;
- they divert resources from activities in the real economy towards financial transactions that are not profitable in their own right; and
- they tend to even out the risks inherent in transactions involving different kinds of financial assets.

Unethical behaviour by financiers for their own benefit and that of their principals is nothing new, nor is it accidental. For centuries, financial advisors have exploited legal loopholes to obtain competitive advantages that enable them to make greater profits than their rivals. In 2003-2007, financial centres (especially those in North America) were swimming in liquidity, and high-yield projects were in great demand. All over the world, institutions involved in financial operations often felt tempted to propose uses of capital that, although unethical, would generate outstandingly high returns – and they often found the temptation too great to resist.

The financial sector's success in providing bonuses, commissions and salaries well above the average in other sectors drew the attention of some of the world's brightest individuals – doctors, mathematicians, economists, biologists and many others. Lured by the prospect of vast returns, experts from all kinds of fields migrated *en masse* into financial firms to become vice-presidents, partners and analysts of derivatives, stocks, securities, foreign exchange and so on – an army of often brilliant minds working out how to exploit opportunities that in common-or-garden ethics would be quite out of bounds.

We can categorise four main kinds of pro-principal unethical behaviour: 1) failure to record losses or profits (of whatever kind); 2) creation of subsidiaries to carry out questionable activities; 3) unsupervised transaction clearances; and 4) appointment of project managers who cannot be held accountable for losses.

Failure to record losses or profits

Failure to record real values on company balance sheets is a common form of unethical behaviour designed to benefit both agents and principals. Negative values can be omitted in order to boost a company's share price or reduce premiums on the securities it issues. Positive values, on the other hand, can be concealed in order to evade tax or facilitate shareholder or credit control by the manipulating party.

In the 1990s, a number of US companies jointly lobbied Congress to be allowed to omit encumbrances on company capital resulting from employee stock options. The lobbyists argued that any reduction in a company's book value would adversely affects its market value and so harm its own shareholding employees – whose welfare was the whole purpose of the policy.

The companies were proposing that a real fall in the total value of their assets should be concealed for the benefit of their shareholding staff and executives.

Something similar is now happening with public-private partnerships set up to help certain companies divest themselves of non-liquid assets, regarding the way in which the assets are priced. The companies in question argue that, if the assets are priced by the market, their value will not be sufficient to cover the companies' urgent need for capital. If, on the other hand, the companies themselves were allowed to price their assets – already due to be purchased with public funds – they could set values high enough to meet their capital requirements.

Once again, noble ends are being used to justify unethical means. Yet ethics cannot prevail – and hence trust among financial operators cannot be restored – unless the rules of the game (which regulate the means) take precedence over all else. It is an ethical principle that the ends do not necessarily justify the means – and, given that the ends are so often claimed to be laudable, ethical regulation of the means becomes all the more essential.

Creation of subsidiaries

When offshore subsidiaries are used to carry out questionable activities, the usual purpose is to help the parent company evade tax. A company sets up branches in other countries where the tax burden is either smaller or easier to avoid (legally or otherwise). The parent company then incurs various fictitious or quite simply unnecessary costs towards its subsidiaries, bringing part of the company's capital under their control, so that it is subject to less tax. In some cases the subsidiaries are set up for the very purpose of generating costs for the parent company, which can then deduct them from its taxable income in the country of origin. Perhaps the most notorious case of tax evasion via subsidiaries involved the Enron company, which for decades devised ways and means of diverting funds to branches abroad simply in order to avoid paying tax. As so often, this was made easier by the existence of tax havens. In some of these countries the level of bank secrecy is such that legal entities can receive sums of foreign currency anonymously – and so the authorities have no way of checking whether the recipient is in fact a branch of the institution that has paid the money.

Since cracking down on tax havens and bank secrecy is now high on the world political agenda, we can focus instead on what makes companies engage in such illicit activities. The level of taxation in the country where the parent company is based may be considered excessive, damaging to the company's progress, and hence an excuse for the illicit practice. However, ethical behaviour – as referred to above – has to apply not only to the ends, but also to the means used to attain them.

Unsupervised transaction clearances

The third kind of unethical behaviour can occur because a number of leading operators are authorised to represent both sides in a financial transaction without any need for third-party supervision. One case in which this played a key part was the company set up by Bernard Madoff, an operator who was licensed to conclude transactions without supervision of any kind. This evident lack of transparency eventually gave Madoff the front he needed for a type of financial scam known as a Ponzi scheme.

Although such practices are not unethical in themselves, they do give rise to situations in which unethical choices are hard to resist. Having the power to determine the value of a financial transaction, even the most well-intentioned operator will tend to underestimate potential risks and the likelihood of their occurring. The final value of the transaction will then be such that the dividends accruing to the principal – and above all to the agent – will be exceptionally high. The discount on these profits that would normally be required to offset the likelihood of various setbacks occurring will be kept to a minimum, resulting in an artificial transaction and surreal values.

Agents may argue that, by underestimating the damaging effects of the risks involved, they are saving both themselves and their principals unnecessary costs and hence achieving an optimum value for the transaction. However, if one lesson can be learned from the current crisis, it is that risks should never be discounted. The more clearly and accurately the risks involved in a transaction are stated, the less likely it is that values will be distorted and hence that resources will be misallocated.

The main violation of ethical standards resulting from unsupervised transactions is not so much misallocation of resources as misapplication of the rules of the game among operators. Those who are licensed to represent both sides in a transaction are in a position to set much lower costs than anyone else, by minimising the risks involved – not because they are actually able to reduce them, but because of a natural tendency for their interests as sellers to interfere with their decisions as buyers.

Lack of accountability

In the opening years of the twenty-first century, i.e. before the current crisis, the real level of risk accepted by the financial sector became exorbitant. Using a vast array of dazzling instruments, financial institutions (and companies acting as such) devised more and more ways of making highly risky offers to investors. During this period, according to sources in the sector, "anybody who could fog up a mirror could borrow money". The results are now only too evident: numerous projects were financed at an unacceptable level of risk, and the risks were seldom properly monitored. Countless debts had to be written off, and the executives directly responsible for approving the loans were not held accountable for the monetary consequences.

This scenario was largely due to the fact that the salaries and bonuses paid to the managers responsible for authorising such financing did not depend on the performance of the securities issued by their companies or the instruments on which loans were based. Such lack of accountability – which is the key issue here – is not in itself unethical. Even if executives who approve loans are not exposed to monetary penalties, their behaviour is perfectly ethical as long as they act with due caution and care.

Nevertheless, the fact that those responsible for financing projects were not subject to penalties led them, even unwittingly, to underestimate the scale of the risks involved. With market liquidity at its height, the temptation to offer instruments that allowed excessively risky projects to be financed was simply too strong to resist. Finance thus became available to agents, principals and entrepreneurs whose profiles and ideas would not normally have qualified for it. In reality, the agents who provided it were unethically committing their companies' resources at lower prices than the risks involved in the various projects would normally have demanded.

Damage to credibility

The four above-mentioned pro-principal unethical practices not only undermine public confidence in the financial sector as a whole, but they also destroy trust between players within the sector.

The omission of values on company balance sheets and the use of subsidiaries to avoid penalties or tax clearly undermine respect for the existing rules. Both practices violate accepted standards on such matters as tax liability and transparency of corporate finance. They therefore run counter to public expectations that every sector of the economy will comply with socially agreed standards of behaviour. At the same time, they destroy one of the preconditions for trust among financial players and institutions, which is that players in the sector must observe the social conventions on which the rules of the game are based.

On the other hand, the unsupervised transaction clearances and the fact that project managers cannot be held accountable for losses are not in themselves direct violations of accepted standards. Nevertheless, they do damage the credibility of the financial sector by creating situations in which agents will unconsciously tend to behave in socially unacceptable ways. In dealing with conflicting interests, all such agents will tend to underestimate the risks and costs arising from prudent management of the transactions entrusted to them. If unsure whether a particular decision will be made, and in the hope that it will not be, the general public and others involved in the financial sector will tend to give agents the benefit of the doubt – hardly a basis for reliability.

A profitability artificially distorted

The four above-mentioned kinds of pro-principal unethical behaviour have one feature in common: a deliberate intention to distort relative prices within the economy. Corporate balance-sheet omissions and the use of subsidiaries to avoid monetary obligations artificially inflate the market value of certain companies. The fact that some operators are unsupervised and that executives' incomes do not depend on the decisions they make will, as we have seen, artificially reduce the values of certain transactions to below what they would be if the risks were properly accounted for.

The basic function of the financial sector is to channel savers' funds towards players whose need for capital, for various reasons, exceeds their present supply of it. There is an optimum state of equilibrium between the minimum that savers are willing to accept in return for lending the capital they have accumulated and the maximum that investors are willing (or able) to pay for the capital they borrow.

When the profitability of certain transactions is artificially distorted, more resources are committed to purely financial activities. This means that less capital is channelled towards investment projects in the real economy, such as capital goods or research into agricultural productivity. One symptom of this is that financial operators rapidly grow rich, despite – or even at the expense of – stagnating or slower-growing incomes in other sectors.

This therefore reduces public confidence in financial institutions, since their activities have been visibly extrapolated and their dividends, which should normally be proportional to those earned in the real economy, are in fact growing much faster than the rest.

Partly because of these unethical practices, excess liquidity in the financial sector not only undermines society's faith in the sector, but also destroys trust among financial players. As the risks involved become more and more evened out, trust among creditors, debtors and intermediaries is eroded.

Market risks and values are evened out

The effect of pro-principal unethical behaviour is to minimise the losses or costs normally faced by companies or investors that seek to comply with ethical standards. The market value of unprofitable companies then approaches that of more cautious ones, and the risks inherent in aggressive transactions appear much the same as in more conservative (but less profitable) ones.

Shrewder market analysts consider this process artificial, misleading, and damaging to the reliability of the financial sector, for there is little way of knowing which companies' market value is attributable to improved performance and which to massaged balance sheets or illegal use of subsidiaries to avoid certain costs, or which transactions involve less risk by their very nature and which have had their risks artificially reduced.

In such an atmosphere of uncertainty and distrust, if just one major investor suddenly backs out, a wave of panic may spread among the rest, bringing much of the financial system to its knees.

Restoring credibility through ethics

The main thrust of this essay is that ethical professional behaviour is not only a virtue in itself, but also provides a way to restore society's faith in financial institutions and trust within the sector itself. Recently, with liquidity at historical levels, countless operators in leading financial markets came up with the most surprising ways of generating exceptionally high returns for their principals.

Even though some of these offers did not violate accepted standards of professional conduct, many of them clashed with the demands of common-or-garden ethics. The cumulative impact of such unethical behaviour on the credibility of the financial sector, and on trust within it, was evident from the rate at which investors liquidated their assets in the second half of 2008.

This paper has discussed a number of unethical practices – supposedly win-win games yielding exorbitant profits for both agents and principals – that have helped to destroy confidence in and among financial institutions. It has also looked at the ways in which such operations have contributed to the collapse. What now remains is to suggest ways of discouraging such practices, or at least cushioning their impact on the credibility of the sector.

The recipe proposed here focuses on expanding the notions of transparency and accountability and their application in the financial sector.

Naturally, the more transparently financial companies and institutions operate, the less likely it is that doubts will arise as to their activities or their compliance with ethical principles. Arrangements such as the extraordinary levels of bank secrecy provided by some countries, and the right of certain bodies not to disclose the nature or value of some of their financial operations, help to reduce transparency and increase distrust between major financial players, as well as in the eyes of society as a whole.

Provide financial players with proper information

Obviously, legislation requiring a higher level of transparency on the part of financial institutions and other bodies that engage in financial activities would be in the interests of every country's tax authorities. Such statutory disclosure requirements for financial operations would encourage compliance with ethical standards and help restore trust among players in the sector, as well as society's faith in it.

It would therefore be a good thing if all the information about every company's financial operations were to be published, rather than just information concerning taxable sums. Such operations would be subject to scrutiny by the market, allowing it to determine, for its own purposes, whether the risks inherent in a given transaction have been underestimated (and, if so, what the probable reasons are); whether the activities of a given subsidiary are legitimate or merely serve the questionable interests of the parent company; or whether the omission of certain costs is justified or is simply a manoeuvre designed to inflate a company's market value; and to draw whatever other conclusions it sees fit.

The purpose of this would be to provide financial players (as well as other interested parties within society) with the information they need in order to keep abreast of each company's activities and the risks it has incurred. This would enable players to place their trust in institutions confidently, rather than just blindly follow the findings of a handful of leading players, based on imprecise reports about key financial transactions.

Incentives to act ethically

Accountability is an important tool for increasing the efficiency of operators and companies, and its role in ensuring compliance with ethical principles should not be underestimated. If the operators responsible for each observable element of the process are actually exposed to penalties, the means used to make exceptional profits will also be subject to scrutiny. They will then be less likely to resort to practices that do not violate accepted standards but are nonetheless unethical, simply for their clients' benefit.

To tackle the fourth above-mentioned kind of pro-principal unethical behaviour, one proposal often made in the media is to tie managers' bonuses and salaries to the performance of the securities issued by their companies. Those responsible for issuing loans will then have a strong incentive to assess the risks inherent in each proposal carefully, since these may do serious damage to their company's position.

One fundamental economic axiom is that people respond to incentives. One way to ensure accountable, responsible behaviour in the long term would be to give players incentives to act that way, rather than merely call them to account after the event. This will mean looking closely at financial operators' personal motives, as well as supervising their activities properly.

Corporate cultures that set out to make employees' personal ambitions coincide with company goals undoubtedly tend (assuming that both are legitimate and ethical) to encourage ethical decision-making. Executives who feel they are part of a team whose work takes account of and helps them attain their own goals will be more inclined to take responsibility for what they do, and hence more likely to work more diligently.

To ensure proper supervision of compliance with ethical standards, under a system of duly attributed accountability, companies can also make use of incentives aimed at the relevant players. One such instrument would be to distribute the penalties imposed for violations of the rules, or for loss of market value, among all the members of the department responsible. Although this may create a climate of hostility and suspicion within each department, it will also give all the players involved the same incentive to find ethical solutions to dilemmas faced by their colleagues.

A long road ahead

Although the links between ethical behaviour and credibility are obvious, the task of analysing how both can be achieved more (or less) effectively is almost endless. This paper has described how, in the midst of the present crisis, failure to comply with ethical standards – and the resulting lack of credibility – have reached a critical point. The new systems of financial regulation that are now being set up will certainly take account of the need to guarantee ethical behaviour, in the interests of greater predictability and credibility among financial players.

For the time being, the public's focus on every last detail of government plans to bail out financial institutions goes to show just how low the sector's reputation has now sunk in society's eyes. The road towards restoring confidence among creditors, debtors and operators will be long and winding, but it is a road that must be travelled. However, the task of consolidating ethical behaviour in a sector that is currently in such desperate need of public funding is proving just as hard.

Bibliography

Dobbs, J., 1997. *Finance ethics: the rationality of virtue,* New York: Rowman & Littlefield.

Lenzner, R., 2008. "Bernie Madoff's $50 Billion Ponzi Scheme", *Forbes,* 12 December.

6

EMOTIONS, PERSONAL ETHICS AND PROFESSIONAL LIFE: THE LOST LINK

Meredith Benton

A description of the current financial crisis does not need to be repeated here. The reverberations of a failed global financial system will be felt for years, if not decades. The reasons for the felling of our global economic system are innumerable. There were many perpetrators, and many more victims still. While retrospective analysis is essential, of far greater import at this juncture in time is understanding how to avoid future transgressions of this scale and impact. Will greater Securities and Exchange Commission (SEC) oversight, mortgage bank policies, or more thorough investigative journalism help us avoid future similar calamities?

These and all similar efforts would not have prevented the current crisis, nor will they, or other prescriptive solutions, prevent future upheavals. Rather, in discussing the bank leverage, collateralised mortgage obligations, or foreign exchange rate, we need to remember that the core of these institutions and concepts are not laws, corporate charters or global treaties. At the core, the financial system was developed by, is stewarded by, and is fully dependant on human decision-making.

Before we create a new financial system, with new loopholes for the creative greedy to slip through, let us ask ourselves: what leads people to act? How do they choose one action over the other? And, are we able to structure our financial system in a way that might encourage ethical behaviour?

The current state of crisis within the financial marketplace exists, in large part, because of a detachment between personal ethics and the professional life.

Who are we?

In 1971, researchers at Stanford University conducted the Stanford Prison Experiment. In this experiment, undergraduate students were assigned either the role of prisoner or guard through the luck of a coin toss. If they were to become guards they were given wooden batons, uniforms and reflective sunglasses. If they were to become prisoners, they were "arrested" at home, stripped of their personal belongings and reassigned identification numbers. The guards, while cautioned not to physically assault the prisoners, were given full power over them. All students participating in the study were screened ahead of time for psychological stability.

This experiment had to be terminated after six days. Conditions had become unsafe for the prisoners. More than a quarter of the guards were deemed to be exhibiting sadistic or dangerous tendencies. This same phenomenon, where ordinary citizens act with extreme cruelty, has, unfortunately, been observed in far less benign situations, such as Abu Ghraib. While it may be reassuring to view the perpetrators of these injustices as aberrations of humanity, the truth is far less reassuring.

In reviewing these and similar scenarii, psychologists have identified a number of elements that contributed to the abuses perpetrated. These included disorientation, depersonalisation and de-individualisation of the victims. Within the prison experiment, authoritarian roles were institutionalised, with a strong power dynamic emphasised.

Understanding, and accepting, the human psyche

To change the financial system, to imbue it with ethics, we must do more than write new rules. We must understand and address who we, as humans, truly are. Rather than discuss idealised versions of the self, we must first acknowledge the capacity for evil and cowardice that exists within all – not just financiers.

We must assume that "good" people have been involved in past finance scandals and ethical transgressions. These perpetrators most likely experienced a level of cognitive dissonance. Cognitive dissonance occurs when holding two conflicting ideas leads to the justification or rationalisation of attitudes or behaviours that would otherwise be considered unethical. This assumes a struggle within the self around ethical beliefs.

To some extent cognitive dissonance is a daily experience. We know that driving is expensive, bad for our health and the environment. But, we have groceries to carry home. Or we need to be somewhere quickly. Or, perhaps, it is too hot, too cold, or raining outside. A rationalisation process may often lead to an exponential pursuit of the behaviour or actions originally identified as dissonant. To continue our example, our rationalisations continue, the weather may be warm and we may be on vacation, but we've fallen into the habit of driving, and so we continue. Perhaps, given the amount of time we spend driving, we upgrade to a nicer model of car. Cognitive dissonance encourages the denial of contradictory data and the development of a confirmation bias. Once in our new car, we rarely, if ever, stop to consider our original oppositions to driving.

Cognitive dissonance and self-rationalisations can take many forms. In experiments where participants who held a particular belief were publicly forced to state something to the contrary, researchers have found that participants often shifted their beliefs to accommodate the statements that they had made. Interestingly, when participants were induced to make public statements in order to receive some form of a reward, the greater the reward, the less of a shift was observed within their personal belief system (Festinger and Carlsmith, 1959).

The implications of this study must be carefully considered, as they infer that those people who modify their beliefs for small rewards are subject to more internal pressure to justify this changed direction. For corporate and public policy this indicates that rather than watching for shifts in corporate culture at the top of the organisation – where there is much to gain by unethical behaviour – attention ought also be carefully focused on the middle ranks, where a combination of powerlessness or minimal authority, small rewards, and cognitive dissonance might combine in very damaging ways.

Moral aspects of choices

Moral decision-making has been considered by two key theories, deontological and consequentialist. The deontological approach, derived from the Greek word for duty, takes the perspective that a particular act or action is right or wrong; the consequentialist considers, of the act, what the consequences of doing something might be (Tanner *et al.*, 2008). Of course these are not mutually exclusive concepts, as the consequence of an act often defines whether it is right or wrong.

From the allegorical narrative of *The Lord of the Flies,* to internet chat rooms, the Klu Klux Klan and masquerade balls, we are well aware that anonymity allows for the expression of the baser, and less culturally supported, human desires. As detailed in the theory of consequentialist decision making, acts are considered with a focus on outcomes – the risks and rewards of the choice. When anonymity is allowed, the risks decline dramatically. With this in mind, a movement has sprung up among the strange bedfellows of institutional investors, environmentalists and human rights activists, aimed at seeking greater disclosure and transparency from companies around their social and environmental programmes and policies. A positive feedback cycle is created, as investors increasingly incorporate these data into their valuations, as strong sustainability programmes are rewarded by greater investor support, which, in turn is rewarded by greater disclosure and stronger programmes.

Research is just now beginning to consider the moral aspects of choice, particularly when trade-offs, or cognitive dissonance, is involved. The term "protected values" has been developed to describe those beliefs that people are not willing to compromise at any price. Protected values have been shown to be highly associated with a deontological orientation. When someone has a protected value, they consider the consequences of their decision to be irrelevant, as long as their protected value is prioritised. A 2008 study found that those people having a deontological orientation were more likely to prefer acts to omissions. That is, they were more likely to respond and be motivated by positive statements such as "bring about good", than negative statements such as "do no harm" (Tanner *et al.*, 2008).

The role of emotion

Another emerging field, moral cognitive neuro-science, provides us with additional insight into the human decision making process. The roles of deliberation, affect and emotion are highlighted through this research. In this field, emotions are defined as somatic changes in response to a stimulus. Feelings, on the contrary, are created by the correlated emotion, as a secondary result. This research field is in direct opposition to the classical Cartesian view of decision-making as a reasoned, emotion-free process. By using brain imaging, positron emission topography and magnetic resonance imaging, researchers have determined that two clear neural processes, cognitive and affective, are involved in decision-making. Business decisions, however, have traditionally assumed a rational and deliberate process – one that is free of the affective.

Current neuroscience research indicates that the mind does not have the ability to compute without emotion. The cognitive system must work through the affective system. While the cognitive system is responsible for the searching of options and predicting consequences, the evaluation of this data must be done by the affective system. Indeed those people with damage to their affective region were both emotionally flat and poor decision makers.

Research indicates, however, that according to the decision at hand, the brain works in different modes. In research studies, brain activity associated with emotion is significantly higher when participants viewed the situation as being "moral personal" versus "moral impersonal". An example of "moral personal" would be one that had direct contact with human suffering, such as deciding who to save from a sinking boat. "Moral impersonal" involved questions around returning money from a lost wallet (Wenstop and Koppang, 2009).

The influence of management

Individual factors identified that influence ethical decision-making includes: gender, moral cognitive development, ego strength, and control. Meanwhile situational factors include: reinforcement, commitment, sense of justice and social pressure. While a company can do little, in legal terms, to address individual factors of ethical decision-making, it can do much to address situational elements.

As demonstrated in Dipanker Ghosh's 2008 research, employees determined to maintain high ethical standards "do indeed become less ethical when corporate management adopts a profit-oriented approach compared to when it values integrity, or when no corporate values are professed". It is important to note that in his study, ethics were assessed as they related to the company's own resources. Therefore, employees at companies with inflexible foci on the bottom line were significantly more likely to behave unethically towards their own employers. Ghosh's study also observed that those employees identified as holding high ethical standards were significantly more likely to demonstrate these standards in workplaces where company management actively encouraged and valued integrity-based decision-making. When corporate management did not seek to create and encourage a public sense of integrity, the discernable difference in behaviour between high and low ethical behaviour in employees was significantly lower. Ghosh's study gives significant credence to the idea that corporate attitudes and intentionally created cultures are of great import in developing an ethically run company.

Further research into workplace environments has demonstrated a strong link between management behaviour, company culture and employees' personal decisions. Studies have shown that employees tend to look to their supervisors for guidance on the appropriateness of certain behaviours. A particularly telling study conducted in 1979 by Hegarty and Sims found that when employees were presented with a letter from the CEO that encouraged ethical behaviour, even using a method as indirect as an expression of enthusiasm about a journal article, the employee was significantly less likely to pay kick-backs. Similarly, a study in 1985 showed that employees at companies where work-life balance was emphasised were far less likely to accept kick-backs than employees at explicitly profit-driven companies (Bailey and Alexander, 1993).

Alternatives to the *status quo*

For a more ethical financial system, the goal must be to empower employees to stand in opposition, to question, to push, and to think creatively about ways to meet corporate goals, rather than developing another set of laws or voluntary codes. It is not feasible to create a universal ethical framework. Any company or oversight body that tries to do so will find itself slighted – if not in the creation of these codes, then certainly in their implementation.

There are significant advantages to successfully implementing a sense of meaning in the workplace. Studies have identified such positive elements as enhanced commitment, performance, motivation, satisfaction, and trust in management.

However, this paper would not be complete without a warning, as was issued in a 2006 study by Sandra Cha and Amy Edmondson. These researchers found that charismatic leadership around shared employee values may inadvertently lead to employee disenchantment. Disenchantment is defined by a feeling of violation, a loss of trust and enthusiasm, the presence of anger, resentment, bitterness and outrage with a sense of being betrayed or mistreated. This may occur should employees perceive any hypocrisy in their leaders' in organisational value statements. Values, by their abstract nature, create the opportunity for multiple interpretations of intention. As such, employees and management may read different commitments between the lines.

In addition, there is often a natural conflict between business and communal values. Management, as occurs when staff cuts must be made, is obliged to choose between strengthened business performance and the employees' sense of community. In order to reduce the perception of hypocrisy, leaders are advised to take a number of steps:

- Explicitly acknowledge tensions between work-place values and business decisions.
- Engage in a thoughtful discussion with employees around the company's values.
- In times of stress, conscientiously affirm the company's ongoing commitment to its values.

- Allow for feedback around areas of employee concern or disappointment. Management is particularly encouraged to discuss feelings arising from unexpected actions or events.

Opportunities for change

Knowing the challenges facing their employees, what other opportunities exist for managers, investors and other stakeholders to encourage ethical financial markets? Innovative thinking is of essence here, and the opportunities for positive change are limitless.

First of all, corporate social responsibility units should not be designated to fall within the purview of only one division or department of a company. While it is essential to have a designated lead in questions of coordination, reporting and management of sustainability, organisations should seek to disallow the rationalisations that we have seen associated with cognitive dissonance. The negative repercussions of creating autonomous corporate citizenship centres allow employees to justify a detachment from their own responsibility to steward the companies' ethics. Their rationalisations can become: "Addressing this is formally the responsibility of someone else, it is not my responsibility, therefore I need not become involved."

The Stanford prison experiment was not terminated on the sixth day because the sponsoring professor was concerned for his students. Rather, he, Philip Zimbardo, acknowledges that in his role of prison supervisor, he was as caught up in the process as the other guards. It was instead a girl he was dating (later to become his wife) who, on visiting the prison, was appalled by the conditions, and who insisted that the experiment ought to be shut down. This anecdote points to the importance of including external stakeholders. Finance institutions should seek to actively build relationships with non-governmental organisations, and actively bring in external viewpoints, perhaps through quarterly open town hall meetings. This would provide relationship-building, communication, an exchange of ideas and culture between people who hold opposing viewpoints. Being directly responsive to external stakeholders would provide a much-needed unmasking of anonymity, the benefits of which were detailed earlier. Management would be stopped, or at least slowed, in slipping down the slope of confirmation bias by receiving occasional external feedback.

Personal meetings and active relationships with stakeholders would also do much to shift decision-making processes from "moral impersonal" to "moral personal". This shift would do more than change the neurological processes seen in financiers' brains from cognitive to affective, it would also address an additional concern highlighted by the Stanford prison experiment: that of the depersonalisation and de-individualisation of the victims. By encouraging, and indeed insisting that employees be more connected to the impacts of their decisions, particularly in how they affect other humans, companies would do much to shift patterns of behaviour.

Finally, management must also be cognizant of its power to create a strong ethical corporate culture. As we have seen, even a casual word of support from the CEO can shift an employee's ethical behaviour in an unrelated activity. More than the occasional sound-byte to the press, or press release, management should recognise and praise those employees who take extraordinary actions to protect the ethics of their organisations. Company leaders need to make daily efforts to build, and re-affirm a culture of employee empowerment. This is particularly important as it is the small, everyday self-rationalisations that shift an ethical compass, not the large, high-reward steps more often associated with financial transgressions.

Integrating ethics in the workplace

The detachment from, and the marginalisation of personal beliefs and values creates an untenable division within the financial markets.

The *New York Times* of May 28th, 2009, reports that more than 20% of Harvard's graduating MBAs have voluntarily pledged themselves to an honour code to serve the greater good. This is a fine gesture. But, what happens when these students are faced with decisions that are incompatible with their morals or ideals? When their hard-won job would be put at risk, should they choose to follow their code and "oppose corruption, unfair discrimination, and exploitation"? It is not enough for financial leaders to espouse a commitment to ethics and point fingers at rogue bad apples. These leaders must take conscientious steps to integrate a culture of ethical behaviour, personal ethics and autonomy into the workplace. If they fail to do this, then these MBAs, however earnest and committed they may currently have made that pledge in vain.

Bibliography

Bailey, J./ Alexander, R., 1993. "Organisational social cues, framing and justice: effects on management's ethical decisions", in: *International Journal of Organisational Analysis 1 (2)*, 133-160.

Cha, S./ Edmondson, A., 2006. "When values backfire: Leadership, attribution, and disenchantment in a values-driven organisation", in: *The Leadership Quarterly 17*, 57-78.

Festinger, L./ Carlsmith J.M., 1959. "Cognitive Consequences of Forced Compliance", in: *Journal of Abnormal and Social Psychology 58 (2)*, 203-210.

Ghosh, D., 2008. "Corporate Values, Workplace Decisions and Ethical Standards of Employees", in: *Journal of Managerial Issues 20 (1)*, 68-87.

Hegarty, H./ Sims, H., 1979. "Organisational philosophy, policies, and objectives related to unethical decision behavior: A laboratory experiment", in: *Journal of Applied Psychology 64*, 331-338.

Tanner, C. *et al.*, 2008. "Influence of deontological versus consequentialist orientations on act choices and framing effects: When principles are more important than consequences", in: *European Journal of Social Psychology 38*, 757-769.

Wenstop, F./ Koppang, H., 2009. "On operations research and value conflicts", in: *Omega 37*, 1109-1120.

7

THE FINANCIAL SECTOR AND THE BEHAVIOUR OF PEOPLE: WHAT TO DO?

Carlos Eduardo Estapé Viana

In recent years there has been much questioning of the conduct of individual actors from the financial sector. In particular, the question has arisen of the behaviour of people who are part of this sector and who have acted wrongly from an ethical point of view, motivated by personal interest detrimental to the institutions for which they worked and to the common good.

This reflection is intended to address some issues related to the financial sector dynamics and to analyse how some behaviour patterns of the institutions and the financial sector itself may affect people's own behaviour and lead to the occurrence of unethical behaviours of people.

Before starting the analysis of the issues mentioned in the previous paragraph and in order to contextualise this paper, I include a comment regarding the ethical behaviour in itself and what it can mean to people, concluding that there is no consensus and that what can be unethical behavior for a given person, can pass as ethical for another. That is the first problem we have to deal with.

In the end, when talking about findings and what to do I, once again stress the importance of people and their values as an essential element to deal with temptations and unethical attitudes that the financial sector tolerates and even seems sometimes to encourage, as well as I invite the institutions to face up to the problem.

It should be noted that throughout this paper, I will make reference to some aspects related to the financial sector in the Republic of Uruguay that provide a basis for reflection and can be extrapolated to the financial sector in general.

Do ethical principles depend on each individual?

Before taking on the financial sector and some of the issues concerning the behaviour of people who are associated with this sector, and since this paper focuses on ethical behaviour, I have to make an attempt to define what I mean by behaving ethically. Of course, there will be endless definitions of ethics (starting from the etymology of this word) that are irrelevant and are not intended to be included in this reflection.

However, what is relevant is to try to understand what can be considered ethics in the financial sector, which won't be different for other activity sectors. In my opinion, to behave in an ethical manner in the workplace means that people in fulfilling their responsibilities will behave in a way that not only does not disobey any formal standard, but also in the absence of standards, but being aware that acting in a certain way is not correct even though it is formally allowed, the person may behave similarly in pursuit of the common good. Will it be considered that a person behaved unethically if she did not contravene any formal standard? In my opinion yes, because although nothing formally prohibits the person to behave that way, in fact, the rules should be reviewed for certain types of conduct that fall outside the rules themselves and such behaviour is not desired to happen again or if it happens, it must be penalised. In the same way, people should be also able to discern the consequences of their behaviour and if their behaviour harms the common good, refrain from it.

Without any doubt, the fact that ethical behavioujr is caused mainly by the inherent resources of each individual and his/her values rather than by formal rules, leaves space for different positions in terms of what can be regarded as ethical behaviour. This diversity of criteria allows for people to behave according to their own understanding of ethical behaviour based on their own values and hence there will be problems to reach consensus. As a result institutions will in the end dictate them on the basis of a value framework and specify the behaviour from an ethical and moral point of view that they expect from their employees. These messages may be deduced from the very mission of the institution and even translated into codes of ethics that seek to regulate the individual behaviour of people. However, whenever there is place for people's interpretation, as there will be a margin of interpretation to move within, because not everything can be regulated. Hence the lack of consensus on what a person can consider as ethical behavior, and showing the complexity of the matter.

The incentive system vs. ethics in the financial sector

It is not surprising that the system of incentives for the people working in the financial sector (especially private banking functions, representations, and brokers) is a matter well studied and reviewed by the institutions with the desire of achieving the best results by encouraging people to pursue certain goals (it may be return on a portfolio for example) so as to pat the objectives of the individual in line with those of the institution.

I do not intend to analyse the incentive systems used by the institutions, or assess the suitability of one or another system. The approach that I will follow will be from the perspective of how the incentives systems can affect the ethical behaviour of people.

There is no doubt that the rewards in the financial sector in general are very important, either being monetary rewards, or promotion opportunities and careers.

These rewards guide the behaviour of certain people who move toward achieving their goals, often without any regard for their behaviour from the ethical point of view as long as they do not contravene any formal legal, regulatory or internal standard to the institution.

This search – sometimes desperate – to achieve some predetermined goals that are often set a priori very high, means that people – deliberately or not – behave in an unethical way. There is no doubt that depending on the person, she will be more or less willing to behave unethically, and it would seem very naïve to consider that there is not a single person who would also behave in an unethical way with incentives or without them. However, most of the people assume that everyone wishes to behave within an ethical framework.

In any case, people can be subject to a system so demanding, that either being conscious or rationalising their behaviour in the situation they are in, they behave in an unethical way motivated by the desire to reach a given goal, or in a way even more critical when in threatened with case of not achieving the goal, it can lead to loss of employment. At this point, the values of the institutions and people take precedence.

The values of the institutions matter, because there will be some people who from their HQ will promote unethical behavior, certainly not illegal or contrary to any formal rule, but clearly pointing to the expected behaviour by people within the institution. Such behaviour can be in competition with other companies from the sector, internal competition between employees or many other issues that are inherent to the institution and that the organisational culture has already determined as a behavior to adopt in a certain way in order to be promoted or even to remain in the institution. It will reside in the values of the person to accept the rules of the game or not, and certainly in this case the option is to get out or not even enter.

However, it can happen that the institution promotes ethical behaviour and really adheres to the values, but the incentive system, or rather we could say, rewards and punishments, determines that a person, in order to get a reward or at least to avoid a punishment, is cornered and encouraged to behave in an unethical way, not because he/she believes that it is the right thing to do (although he/she can rationalise it given the situation) but because he/she considers that there is no other alternative. Some examples of unethical behaviours that may occur in these situations are abuse of available information, abuse of client funds, and inappropriate attitudes towards colleagues to mention some of the most common cases. In cases like those, the values of a person must be clear and strong to be able to act accordingly despite the situation where he/she is.

Without any doubt, it will not be easy to do it if this is unavoidable. What is desirable is that before being in an objectionable situation, the person seeks to prevent it and eventually finds an alternative route that does not involve bad behaviour.

In short, can incentive systems and ethical behaviour in the financial sector coexist? Undoubtedly yes. However, precautions must be taken when designing incentive systems in order that individuals who share the values of the institution won't be compelled to misbehave for not being able to achieve predetermined goals. Of course, I have left aside those who do not reach the goals for poor work or incompetence. I refer to those cases when the goal is so high and the penalty for not achieving it is so great as to push the person to behave unethically to avoid punishment (by punishment we can include not to move up on the career, stay out of it or having to leave the institution). It will be people's own responsibility to make sure they are not becoming involved in extreme situations that bring into play their ethical principles. That care should begin with the institution they choose to join, and then negotiating the goals. If a person joins an institution that from the beginning, she/he is aware encourages and rewards behaviors not being shared by him/her because he considers them to be unethical, that person should immediately refrain to become a member of that institution since sooner or later his/her values will collapse or, much worse, she/he will change to adapt to the rules of the game.

Labour market dynamics in the financial sector and possible unethical conducts

A situation that has caught my attention and even surprised me from the beginning of my career is the income level of some employees of financial institutions, particularly in my country. Without getting into a historical analysis of the financial sector and the economy it is clear that due to the fact that being a very sensitive sector in the economy as a whole as well as for individuals because they manage their funds and savings, and everything related to the trust between investor – Institution, the people working in the financial sector earn reasonably high incomes compared to other sectors in general, whatever their position, particularly those who work in private banking as investment brokers.

I do not try to argue if that is right that those persons should have high incomes nor from a standpoint of merit or anything else, but rather try to understand how the dynamics of the labour market promotes some behaviours that from my point of view are unethical.

The political and economic conditions in Uruguay as well as an increasing globalisation have helped in recent years the establishment of several financial institutions that previously weren't present, and also to increase the activities of other institutions that were already present, resulting in a labour market, especially in regards to investment banking, with important dynamics.

That movement of people working in investment banking is one of the issues in the financial sector that although totally justified from the point of view of supply and demand of labour, may induce,unethical behaviours.

In order to expand, investment banks typically recruit investment brokers with their own portfolios of customers. The first dilemma that is widely discussed but that we won't address in depth here is whether clients in this sector of activity belong to financial institutions or to the persons. I can conclude that they are a little of both. There will be clients who are loyal to a particular institution, regardless of the agent who provides service. They must feel some kind of connection with the agent on duty, but once that relationship is established they would rather not change it. Other customers are loyal to the person who advises them regardless of the institution for which he/she works as long as the institution provides enough support.

That coming and going of investment brokers with their own portfolio can generate unethical behaviour in institutions such as the theft of investment agents by another institution. Although it is the law of the labour market and the parties are free to compete, the methods used to come by people on demand are often unethical. In addition, once the investment agent has moved from a financial institution to another, the latter engages in an effort to attract the customers together with the broker, inducing them to leave the former financial institution for the new one. At this stage, the values of the person to communicate a clear message in an ethical manner take relevance because there are many cases where in an effort to move his/her clients, the broker reveals business secrets from the previous institution or mentions problems that had never surfaced previously.

These financial sector labour market dynamics, in which each change of institution produces a substantial increase in the income of the investment broker is a major cause of unethical behaviours of people who either rationalise their actions with the premise that the end justifies the mean and that everyone in the sector make it, or induces them to unethical behaviors that generate an internal conflict in the person who knows he is acting wrongly. It depends again on the values of the institutions and individuals to put a framework for behaviours, and the nuances of behaviours encouraged by the institutions emerge again as well as how a person must act within such a framework

Controls have been implemented, but it is not enough: What else can be done?

We have pointed out the issue of unethical behaviours of people working in the financial sector and how certain actions of institutions and markets act as a stimulus for the occurrence of these behaviours. There is no doubt that the behaviour of people in financial institutions has been and will be subject of widespread communications especially when cases of public notoriety come to light as in the Madoff case, the downfall of Bear Stearns or, in Uruguay, the cases of Banco Comercial or Banco de Montevideo.

Various controls of a formal nature have been implemented with the purpose of controlling the behaviour of financial institutions (such as the Sarbanes Oxley Act regulating financial functions in the United States of America, or the increased control from the central bank of Uruguay) that allow to have greater control of the financial institutions and to penalise them in the event of contravening any norm. However, they are not enough to prevent unethical behaviours of institutions or individuals when these are not in formal breach of the rules.

In the same way, the financial institutions have worked for the commitment of their individuals providing messages from the centre that are translated into values, and have developed codes of ethics. However, it is not enough to eliminate the non-desired behaviours. One element that I consider very important is the fact that the institution itself had an ethical code as well as the people who run it. This is essential so the message won't be contradictory and the institution will be running within a really ethical framework and all must ensure its care. Of course, it will be convenient to have the desired behaviour explicitly stated, but it is not enough unless it is communicated properly and then enacted accordingly, punishing harshly those who deviate from the desired ethical behaviour so it shows evidence that it is an important matter and that the institution's life can depend on it.

Financial institutions are the ones who must take charge of this issue, leading the fight against unethical behaviour, because as we saw, the financial institutions themselves in one way or another define the conditions under which people can be incentivised to behave unethically.

Regulating entities will be in charge of monitoring the compliance of institutions with formal standards but they cannot get into managing the behaviour of the people within the institutions, which will be provided by the institutions themselves.

Finally, we emphasise once again the indispensable role of people and their values, which will ultimately be the limit that each person will have in front of the temptation to behaving unethically. Of course this can have a more profitable short-term outcome even with the assurance that sometimes they won't see any negative consequences from their actions. Therefore, institutions when selecting people who will join them, or train those already within, should pay special attention to the ethical aspects and analyse the resources that the person has to deal with difficult situations and under pressure. Without being an expert in the matter, I know that the psychological tests that are used in many places before incorporating an employee, strongly test the resources that a person has to tolerate pressure and that is at least a starting point.

In short, financial institutions must take care of this issue. This is not something unknown to them and their policies can lead people to undesirable behaviours beyond the codes of ethics they have. They must work in the selection of personnel to be hired and monitor them permanently. Of course it is not easy and it would be ideal to find a magic formula or an indicator to be monitored but since there is not one, then at least we must be aware of the problem addressing it at the outset which is the institution itself.

8

DECISION: THE SPACE BETWEEN THE CODE OF ETHICS AND ETHICAL BEHAVIOUR

Carmen Lucia Carmona Paredes

The financial crisis and frauds that have occurred in the last decade have inspired an extraordinary wave of regulatory reforms, changes in corporate governance structures, adoption of codes of ethics, and implementation committees (Dominguez, Alvarez and Sanchez, 2009). However, despite these clear efforts that promote ethical behaviour in the financial world, the fact is that the link between preventive solutions and a reduction in the number of scandals is not clear. (Huse, 2005; Roberts et to the, 2005; Hans et to the, 2009; Schwartz, 2005; Bonn and Fisher 2005). There is still a gap between what it is said and what it is done.

Therefore, the new question that arises is how to form this bond and transform a code of ethics in ethical actions? The answer lies in a change in the decision making process since the decision is the time bag between reflection and action, that is, between the code of ethics and the ethical behaviour.

A good decision qualifies as such when it carries out a procedure of analysis that takes into account certain principles (Howard, 1976).

Therefore, the quality of analysis in the decision-making of a manager is of fundamental importance to the transformation of corporate plans and strategies. This, in turn, framed in the context of business growth, embodies the essential need to fit the decision analysis approach into the corporate internal financial perspective because it is almost impossible to think about strategic decisions regardless of from the allocation of resources.

It is common to observe the continued discussion among financial people and ethics teachers trying to give an answer to the dilemma as to whether the goal of corporations is or is not to maximise shareholder value. To account for this debate very present in the literature, it is necessary as a first step to clarify the value or values that want to be maximised. Only that way, with the formalisation of the ethics in a tangible value or values, a new sense to the analysis and a specific meaning to this universal concept may be given.

Recognising the true values of a company goes beyond reading its corporative social report, its mission, and even its code of ethics. Adam and Shavit (2008) suggest to analyse the way in which the company carries out the assessment of the investment options and to observe the criteria used for the allocation of resources. These criteria are a more realistic demonstration of corporate values because decision makers use them to judge whether a proposal is good or bad for the business context. In many companies the evaluation of investment options is a fundamental part of the process of Portfolio Management of Strategic Projects (CPM for short English Corporate Portfolio Management).

Throughout this process, the decision-maker constantly faces difficult choices mainly by selecting projects that fulfill the growth target of the company without contradicting the ethics of the business. The reality is that the evaluation of investment options that maximise these two types of values involves a complex thought process filled by a tangle of interactions. An effective technique for addressing the complexity of this type of situations is the use of Analysis for Decision Making with Multiple Criteria (MCDA) as an internal procedure for making strategic investment decisions. The implementation of this method allows to transform the approach to Project Portfolio Management by translating a general concept of ethical values into tangible and specific values, and by providing a useful learning tool for achieving better decision-makers education, and as a result to achieve more ethical actions.

Value vs. investment values

If we pay attention to recent changes in regulations (Somarnes Oxley Act in the United States and Bribery Act in the United Kingdom, etc.) and to the changes in corporate governance schemes, it can be observed that the efforts of recent years have seen monitoring and auditing as an universal solution for the reduction of cases of unethical behaviour. One consequence of this type of solution is the tendency for companies to consider ethical behaviour from a legal compliance point of overs. In this respect, a recent survey of the FTSE350 (Barma, 2010) confirms this tendency by showing that about 70% of participants identified the Internal Audit Committee as responsible for ethical behaviour.

The challenge is to get companies to depart from this policy and to move on from delegating the topic to a specialist, or a committee of the Board of Directors, or to a group of consultants to making ethics an integral pert of their business models, included into strategic processes and hence investments evaluation.

For this to happen, the first step is to define ethics in a way that is congenial with a specific business pattern. With a substantive definition I do not mean a code of ethics or a list of business values because too often we think that these efforts are enough to create an organisational culture. However, the expert in CPM, Kevin Bossley (Catalyzed[1] Consult-

---

[1] *www.catalyze.co.uk*

ant) who has participated in dozens of strategic decisions, in an interview described otherwise. When asked how often is expressed and taken into account in decisions the commitment that some companies have to preserve the environment, human rights or a particular community, he, surprinsingly, pointed out the lack of inclusion of these values in the evaluation of strategies.

Unfortunately, these observations are not surprising from a personal point of view, if one takes into account that a company's growth, the success of a product, the value of the shares, and so on, is epitomised only in financial values or indexes that represent them. Consequently, this way of reporting and measuring success is a source of pressure for decision-makers. In a way, this is what the survey by AMA (2006) reveals, in which two-thirds of the participants responded that the pressure to meet unrealistic business goals is the most likely cause for making the ethical standards of an organisation irrelevant.

This kind of pressures could be alleviated if corporate employees had a tool to show to managers in a frank way the challenges involved in making decisions, particularly when you need to decide where to invest money often in millions dollars amounts. Hence, the importance of a process allowing the definition of values that are real business goals and explicitly relevant for the investors.

One practical manner in which we can identify the investment priorities of a company is through the decisions taken pursuant to the Portfolio Management of Strategic Projects. This function is an internal financial process that can be defined as a sequence of decisions seeking the best combination of projects and programmes ensuring business growth. This sequence of decisions includes identification, prioritisation, authorisation, and project management (Sanwal, 2007).

In theory, a Portfolio of Projects at the highest level is designed to define strategies and give a direction to financial decision making. A typical life cycle of a project portfolio begins with the introduction of the strategic plan from which we derive the determining criteria for the allocation of resources. (Sanwal, 2007). We would expect that the mission and vision could give specific clues about the criteria for making decisions and provide guidance as to the values to be maximised through investments, i.e, which value or values it will give value through money. Under this premise it is said that a strategic project portfolio shows the real interest behind the investment.

Ethical dilemmas are complex decisions

The reality is that if a project is preferred over another it is because it is valued for more than one reason. This statement by Ralph Kenney is the premise on which the Analysis for Decision Making with Multiple Criteria (MCDA) is based, which, as its name indicates, allows evaluating options taking into account multiple criteria. Its main feature is that it enables the decision-maker criteria to include "soft" criteria, to resort to trials to evaluate the differences between options, and uses preference values for measuring the degree to which the options (projects, programmes and strategies) achieve the goals put forth in the criteria. It is a process that helps giving structure to the coherence of thought (Howard, 1976).

The MCDA method builds on a set of consistent judgments in a preference scale that allocates scores to each option. These scores constitute a single numerical scale that allows comparison of options with different units. This is possible because the methodology does not evaluate the importance of one criterion against another, but it compares the value of the change in units of one versus another. This methodology has been used as part of Portfolio Management of Strategic Projects (CPM) in various processes in the private and public sectors and its popularity emerges from the consistency of judgments made and the transparency of the analysis that combines social with technical elements. (Phillips, 2002).

The objective of the analysis is to provide an overall ranking of the options and consists of five steps illustrated in table 1. The first step has its basis in the utility theory. Utility is understood to reflect the inherent value that the decision-maker gives to the alternatives and on which depends the final decision (Howard, 1976). Basically, this step identifies and defines guidelines for evaluating the options (investments, programmes and projects) and in particular, it is the space in which the company can translate the meaning of ethics in a business context through explicit values.

MCDA Stages
1. Identification of objectives or criteria
2. Identification of options
3. Evaluation of options
4. Sensitivity analysis

Table 1: MCDA Stages

It is important to note that MCDA has no commutative property so that the order of the steps alters the result. Carrying out the identification of objectives as the first step before considering possible solutions avoids unnecessary ethical dilemmas.

Once these criteria and alternatives have been identified, they need to be evaluated. (step 4, Table 1). This procedure is performed by comparing all alternatives within each criterion, one at a time, in order to define the difference between the alternatives. This technique clarifies the situations in which there is an investment option X that is better at certain value, an option Y that give a best result at another value and an option Z that has the potential to give good results at both values but with a high level of risk.

In many cases the ethical dilemmas faced by decision-makers arise out of this tangle of interactions. The MCDA methodology is an effective tool to reduce complexity because the analysis is focused on answering what you value and how much you value each situation.

The MCDA methodology does not change the mentality of the decision maker. It is a process that can zoom in the decision-making and transform a process that in many occasions takes place unconsciously into an explicit sequence that moreover, is also transparent, auditable and systematic.

MCDA: A tool for learning

Decision making is a skill that is learned by doing, so having a tool that allows a continuous learning is essential to develop better decision makers. The MCDA is an effective learning tool because it meets the two requirements for authentic learning of complex situations (Sterman, 1994). On the one hand, the methodology allows for obtaining the knowledge and perceptions of decision makers and also allows for creating feedback structures on these knowledge and perceptions. This is important because we must not forget that decision-makers of a company are improvising in the sense that the problems they are facing are never the same since business context is in constant motion.

Therefore the MCDA processes allows for capturing the context of each decision, and permits decision makers to look back and compare information, perceptions and understanding of the reasons why certain courses of action have been chosen. This learning and continuous improvement cycle is achieved because there is real transparency in the evaluation of the options, and this goes beyond the simple formulation of possible business options. It means transparency in the participants, even including their different points of view, the flow of information, the definition of monitoring indicators and mainly the allocation of resources to implement strategies (Adam and Shavit 2008).

The crucial factor is that the integrity of decision makers will result from following rules of conduct consistently. The impartiality of the decision makers will emerge in the repetition of these rules, the result being a pattern of ethical decisions, while habits are not achieved by thinking or writing codes of ethics, but through actions. Consequently, integrity will affect both the decisions made as well as the action that they generate and that will define the strategy of the company.

This learning cycle has potential for success even in extreme cases in that there is no clear translation of ethics in explicit decision values because, like any addiction, the first step is to accept the problem and recognise that values are not put into practice and that for example, short term interests of investors are consistently put in the first place.

Conclusion

It is important not to confuse good decisions with good results. None of us can know the future, which means that we can take a decision that result in a bad outcome or vice versa. Of course, mistakes can happen but they will be less frequent and they won't be due to a limited analysis. What we do know with certainty is that the lower the quality of decision analysis, the worse the outcomes.

The proposed inclusion of a MCDA methodology has as an objective to zoom in on decision-making by allowing the definition of the values, measuring them on a common scale that permits comparison with each other. It is a practical alternative to address the complexity of the assessment of strategy and an honest way to put on the table the true motivation behind the investments and thereby give a way out of the conflict of interests or values that constantly are joined.

The real effort should not be focused on regulations or monitoring, if it is actually looking for creating values for the individual and develop decision makers that have integrity, and that are motivated by values not by rules and incentives; and with the courage and conviction to resist temptations. It is true that the learning and improvement of analysis in decision-making will grow gradually, but it will not take place if the first step that requires recognition of the true values of investment is not taken.

In my vision of future corporate practices, I see that MCDA

- is the method most often used for corporate representatives as a methodology of analysis of decisions during strategic planning and budget allocation.
- is a standard on the Boards of Directors and is known among its members as the method "multi-criteria" referring to the way in which directors account for the decisions that have been taken; i.e. the MCDA is the way in which information is shared and reports are given to investors about the reasons behind the evaluations made, the obstacles they face at the time and alternative actions that have been taken into account.

Bibliography

Adam, Avshalom/ Shavit, Tal, 2009. "Roles and responsibilities of boards of directors revisited in reconciling conflicting stakeholders interests while maintaining corporate responsibility", in: *Journal of Management and Governance 13 (4)*, 281-302.

American Management Association/ Human Resource Institute, 2006. *The Ethical Enterprise, Doing the Right Things in the Right Ways, Today and Tomorrow.*

Barma, Hanif, 2010. "Culture Clash: Policies and procedures are useless if your culture is wrong", in: *Internal Auditing 34*: 11.

Bonn, I./ Fisher, J., 2005. "Corporate governance and business ethics: Insights from the strategic planning experience", in: *Corporate Governance: An International Review 13*, 730-8.

Dominguez L. *et al.*, 2009. "Corporate Governance and Code of Ethics", in: *Journal of Business Ethics 90*,187-202.

Howard, Ronald, 1976. *Readings in Decision Analysis,* Part III, Decision Analysis Group, Stanford Research Institute, 491-520.

Huse, M., 2005. "Accountability and Creating Accountability: A Framework for Exploring Behavioural Perspectives of Corporate Governance", in: *British Journal of Management 16*, 65-79.

Phillips, Larry, 1984. "A theory of requisite models", in: *Acta Psychologica 561 (3)*, 29-48.

Roberts, J. *et al.*, 2005. "Beyond Agency Conceptions of the Work of the Non-Executive Director: Creating Accountability in the Boardroom" in: *British Journal of Management 16*, S5-S26.

Sanwal, Anand, 2007. "Get Sustained Growth by Savvy Portfolio Management", in: *Journal of Corporate Accounting and Finance 19 (1)*, 3-10.

Sterman, John, 1994. "Learning in and about complex systems", in: *Systems Dynamics Review 10*, 291-330.

Schwartz M. *et al.*, 2005. "Tone at the Top: An Ethics Code for Directors", in: *Journal of Business Ethics 58*, 79-100.
Van Ees, Hans *et al.*, 2009. "Towards a Behavioural Theory of Boards and Corporate Governance", in: *Corporate Governance: An International Review 17 (3)*, 307-319.

9

ETHICS: AN ESSENTIAL PREREQUISITE OF THE FINANCIAL SYSTEM

David Sifah

Ethics in general deals with human behaviour that is acceptable or right or is not acceptable or wrong according to conventional morality. General ethical norms encompass truthfulness, honesty, integrity, respect for others, fairness, and justice. They relate to all aspects of life, including business and finance. Financial ethics is, therefore, a subset of general ethics.

Ethical norms are essential for maintaining stability and harmony in social life, where people interact with one another. Recognition of others' needs and aspirations, fairness, and co-operative efforts to deal with common issues are an example of aspects of social behaviour that contribute to social stability. In the process of social evolution, we have developed not only an instinct to care for ourselves but also a conscience to care for others.

However, situations may arise in which the need to care for ourselves runs into conflict with the need to care for others. Then ethical norms are needed to guide our behaviour. As Dempsey (1999) puts it: "Ethics represents the attempt to resolve the conflict between selfishness and selflessness; between our material needs and our conscience".

An inconsistency at the heart of finance

Ethical dilemmas and ethical violations in finance can be attributed to an inconsistency in the conceptual framework of modern financial-economic theory, and the widespread use of a principal-agent model of relationship in financial transactions. The financial-economic theory that underlies the modern capitalist system is based on the rational-maximiser paradigm, which holds that individuals are self-seeking (egoistic) and that they behave rationally when they seek to maximise their own interests. The principal-agent model of relationships refers to an arrangement whereby one party, acting as an agent for another, carries out certain functions on behalf of that other. Such arrangements are an integral part of the modern economic and financial system, and it is difficult to imagine it functioning without them.

The problem is that the behavioural assumption of the modern financial-economic theory runs counter to the ideas of trustworthiness, loyalty, fidelity, stewardship, and concern for others that underline the traditional principal-agent relationship. The traditional concept of agency is based on moral values. But if human beings are rational maximisers, then agency on behalf of others in the traditional sense is impossible. As Duska (1992) explains it: "To do something for another in a system geared to maximise self-interest is foolish. Such an answer, though, points out an inconsistency at the heart of the system, for a system that has rules requiring agents to look out for others while encouraging individuals to look out only for themselves, destroys the practice of looking out for others."

The ethical dilemma presented by the problem of conflicting interests has been addressed in some areas of finance, such as corporate governance, by converting the agency relationship into a purely contractual relationship that uses a carrot-and-stick approach to ensure ethical behaviour by agents. In corporate governance, the problem of conflict between management (agent) and stockholders (principal) is described as an agency problem. Economists have developed an agency theory to deal with this problem.

The agency theory: a structured relationship

The agency theory assumes that both the agent and the principal are self-interested and aim to maximise their gain in their relationship. A simple example would be the case of a store manager acting as an agent for the owner of the store. The store manager wants as much pay as possible for as little work as possible, and the storeowner wants as much work from the manager for as little pay as possible. This theory is value-free because it does not pass judgment on whether the maximisation behaviour is good or bad and is not concerned with what might be a fair wage for the manager.

It drops the ideas of honesty and loyalty from the agency relationship because of their incompatibility with the fundamental assumption of rational maximisation. "The job of agency theory is to help devise techniques for describing the conflict inherent in the principal-agent relationship and controlling the situations so that the agent, acting out of self-interest, does as little harm as possible to the principal's interest" (DeGeorge, 1992).

The agency theory turns the traditional concept of agency relationship into a structured (contractual) relationship in which the principal can influence the actions of agents through incentives, motivations, and punishment schemes. The principal essentially uses monetary rewards, punishments, and the agency laws to command loyalty from the agent.

A paradoxical situation

Most of our needs for financial services – management of retirement savings, stock and bond investing, and protection against unforeseen events, to name but a few – are such that they are better entrusted to others because we have neither the ability nor the time to carry them out effectively. The corporate device of contractualisation of the agency relationship is, however, too difficult to apply to the multitude of financial dealings between individuals and institutions that take place in the financial market every day.

Individuals are not as well organised as stockholders, and they are often unaware of the agency issue. Lack of information also limits their ability to monitor an agent's behaviour. Therefore, what we have in our complex modern economic system is a paradoxical situation: the ever-increasing need for getting things done by others on the one hand, and the description of human nature that emphasises selfish behaviour on the other. This paradoxical situation, or the inconsistency in the foundation of the modern capitalist system, can explain most of the ethical problems and declining morality in the arena of modern business and finance.

Ethical violations…

The most frequently occurring ethical violations in finance relate to insider trading, stakeholder interest versus stockholder interest, investment management, and campaign financing. Business in general and financial markets in particular are replete with examples of violations of trust and loyalty in both public and private dealings. Fraudulent financial dealings, influence peddling and corruption in governments, brokers not maintaining proper records of customer trading, cheating customers of their trading profits, unauthorised transactions, insider trading, misuse of customer funds for personal gain, mispricing customer trades, and corruption and larceny in banking have become common occurrences.

Insider trading is perhaps one of the most publicised unethical behaviours by traders. Insider trading refers to trading in the securities of a company to take advantage of material inside information about the company that is not available to the public. Such a trade is motivated by the possibility of generating extraordinary gain with the help of non-public information (information not yet made public).

It gives the trader an unfair advantage over other traders in the same security. Insider trading was legal in some European countries until recently. In the United States, the 1984 Trading Sanctions Act made it illegal to trade in a security while in the possession of material non-public information. The law applies to both insiders who have access to non-public information and those with whom they share such information.

… And ethical codes

Approaches to dealing with ethical problems in finance range from establishing ethical codes for financial professionals to efforts to replace the rational-maximiser (egoistic) paradigm that underlies the modern capitalist system by one in which individuals are assumed to be altruistic, honest, and basically virtuous.

It is not uncommon to find established ethical codes and ethical offices in American corporations and in financial markets. Ethical codes for financial markets are established by the official regulatory agencies and self-regulating organisations to ensure ethically responsible behaviour on the part of the operatives in the financial markets.

One of the most important and powerful official regulatory agencies for the securities industry in the United States is the Securities and Exchange Commission (SEC). It is in charge of implementing Federal securities' laws, and, as such, it sets up rules and regulations for the proper conduct of professionals operating within its regulatory jurisdiction. Many professionals play a role within the securities industry. The most important of these are accountants, broker-dealers, investment advisers, and investment companies.

Any improper or unethical conduct on the part of these professionals is of great concern to the SEC, whose primary responsibility is to protect investor interests and maintain the integrity of the securities' market.

The SEC can censure, suspend, or bar professionals who practice within its regulatory domain for lack of requisite qualifications or unethical and improper conduct.

The SEC also oversees self-regulatory organisations (SROs), which include stock exchanges, the National Association of Security Dealers (NASD), the Municipal Securities Rulemaking Board (MSRB), clearing agencies, transfer agents, and securities information processors. An SRO is a membership organisation that makes and enforces rules for its members based on the Federal securities' laws. The SEC has the responsibility of reviewing and approving the rules made by SROs.

Other rule-making agencies include the Federal Reserve System, the Federal Deposit Insurance Corporation (FDIC), and state finance authorities. Congress has entrusted to the Federal Reserve Board the responsibility of implementing laws pertaining to a wide range of banking and financial activities, a task that it carries out through its regulations. One such regulation has to do with unfair or deceptive acts or practices. The FDIC has its own rules and regulations for the banking industry, and it also draws its power to regulate from various banking laws passed by Congress.

Professional codes of good conduct

In addition to federal and state regulatory agencies, various professional associations set their own rules of good conduct for their members. The American Institute of Certified Public Accountants (AICPA), the American Institute of Certified Planners (AICP), the Investment Company Institute (ICI), the American Society of Chartered Life Underwriters (ASCLU), the Institute of Chartered Financial Analysts (ICFA), the National Association of Bank Loan and Credit Officers (also known as Robert Morris Associates), and the Association for Investment Management and Research (AIMR) are some of the professional associations that have well-publicised codes of ethics.

By joining their professional organisations, people who work in the field of accounting agree to uphold the high ethical standards of their profession. Each of the major professional associations for accountants has a code of ethics. The Code of Professional Conduct of the American Institute of CPAs (AICPA), the national professional association for CPAs, sets forth ethical principles and rules of conduct for its members.

The principles are positively stated and provide general guidelines that CPAs (or any professionals, for that matter) should strive to follow. The rules of conduct are much more explicit as to specific actions that should or should not be taken. The Institute of Management Accountants (IMA) Standards of Ethical Conduct applies to practitioners of management accounting and financial management, and the Institute of Internal Auditors (IIA) Code of Ethics applies to its members and to Certified Internal Auditors (CIAs).

Towards a paradigm shift?

The other approach to address the ethical problems in business and finance consist in re-examining the conceptual foundation of the modern capitalist system and changing it to one that is consistent with the traditional model of agency relationship. The proponents of a paradigm shift question the rational-maximiser assumption that underlines the modern financial-economic theory and reject the idea that all human actions are motivated by self-interest.

They embrace an alternative assumption – that human beings are to some degree ethical and altruistic – and emphasise the role of the traditional principal-agent relationship based on honesty, loyalty, and trust. Duska (1992) argues: "Clearly, there is an extent to which [Adam] Smith and the economists are right. Human beings are self-interested and will not always look out for the interest of others. But there are times they will set aside their interests to act on behalf of others. Agency situations were presumably set up to guarantee those times."

The idea that human beings can be honest and altruistic is an empirically valid assumption; it is not hard to find examples of honesty and altruism in both private and public dealings. There is no reason this idea should not be embraced and nurtured. As Bowie (1991) points out: "Looking out for oneself is a natural, powerful motive that needs little, if any, social reinforcement. [...] Altruistic motives, even if they too are natural, are not as powerful: they need to be socially reinforced and nurtured."

If the financial-economic theory accepts the fact that behavioural motivations other than that of wealth maximisation are both realistic and desirable, then the agency problem that economists try to deal with will be a non-problem. For Dobson (1993), the true role of ethics in finance is to be found in the acceptance of the internal good (good in the sense of "right" rather than "physical product"), which, he adds, is what classical philosophers describe as "virtue" – that is, the internal good toward which all human endeavour should strive. He contends: "If the attainment of internal goods were to become generally accepted as the ultimate objective of all human endeavours, both personal and professional, then financial markets would become truly ethical."

Ethical responsibilities and professional reputation

A distinguishing mark of professions such as medicine and accounting is acceptance of their responsibilities to the public. The AICPA Code of Professional Conduct describes the accounting profession's public as consisting of "clients, credit grantors, governments, employers, investors, the business and financial community, and others who rely on the objectivity and integrity of Certified Public Accountants (CPAs) to maintain the orderly functioning of commerce". Many, but not all, CPAs work in firms that provide accounting, auditing, and other services to the general public; these CPAs are said to be in public practice.

Regardless of where CPAs work, the AICPA Code applies to their professional conduct, although there are some special provisions for those in public practice. Internal auditors, management accountants, and financial managers most commonly are employees of the organisations to which they provide these services; but, as professionals, they, too, must also be mindful of their obligations to the public.

The responsibilities placed on accounting professionals by the three codes of ethics and the related professional standards have many similarities. All three require professional competence, confidentiality, integrity, and objectivity. Accounting professionals should only undertake tasks that they can complete with professional competence, and they must carry out their responsibilities with sufficient care and diligence, usually referred to as *due professional care* or *due care*.

The codes of ethics of the AICPA, IMA, and IIA all require that confidential information known to accounting professionals not be disclosed to outsiders. The most significant exception to the confidentiality rules is that accounting professionals' work papers are subject to subpoena by a court; and that nothing analogous to attorney-client privilege exists.

To a large extent, the accounting profession is self-regulated through various professional associations rather than being regulated by the government. The AICPA, the IMA, and the IIA have internal means to enforce the codes of ethics. Furthermore, the professional organisations for CPAs in each state, known as *state societies of CPAs*, have mechanisms for enforcing their codes of ethics, which are usually very similar to the AICPA Code.

Violations of ethical standards can lead to a person being publicly expelled from the professional organisation. Because of the extreme importance of a professional accountant's reputation, expulsion is a strong disciplinary measure. However, ethical violations can lead to even more adverse consequences for CPAs because of state and Federal laws.

Self-regulation of accounting professionals?

The state government issues a CPA's license to practice, usually through an organisation known as the *state board of accountancy*. Since state laws governing the practice of accountancy typically include important parts of the AICPA Code, the Code thus gains legal enforceability. Consequently, ethical violations can result in the state decision to revoke a CPA's license to practice on a temporary or even permanent basis. Because a licensed CPA is also likely to belong to the AICPA and the state society of CPAs, investigations into violations of ethics may be carried out jointly by the AICPA, the state society, and the state board of accountancy.

CPAs in public practice that audit the financial statements of public corporations are subject to Federal securities' laws and regulations, including the Securities Exchange Act of 1934. The Securities and Exchange Commission (SEC), which administers these laws, has broad powers to regulate corporations that sell their stock to the public. One important SEC requirement is that an independent CPA carries out audits of these corporations' financial statements. The SEC has the authority to establish and enforce auditing standards and procedures, including to determine what constitutes independence for a CPA.

The SEC has largely delegated the setting of standards to the private sector but retains responsibility for overseeing and enforcement. In 1998 the SEC and the AICPA jointly announced the creation of the Independence Standards Board (ISB), a private-sector body whose mission is to improve auditor independence standards. In announcing the formation of the ISB, the SEC reaffirmed the crucial importance of the CPA's independence: "[M]aintaining the independence of auditors of financial statements [...] is crucial to the credibility of financial reporting and, in turn, to the capital formation process" (SEC Release FRR-50, 1998).

There are many occasions when proper business ethics are exercised by organisations and commercial firms that consider themselves socially responsible and viable. Most financial organisations value their investors as a way of exercising ethics in their business. They call this the Human Capital Value. By considering people as their prime asset, businesses around the world scale their way to success. Those involved in the organisation may include employees, investors, stakeholders, contractors and suppliers.

However, in this age of global competition, modern businessmen believe that ethics do not help the business to succeed and prosper, but rather that they limit its resources. The new business age has given birth to a new set of business ethics that are in the best interest of the business itself, these ethics include: valuing diversity, distributed power, reality testing etc. These ethics are further known to be global ethics.

Current trends

Opportunistic agents try to maximise their wealth, even at the expense of others. Since to maximise wealth, agents may act with guile and deceit, agents no longer trust each other. This may for example lead to lenders charging higher rates of interest on their loans because they cannot trust borrowers to invest fully in the most profitable projects. The result is at best a makeshift balance, one that maximises nobody's wealth. On this point, Dobson (1993) quotes the business ethicist, Norman Bowie: "The conscious pursuit of self-interest by all members of society has the collective result of undermining the interests of all."

In today's globalised world of finance, where businesses often deal with each other often without any personal contact, the need for enforceable contracts is crucial, if the whole system is to avoid failure. Furthermore, the problem of enforcing contracts is not purely external to the business. The now prevalent view of the firm is as a nexus of contracts, containing within it people with very different and sometimes conflicting objectives. When one takes this view of the corporation, it begins to look much more like a structured market, structured so as to minimise costs and maximise efficiency.

The problem of enforcing contracts is not therefore merely one of the firm's interactions with other entities, but one that touches the very heart of the firm. Explicit contracts can be enforced through the courts (at a cost), but implicit contracts require trust and mutual good will for their enforcement. It would seem, then, given the importance of contracts for the functioning of the financial system, that building trust could be considered a central ethical requirement.

Trust for trust's sake is irrational in finance

Unfortunately, the finance paradigm has already decided that to pursue trust for more than merely materialistic, opportunistic ends is irrational. As Dobson says: "But for trust to work, agents must be intrinsically trustworthy. They cannot merely act in a trustworthy manner when it suits their material ends. What is required is trust for trust's sake. But clearly "trust for trust's sake" is irrational within the finance paradigm… an individual who forgoes material gain in order to honour some trust-based agreement would be as irrational as an individual who forgoes material gain because the moon happened to be full…. Within the finance paradigm, the act of honouring trust *in and of itself* has absolutely no value" (italics in the original).

Firms try to create confidence in what they are doing by sending out signals that may or may not convince the market that they are trustworthy. "Good" firms need to send out signals that cannot be mimicked by "bad" firms if they are to be effective. If giving such a signal is not too costly, the good firm that gives it creates a "separating equilibrium" in which it is clear who is who to outside agents. However, such signals do have some cost, and this reduces the efficiency of the good firm. Again, at best we can have a second-best outcome, with a "residual loss" due to the contractual enforcement problem between agents.

Opportunistic agents cannot be trusted

It is important to realise here that we are not dealing with a redistribution of income from principal to agent, but with an absolute loss from which no one gains. Lack of information or "information asymmetry" can make it difficult for principals to know in advance whether they can trust agents, and "moral hazard" describes the situation where it is uncertain whether agents will honour or abuse the trust placed in them. In both cases, proponents of finance theory would argue that firms could build a reputation of trustworthiness that is consistent with the opportunistic and maximising assumptions of the finance paradigm.

Reputation is not well defined in the literature of finance; but by extrapolating from the annual *Fortune* survey to rank companies by their reputation and a number of other sources: reputation is a behavioural trait. A firm builds its reputation by demonstrating a consistent mode of behaviour through a series of contractual situations. Once built, a reputation increases the value of the implicit claims sold by the firm to stakeholders. Thus, a firm's desire to earn future profits by maintaining its reputation may act as an implicit contractual enforcement mechanism.

Yet we still hear of financial scandals, even among the most respectable of banks and financial agencies. Furthermore, firms like Salomon brothers that were the subject of a serious fraud, seem to bounce back into action after a short period of re-organisation and knocking heads together. From the point of view of the finance paradigm, there was a fundamental flaw: opportunistic agents cannot be trusted.

Challenging the financial paradigm

The first challenge offered to the finance paradigm comes from the way financial markets themselves operate. After Salomon brothers were involved in stitching up the market for US Treasury bonds, an expert on the incident, Clifford Smith, claimed that Salomon was *punished* for its *unethical* behaviour by the financial markets. This implies that there was some moral basis to the punishment, which took the form of economic sanctions incurred by Salomon brothers as a result of the scandal. However, to see whether there was a moral basis to this censure and not purely a financial one, the underlying motivation for the censure needs to be established.

In an indirect way, this information was forthcoming through the approval that the new chief executive, Warren Buffett, received when he stated: "If I hear of an employee losing the company money, I'll understand. However, if I hear of any employee losing Salomon one shred of reputation I'll be ruthless!" This statement is important because it separates the loss of reputation from the loss of money, with the implication being that reputation is not purely an instrument used in the maximisation of wealth. In other words, an employee who makes a technical error, losing money for Salomon Brothers, will be treated with understanding, but an employee who sets out to exploit other agents in the market, gaining money for Salomon Brothers but tarnishing the reputation of the firm's honesty, will be treated severely. This is clearly in open contradiction with the tenets of the finance paradigm.

This discussion still leaves aside the motivation that any given employee might have for not tarnishing the company's reputation. After all, many would maintain, what matters is what the person does, not why they do it. However, this "practical" argument includes a fatal inherent weakness: "An agent who is not motivated to act ethically will sooner or later act unethically". The last-ditch stand of the finance paradigm against this thinking is the "confidence school" position: scandals undermine confidence in financial markets, which may reduce the number of participants in the market and reduce the efficiency of the market.

This explains why ethical behaviour is important: it maintains confidence in the market. This justification of ethics only supports the position that unethical behaviour is unacceptable if it undermines confidence in the market. The obvious implication is that if something can be done in such a way as to not undermine such market confidence, the behaviour is acceptable, on condition it maximises wealth.

This connects what may well seem to be a very distant ethical tradition and language to the notion of quality control and procedures, something familiar to all business people in the post-Japanese technological era. It was proven during the industrial revolution that the traditions of business that survived were those that maintained a more virtue-based approach. Only later were these eclipsed by the forms that are more familiar to us today. It has also been proven that businesses that operate on the virtue of ethics and compete efficiently in financial markets, even if there are opportunistic agents. Furthermore, markets cannot operate without such virtuous agents.

When Aristotle described life's ideal as one of intellectual pursuit or contemplative enquiry, he accepted that the material wealth of his society was sufficient for only a fraction of its inhabitants to realise this ideal. The triumph of our age is that the wealth generated by the firm through the market system has freed the majority of humanity from the fetters of material servitude. But the victory has been Pyrrhic.

Ethics as the essential condition for finance

It would be an understatement to say that the discipline of finance has not been strongly associated with ethics; if anything, the two areas have been opposed to each other as mutually exclusive. Even where such an opposition is not maintained, it remains true that the ethics of finance is underdeveloped compared to the fields of business ethics or professional ethics. Most financiers have not had in-depth ethical training, whereas ethicists lack an understanding of the technicalities of financial management. The situation is thus self-perpetuating.

In recent years, however, following a series of stock market crashes, bank scandals and the present general financial instability, there is a renewed interest in the interface between ethics and finance. Within the field of Catholic Social teaching, an important step was taken in 1994 with the publication of the booklet *Modern Financial Systems and the Ethical Imperatives of Christianity* (original in French), written by two members of the French Treasury. Its publication followed a series of meetings between top financiers under the auspices of the Pontifical Council for Justice and Peace.

The ethics of finance has thus arrived at an auspicious time, and it merits considerable attention. Its central aim is to show that the theory of finance, with its assumption of self-interested opportunism and maximisation of wealth on the part of every agent, cannot explain what really happens in financial systems. Additionally, taught in a fundamentalist and uncritical way in business schools, the ideology behind the theory of finance leads to the distortion of agents' behaviour in practice, and the undermining of the proper functioning of a healthy financial system.

It is worth noting that a proper theoretical understanding of finance requires a necessary foundation in some set of ethical assumptions that reach beyond the sphere of technical financial. In other words, an ethical basis to the operation of finance is not a constraint or a limitation placed on financial agents, but rather the prerequisite condition that will allow the financial system to continue to exist.

Bibliography

Bowie, N., 1991. "Challenging the Egoistic Paradigm", in: *Business Ethics Quarterly 1.*

DeGeorge, R., 1992. "Agency Theory and the Ethics of Agency", in: Bowie, N. and Freeman, E. (eds.), *Ethics and Agency Theory: An Introduction*, New York: Oxford University Press.

Dempsey, M., 1999. "An Agenda for Window-Dressing or for Radical Change?" Working Paper, Nathan, Griffith University.

Dobson, J., 1993. "The Role of Ethics in Finance", in: *Financial Analysis Journal*, November-December.

Duska, R., 1992. "Why Be a Loyal Agent? A Systematic Ethical Analysis", in: Bowie, N./ Freeman, E. (eds.), *Ethics and Agency Theory: An Introduction*, New York: Oxford University Press.

PART II

STANDARDS AND VALUES

10

SOCIAL IMPACT RATINGS HOW TO MAKE RESPONSIBLE INVESTMENT APPEALING

Jonathan M. Wisebrod

The investment sector plays a unique role in promoting ethical practices throughout the economy. With well over three trillion dollars invested in socially responsible investments (SRI) worldwide, environmental, social, governance and ethical factors (collectively, "social impact factors") have a demonstrable impact on investment practices. SRI investors utilise various methods of influencing corporate practice, including social screening of investments, that can ultimately reward positive social impact with greater access to financing. This paper proposes a method for incorporating social impact factors as a quantitative parameter in investment analysis and a means of facilitating such analysis in practice. These proposals have the potential to integrate social impact factors into quantitative portfolio management techniques that have traditionally been based only on risk and return.

Social screening techniques within SRI

Very broadly, SRI is the inclusion of any social or ethical criterion in the investment decision-making process. The first instances of socially responsible investing may be the Quakers' rules against investing in arms companies and engaging in the business of slavery as early as the mid-eighteenth century (Kinder, 2005; Kinder and Domini, 1998). Ethical exclusions remain common to this day, as they are applied by investors seeking to avoid companies that manufacture products such as weapons, tobacco, alcoholic beverages, gambling and controversial media. One shortcoming of this mode of SRI is that it is not often clear exactly which companies ought to be excluded from investment. Particularly as companies become larger, more global and increasingly diversified, it is not clear where to draw the line from an SRI perspective.

For instance, a large printing company that makes labels for cigarette cartons might be excluded by an absolute screen on tobacco if even a minuscule percentage of its profits are derived from such products. Furthermore, a company may be legally prevented from refusing to do business with a tobacco company, such as companies that are granted legally-protected monopolies (often in the transportation and telecommunication sectors) and can be required by law to serve all comers. The absolute nature of traditional ethical exclusions makes it increasingly difficult to apply them in a manner that reflects investors' intentions without overly restricting the pool of investment opportunities for socially conscious investors.

Towards the end of the twentieth century the introduction of relative social impact ratings (in contrast with absolute ethical exclusions) enabled more fulsome comparisons of companies on the basis of their social impact. SRI research firms evaluate companies on the basis of a variety of non-financial criteria from a broad stakeholder perspective. Social impact ratings can incorporate environmental sustainability, labour relations practices, community involvement and corporate governance, among other factors. By relying on these broader social impact ratings, positive screening is able to overcome the identification problem encountered with ethical exclusions.

For instance, the social impact rating of a company that manufactures and promotes cigarettes would certainly suffer as a result of its product, while the social impact rating of a company that merely packages or transports the product may suffer only marginally, if at all. In addition, a relative social impact approach rather than ethical exclusion makes it possible to incorporate complex social and environmental factors that are not conducive to absolute determination of investment eligibility. Positive screening based on social impact ratings enables companies to be ranked along a spectrum of relative social responsibility.

A variety of social impact rating systems

Despite significant overlap in the factors assessed by social impact rating providers, the criteria and rating systems differ substantially among providers. Some examples are a numerical system of scores up to twenty (the Total Social Impact Foundation's TSI™ Ratings for S&P 500 companies), a letter category system ranging from AAA to D (Reputex Ratings & Research Services' ratings for Australian companies) and a numerical range of positive and negative social impact ranging from +5 to -5 (dotherightthing Inc. ratings for specific events involving a given company). Other research providers offer a narrative assessment of a variety of social impact criteria for rated companies, rather than distilling the rating to a number or letter (e.g. KLD Research and Analytics, Inc. ratings for S&P 500 and Russell 3000 companies). A proposed means of moving toward a uniform social impact rating system is set forth below.

Social impact ratings can facilitate socially conscious portfolio management based on quantitative methods. In 2001, Summit Mutual Funds, Inc. introduced the Summit Total Social Impact (TSI) Fund. Rather than resorting to ethical exclusions, the fund weighted its investments based on companies' TSI Ratings. The fund included all S&P 500 stocks but re-weighted them on the basis of a social impact multiplier consisting of each company's TSI Rating divided by the median S&P 500 score. Thus, the fund over-weighted companies with higher social impact ratings and under-weighted those with lower ratings. Prior to its closure in 2005, the fund consistently outperformed the S&P 500 Index by about fifty basis points.

Portfolio social impact ratings

The assumption that investors make decisions on a portfolio basis is central to modern portfolio theory because the overall risk of a portfolio changes with the addition of investments that are not perfectly correlated. Hence the benefits of diversification, which can reduce portfolio risk without compromising the expected return of the portfolio. For socially conscious investors who adhere to modern portfolio theory, the introduction of portfolio social impact ratings can permit investment decisions made on a portfolio basis to consider social impact ratings as well as risk and return.

Unlike portfolio risk, which is a function of the correlation of returns from assets in the portfolio, the social impact ratings of individual companies are independent and uncorrelated. A portfolio social impact rating can be calculated simply as the weighted average social impact rating of the companies represented in the portfolio. Some issues that could make this calculation more complicated are whether equity and debt investments should be treated in the same manner, whether short positions should offset long positions in calculating social impact ratings and the treatment to be afforded to derivatives. Although these specific questions are outside the scope of this paper, the answers and the general calculation of social impact ratings would benefit from standardisation in order to achieve the full quantitative potential of social impact ratings.

Positive screening techniques demonstrate that social impact ratings can facilitate relative social impact weightings within portfolios rather than resorting to absolute ethical exclusions. Portfolio social impact ratings have the potential to promote a similar transition for the field of fund management as a whole, by facilitating social impact comparisons of all managed investment portfolios including SRI and mainstream investments. For example, retail SRI is presently dominated by a limited, albeit growing array of SRI mutual funds, so that there is an absolute distinction between SRI and mainstream investments for retail investors. The application of social impact ratings to retail investments is particularly relevant, as SRI mutual funds have recently been the fastest growing segment of SRI in the United States. As there is already competition among SRI and mainstream fund managers for the attention of socially conscious investors, the ability to make social impact comparisons on the basis of portfolio social impact ratings could encourage mainstream fund managers to consider social impact in their portfolio management decisions, though not necessarily at the expense of traditional risk and return criteria.

The identification of a "socially dominant portfolio"

When selecting from among multiple portfolios with similar risk/return characteristics, the socially conscious portfolio investor prefers the portfolio with the highest social impact rating. In other words, a portfolio with a higher social impact rating and given risk/return characteristics dominates (is preferred to) a portfolio with a lower social impact rating and the same risk/return characteristics. Similarly, a portfolio with a given social impact rating and more favourable risk/return characteristics dominates a portfolio with the same social impact rating and less favourable risk/return characteristics.

In practice, the socially conscious portfolio investor first identifies the risk-efficient portfolio(s), relying on modern portfolio theory. Given multiple portfolios with a similar degree of risk, the portfolio with the highest expected return dominates. Given multiple portfolios with the same expected return, the portfolio with the lowest degree of risk dominates. The Sharpe ratio is a convenient tool for analyzing expected return and risk in a single measure of the risk-adjusted performance of an asset, portfolio or trading strategy. The Sharpe ratio measures excess returns over the risk free rate divided by the variability of those excess returns, as measured by their standard deviation. According to modern portfolio theory, a portfolio with a higher Sharpe ratio dominates one with a lower Sharpe ratio, subject to any independent parameters, such as the investor's minimum required return and/or maximum level of acceptable risk. The rational investor selects the portfolio with highest Sharpe ratio among those that satisfy the independent parameters, if any.

If multiple portfolios offer the same risk-adjusted returns as measured by the Sharpe ratio, those portfolios are equally risk-efficient. Provided more than one of these portfolios meets any applicable required return and/or maximum risk parameters, the investor must select from among multiple portfolios. In such cases, portfolio social impact ratings can facilitate the identification of a "socially dominant portfolio". The socially conscious investor selects the portfolio with the highest portfolio social impact rating from the risk-efficient portfolios.

In search of social impact rating standards

Despite the analytical potential of social impact ratings, most investors are unable to implement even the simple portfolio management technique described above. Because fund managers generally do not release detailed information regarding their portfolio holdings, most investors lack the information necessary to calculate portfolio social impact ratings. Furthermore, the process of obtaining social impact ratings and most underlying company data can be time-consuming and costly, even in cases where it is publicly available. Finally, ratings prepared by different social impact researchers are not generally comparable, as there is no universal standard for the criteria and calculation methodology of social impact ratings. In order to fully harness the quantitative potential of social impact ratings, it is necessary to develop a widespread, standardised rating system.

The United Nations' Principles for Responsible Investing (the "UN Principles", launched in 2006 as an initiative of the UNEP Finance Initiative and the UN Global Compact) have been signed by over 150 signatories including institutional asset owners controlling over two trillion dollars, investment managers managing over three trillion dollars and professional service partners. The UN Principles could form the foundation for standardised social impact ratings. The first and third UN Principles (UNEP Finance Initiative and UN Global Compact, 2006) read, in part, as follows:

1. We will incorporate ESG [environmental, social and governance] issues into investment analysis and decision-making processes.

   Possible Actions:

- [...] Support the development of ESG-related tools, metrics and analyses [...];
- Ask investment service providers (such as financial analysts, consultants, brokers, research firms, or rating companies) to integrate ESG factors into evolving research and analysis [...].

3. We will seek appropriate disclosure on ESG issues by the entities in which we invest.

   Possible Actions:

- [...] Ask for standardised reporting on ESG issues (using tools such as the Global Reporting Initiative);
- Ask for ESG issues to be integrated within annual financial reports [...].

The signatories to the UN Principles clearly acknowledge that social impact factors are relevant to investment analysis. However, being basic principles rather than clear rules, the UN Principles are not specific enough per se to facilitate the incorporation of social impact ratings into the quantitative methods that are central to contemporary investment management. The following discussion proposes a voluntary compliance system of uniform global social impact rating standards (the "Standards") designed to standardise the criteria and calculation of social impact ratings in order to supplement these aspects of the general UN Principles with specific Standards. The Standards would afford incentive for companies and fund managers to comply voluntarily, despite the associated costs. By setting out clear requirements for compliance, the Standards would also provide a convenient avenue for focused investor pressure to encourage compliance by companies and fund managers.

Rules rather than principles

The most viable means of encouraging uniform social impact ratings and disclosures would be a system of voluntary compliance, similar to that employed by the existing UN Principles, but based on specific rules rather than broad principles. This means of implementation could be conceptually based on the Global Investment Performance Standards (GIPS®), which were introduced in 1999 and are administered by the CFA Institute's Centre for Financial Market Integrity. The GIPS are based on rules rather than principles and are widely recognised as the current global best practice in investment performance reporting. While compliance is not mandatory, investment managers claiming compliance with the GIPS must make a variety of prescribed disclosures, avoid other prohibited disclosures and rely on pre-defined uniform calculation methodologies in reporting past performance. The GIPS have fostered investor confidence throughout the world by ensuring "fair representation, full disclosure and apples-to-apples comparisons" (CFA, 2005) among compliant fund managers. They have been adopted as the country standard for performance reporting in 26 cases, including several developing countries.

The issue of compliance

The proposed Standards would require companies claiming compliance to publicly disclose a standardised rating calculated according to the prescribed methodology together with certain underlying factual disclosures (e.g. workforce demographics, details of environmental impact etc.). Like the GIPS, the Standards would be based on rules rather than principles. In practice, companies could engage independent rating providers to produce these ratings in much the same manner as companies engage credit rating providers to assess their creditworthiness. In turn, investment managers could claim compliance with the Standards only if the underlying company social impact ratings and the methodology used to compile the portfolio social impact ratings are prepared in accordance with the Standards. To be successful, the Standards would have to be general enough to provide meaningful data for comparisons among companies and fund managers yet specific enough for those comparisons to offer substantive value to socially conscious investors. They would also have to be adopted by a critical mass of companies and fund managers.

Voluntary compliance would allow market forces to govern the pace of adoption of the Standards. Positive externalities could lead to broad compliance with the Standards despite their voluntary nature. When a voluntary compliance scheme is successful, the value of compliance increases as more entities claim compliance. Based on the increase of SRI funds as a proportion of total investment funds, and particularly the rapid growth of SRI mutual funds, compliance with the Standards could afford a competitive edge to compliant companies with respect to their financing options and to investment managers with respect to their assets under management. In the extreme case, compliance with the Standards might ultimately be regarded as a necessary cost of obtaining corporate financing or assets under management, much as many companies and fund managers are willing to incur the high cost of securities regulatory compliance in order to be eligible for public investment. Thus, if the Standards are appropriately defined, natural market forces could eventually lead to widespread adoption without legally mandating compliance.

Natural market forces will set the pace of adoption

The law is not a viable means of implementing well-formulated global social impact rating standards. Foremost, the large number of legal jurisdictions and securities regulators and the persistent lack of harmonisation make it logistically unfeasible to require globally uniform social impact ratings and disclosures for all regulated companies and fund managers. If mandatory Standards were implemented with due attention to the variations among existing regulatory regimes, they would be too broad to offer useful information for investors. On the other hand, if mandatory Standards were specific enough to be valuable for investors, broad legally-mandated compliance would disturb the capital markets by imposing uniform standards through otherwise unharmonised regulatory regimes. Neither of these options could satisfy both investors and regulators. Despite the present trend in some jurisdictions in Europe and, to a lesser degree, in the US, that requires disclosure of some social impact factors, uniform rules-based global social impact rating standards are not a good candidate for implementation through legislation.

Furthermore, avoiding a legally mandated compliance model could help to ensure that developing countries are not left behind. If compliance with the Standards was mandated by law, it is conceivable that the less developed capital markets and less robust regulatory regimes that exist in some developing countries could cause these markets to be left out of the initiative altogether. An implementation mechanism that relies on voluntary compliance is more capable of permitting companies and fund managers in each market and jurisdiction to comply with the Standards at a pace that is dictated by natural market forces. With globalisation of the capital markets and the investment sector, respectively, companies and fund managers increasingly compete for financing and assets under management throughout developed and developing markets. For this reason, implementation through voluntary compliance rather than legislation is the best means of ensuring truly global standards that are eventually adopted by a critical mass of companies and fund managers in all markets.

Notwithstanding the problems inherent to legally mandated compliance, companies and fund managers could still be encouraged to claim compliance with the Standards and provide the relevant disclosures in their regulatory filings as a best practice (e.g. in annual reports, as suggested in the third UN Principle, above). This would invite regulatory sanctions for false claims of compliance, due to the severe repercussions of including misleading information in a regulatory filing. This means of guarding against false claims of compliance is similar to that employed by the GIPS. While refusing to comply with the GIPS does not violate any law, a false claim of compliance can lead to sanctions. For example, according to the CFA Institute's Centre for Market Integrity, the United States Securities and Exchange Commission has sanctioned investment managers for falsely claiming compliance with the GIPS. Similar to the GIPS, the most viable means of implementing the Standards is a voluntary compliance scheme that relies on regulatory force only to avoid false claims of compliance without actually making compliance mandatory.

Arguments for standardised ratings

At present, a social impact rating provider must define its own rating criteria and calculation methodology, gather relevant information for each company to be rated and calculate and update the social impact rating according to the calculation methodology. This process is complicated and expensive due to the diversity of existing rating systems and limited publicly available information about relevant corporate practices. Widespread adoption of the Standards could be expected to reduce these costs due to standardisation and economies of scale.

Standardised ratings would eliminate the need for each rating provider to develop its own rating scheme and for each company to be rated by several providers. The burden of turning up data relevant to a company's social impact rating would fall to the company seeking to claim compliance rather than external rating providers. The company is in the best position to gather the relevant data, while an independent rating provider is in the best position to provide unbiased evaluations of that data. In this manner the role of the rating provider could evolve from a research function to a corporate service function whereby the rating provider produces ratings in accordance with the pre-defined Standards using data that is furnished by the company. Independent audits are already the norm for environmental sustainability reports and it is quite conceivable that the audit methodology could be standardised and extended to include other social impact factors.

Furthermore, as noted above, there are positive externalities associated with a voluntary compliance scheme because the value of compliance increases as more companies and fund managers comply. The pace of adoption by companies and fund managers can be expected to accelerate with time. Due to standardisation, a social impact rating prepared in accordance with the Standards would be an undifferentiated product. As the market for this product grows, an economy of scale would result. In contrast with the present growth of SRI, which has led to more research providers offering competing rating schemes, the service of producing social impact ratings could be commoditised through standardisation. The cost of obtaining social impact ratings could reasonably be expected to fall as rating providers compete to offer a standard service in contrast with the present competition to offer a custom product.

Similar to the GIPS, a key benefit of the proposed Standards would be the uniformity of social impact disclosures, which would facilitate reliable comparisons. If widespread voluntary compliance with the Standards can be achieved, the proposed portfolio social impact ratings and the method for identifying socially dominant portfolios described above would be much more practical for most investors. Further to these simple proposals for socially conscious portfolio management, more complex quantitative social impact metrics could also be developed once standardised ratings are widely available. Given accepted techniques for the incorporation of social impact ratings into quantitative investment analysis, investors would have the necessary information to make informed socially conscious investment decisions among all available investment portfolios. By facilitating comparisons among a wide variety of mainstream and SRI investment portfolios on the basis of social impact, the Standards would expand the scope of investment opportunities that are available for consideration by SRI investors.

A great potential

For investors seeking to consider social impact in addition to return and risk, social impact ratings can enable all of these factors to be incorporated into quantitative investment analysis. Portfolio social impact ratings and the concept of socially dominant portfolios supplement modern portfolio theory with an analytical technique for socially conscious investors. Just as the reliance on standard deviation as a quantifiable risk measure has facilitated quantitative risk analysis, social impact ratings have the same potential to apply a quantitative analytical approach to SRI. Some SRI investors, particularly those who base social screens on religious beliefs, may be committed to absolute ethical exclusions. However, positive screening and quantitative analysis based on relative social impact ratings still hold great potential for a large segment of the SRI investing world.

For this potential to be fully realised there must be a uniform social impact rating system. The UN Principles have laid the groundwork for incorporating social impact into investment decisions but specific rules-based standards are necessary to fully realise the analytical value of social impact ratings. Global social impact rating standards could be developed from the UN Principles if the signatories to the Principles are committed to incorporating social impact factors in quantitative investment analysis. The CFA Institute's GIPS are a good model for voluntary compliance with clear, pre-defined rules that facilitate reliable comparisons. If properly formulated, the Standards could play an important role in bridging the gap between traditional SRI and the quantitative techniques that lie at the root of modern portfolio management.

Appendix: Quantitative application of social impact ratings for a two stock portfolio

The following is an illustration of the quantitative concepts discussed in this paper, based on a simple two stock portfolio of financial services companies using actual economic data. All figures are rounded to two decimal places.

The first table sets forth the assumptions used in this model. Fannie Mae (FNM) and Morgan Stanley (MS), respectively, received the highest (14.6) and lowest (8.2) TSI™ Ratings for financial services companies in the S&P 500, as rated by the Total Social Impact Foundation, an American not-for-profit organisation (these ratings are from 31 December 2003, which is the last time for which TSI™ data is available). The expected annual return for each stock is based on analysts' average 2007 target prices and the risk free rate is assumed to be the yield on a 10-year United States Treasury bond at the time of writing (4.69%). The stocks' expected excess returns are their respective expected returns minus the risk free rate. The stocks' standard deviation and correlation are calculated based on their respective excess stock returns over the last ten years. The Sharpe ratio is calculated from this data.

ASSET CHARACTERISTICS AND RISK FREE RATE

	FNM	MS	General
Expected Return	8.60%	13.90%	
Risk Free Rate			4.69%
Expected Excess Return	3.91%	9.21%	
Standard Deviation	0.26	0.38	
Sharpe Ratio	0.15	0.24	

CALCULATIONS FOR VARIOUS PORTFOLIOS OF FNM AND MS

Portfolio	FNM Weight	MS Weight	Expected Return
1	0%	100%	13.90%
2	10%	90%	13.37%
3	20%	80%	12.84%
4	30%	70%	12.31%
5	**40%**	**60%**	**11.78%**
6	50%	50%	11.25%
7	60%	40%	10.72%
8	70%	30%	10.19%
9	80%	20%	9.66%
10	90%	10%	9.13%
11	100%	0%	8.60%

Portfolio	Expected Ex-cess Return	Standard Deviation	Sharpe Ratio	Social Impact Rating
1	9.21%	0.38	0.24	8.20
2	8.68%	0.35	0.25	8.84
3	8.15%	0.33	0.25	9.48
4	7.62%	0.30	0.25	10.12
5	**7.09%**	**0.29**	**0.25**	**10.76**
6	6.56%	0.27	0.24	11.40
7	6.03%	0.26	0.23	12.04
8	5.50%	0.25	0.22	12.68
9	4.97%	0.25	0.20	13.32
10	4.44%	0.25	0.17	13.96
11	3.91%	0.26	0.15	14.60

This second table includes the relevant calculations for each of 11 different combinations of the two stocks, ranging from the portfolio that is 100% invested in MS (portfolio 1) to the one that is 100% invested in FNM (portfolio 11). It illustrates how the proposed quantitative concepts can be applied in practice.

Portfolio social impact ratings

For each portfolio, the final column calculates the portfolio social impact rating based on the weighted average social impact ratings of FNM and MS.

Socially dominant portfolios

Pursuant to modern portfolio theory, portfolios 2, 3, 4 and 5 are risk-efficient portfolios insofar as they offer higher risk-adjusted returns than all other portfolios (i.e. they have the highest Sharpe ratio, 0.25 after rounding). However, assuming each portfolio satisfies any applicable required return and/or maximum risk parameters, these portfolios are equally preferred because they offer a similar Sharpe ratio. Portfolio 5 has a higher portfolio social impact rating (10.76) than each of portfolios 2 (8.84), 3 (9.48) and 4 (10.12). On this basis, portfolio 5 is the socially dominant portfolio and is preferred by the socially conscious investor.

The author gratefully acknowledges contributions from the Total Social Impact Foundation Inc. and KLD Research & Analytics, Inc., which were kind enough to provide samples of their proprietary research for the purposes of this paper.

Bibliography

CFA Centre for Financial Market Integrity, 2005. *GIPS Fact Sheet*, *www.cfainstitute.org/aboutus/press/pdf/GIPSfactsheet2005.pdf.*

Kinder, P.D., 2005. *Socially Responsible Investing: An Evolving Concept in a Changing World*, Boston: KLD Research & Analytics, *www.kld.com/resources/papers/SRIEvolving070109.pdf.*

Kinder, P.D. and Domini, A., 1998. *Social Screening: Paradigms Old and New*, Investment Research Guide to Socially Responsible Investing, Plano (Texas), Investment Research Forums.

UNEP Finance Initiative and UN Global Compact, 2006. *The Principles for Responsible Investment*, *www.unpri.org/files/pri.pdf.*

11

THE RECONCILIATION OF FINANCE AND ETHICS: INTEGRATING THE INTERIOR AND EXTERIOR DIMENSIONS OF REALITY

Faly Ranaivoson

Finance and… ethics. As you see these two words next to each other, you may feel some tension, or even a slight discomfort. Or you may even smile coyly, thinking they do not belong together. You may spontaneously remember the global financial crisis and shake your head in disbelief thinking of the damages that are still felt across nations and organisations. Or you may belong to a large portion of the population that does not trust institutions, corporations, politics, business people and finance professionals. Even before the crisis reached its pinnacle, a US Roper poll conducted in 2005 showed that close to three quarters of respondents believed wrongdoing was widespread in industry. Only 2% felt that leaders of large firms were "very trustworthy." Recent events have certainly not improved their image.

In this paper, I attempt to convey that what I've just described are only symptoms of a much deeper issue. We built a global framework of scientific, industrial, financial, economic, and informational systems. Yet we lost meaning, value, and ethics in the process.

By holding both finance and ethics in my consciousness, I feel an invitation to recover what has been broken, to integrate what has been fragmented. I extend this invitation to finance professionals – who are usually very at ease with the tangibles – to explore the intangibles and to integrate the world of the visible and the world of the invisible.

Derivatives gone mad

Indeed, we did master the technical or *exterior* dimension of doing business and finance. I'll just use the example of derivatives to illustrate this point.

The derivatives market has grown from $100 trillion to $500 trillion in 2007. "The total world derivatives market has been estimated at about $791 trillion face or nominal value, that's 11 time the size of the entire world economy" *(en.wikipedia.org/wiki/Stock_market*). In July 2008, the Jutia Group reported that global derivatives had reached more than one quadrillion dollars (that's one followed by 15 zeroes!): $548 Trillion in listed credit derivatives and $596 trillion in notional/OTC derivatives. And if these raw numbers still do not talk to you, just take a look at the following graph:

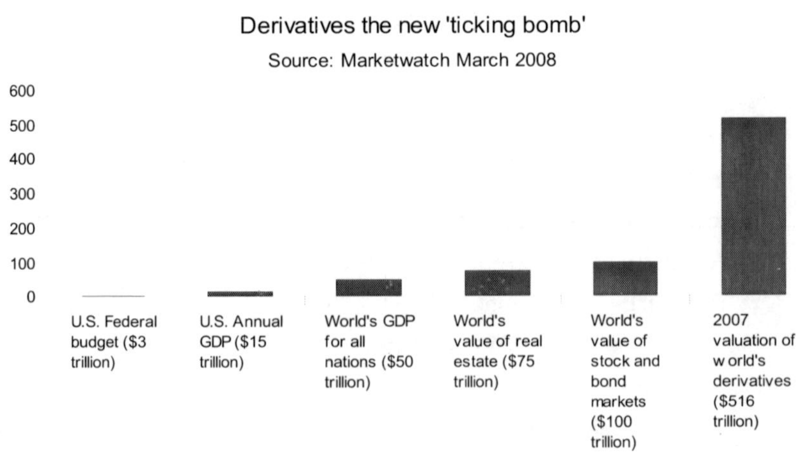

Very much like Dr. Frankenstein, we have designed our very own monster and it is now getting out of hand. William H. Gross founder of Pimco, a global investment management firm, employed the term "shadow banking system" to describe the system whereby "derivatives are a means to creating money outside the usual central bank boundaries, simply because they're bilateral contracts between institutions or companies."*(www.marketwatch.com/story/derivatives-are-the-new-ticking-time-bomb)*

And Warren Buffet almost compared the highly technically sophisticated financial engineers who developed derivatives to mad scientists designing a nuclear bomb when he wrote in his 2002 letter to Berkshire shareholders: "We try to be alert to any sort of mega-catastrophe risk, and that posture may make us unduly appreciative about the burgeoning quantities of long-term derivatives contracts and the massive amount of *uncollateralised* receivables that are growing alongside. In our view, however, derivatives are financial weapons of mass destruction, carrying danger that, while now latent, are potentially lethal."

We know the rest of the story…

Modernity gone mad

The derivatives bubble, cultural taboos around money, our own personal tension around ethics and finance… all of these symptoms, in a way, can be traced back to what the philosopher Ken Wilber calls the "disaster of modernity."

But first let's quickly clarify what we mean by *modernity*, as it is one of these words to which many meanings can be attached. Historically, modernity loosely starts at the Renaissance and continues in some ways to this day. Philosophically, it refers to our attempt to understand and represent nature as accurately as possible. Scientifically, modernity is about measuring nature and discovering the mechanisms that causes its functioning. Politically, it marked the rise of human rights (equality before the law, outlawing of slavery, women's rights, and so forth). From a techno-economic structure standpoint, it is associated with industrialisation.

Before we investigate the bad news of modernity, first let's acknowledge its good news. Wilber reminds us that "the *governing principles* of the hundred or so democratic nations in today's world are in fact the *principles of modernity* – that is, the values of the liberal Western Enlightenment." (Wilber, 1998.) We have to remember that these human rights that are so dear to us (freedom of speech, religion, assembly, etc.) did not exist on a global scale before the Enlightenment – though they still have to be adopted more universally.

Another way of characterising the dignity of modernity is through the separation of church and state. This is a direct manifestation of what Max Weber called "the differentiation of the cultural value spheres – that is *the differentiation of art, morals, and science*." What happened typically during the Middle Ages is that someone such as Galileo would clash with the church because the spheres of science and religion were not differentiated and the latter prevailed. It was not a healthy integration of these value spheres but rather an unhealthy fusion. What differentiation permitted is for someone such as Galileo to pursue his endeavours without being persecuted by the Inquisition.

But then, this differentiation went too far into disassociation. Dignity turned into disaster. What happened is that the value-sphere of science took over as the value-spheres of aesthetics and morals were reduced to a monological view. Art, morals and science went their separate ways. And science unfortunately turned into scientism by dismissing all the interior aspects of consciousness, soul, art, morals, and ethics, arguably because none of these subjective domains can't be apprehended by the "eye of flesh" of empirical science.

So what was declared real, was anything that could be described in an empirical fashion; as all phenomena investigated by empirical science all have what Alfred North Whitehead called a simple location: meaning that you can literally put your finger on them. Therefore, the brain is real, galaxies are real. Yet you can't put your fingers on goodness, nor on consciousness (the disaster of modernity has reduced it to brain waves), nor on ethics. Our sense of discomfort has profound roots indeed.

Unfortunately, our conversations around finance have followed the trend set by the disaster of modernity by almost solely focusing on the quantifiable exterior, which is the domain of indexes, statistics, and measurement systems for accounting. While we have no issues speaking intelligently to the quantifiable, we haven't reached the same level of complexity in our interior dimension. And our ethical relationship with finance and money has suffered. We are definitely ill-equipped to address hard-to-measure data such as goals and motivation, not to mention meaning-making and culture. To this day, finance professionals lack words for these conversations. They are reduced to using terms such as "life planning" or "soft side."

The paradox of money

It's almost funny to think that we apply the principles and methodologies of exact science to finance when we think of the nature of money. Indeed, when we attend a course in finance, read the economics section in the journal, or watch CNBC, it might seem that finance is akin to a hard scientific discipline. And in a way it almost is, when we look at all the charts and numbers. Yet it would be foolish to believe we're really in the realm of strict calculus and exact science.

Bernard Lietaer reminds us that money is actually not a thing; "it's a combination of beliefs, promises, and commitments anchored to some principle upon which enough people rely on so that it can be used to support different types of exchange." (*www.lietaer.com/2010/09/what-is-money/*)

And so there lies the paradox of money: Trapped in the disaster of modernity, some finance professionals and economists continue to treat finance as a big machinery and people as routine operators. Yet we just saw money is not only the result of physical workings. It primarily requires subjective integrity and intersubjective ethical agreement. Certainly by looking at charts, we might observe some trends. But these trends are the results of aggregations of human interactions based on agreements. And we should not forget that humans are even less predictable than natural elements, even though classical economists might argue the contrary.

In the end, we can't predict what will happen in finance. Its principles are as much of the social as they are of the hard sciences, hence their inexactitude. We shouldn't be surprised then that money is the second most addressed topic in the Christian Bible (Wagner, 2006). Money is both from interior and exterior, hearts and hands.

Rehabilitating the interior

The task that lies ahead of us is not to merely promote ethics in finance. Doing so may lead us to think of ethics as a band aid to partially cover the deep wounds left behind by the excesses of finance. No. Our task is to rehabilitate the interior dimension of reality thereby putting as much attention on ethics as we do on [the technical side of] finance.

One of the main lesson of post-modernity – we'll refer very broadly to it as to what emerged in the wake of modernity – is that "reality is not in all ways pre-given, but in some significant ways is a construction, an interpretation (…); the belief that reality is simply given, and not also partly constructed, is referred to as the myth of the given." (Wilber, 1998).

Immanuel Kant was one of the first philosopher to fight the myth of the given. In *Critique of Pure Reason*, he demonstrated that science wasn't able to come to the conclusion that the interior dimensions of soul, morals, and ethics existed. Furthermore, he demonstrated that science wasn't able to conclude that these interior dimensions *didn't* exist either. Next, in *Critique of Practical Reason*, he went on to demonstrate that indeed the interior dimension could not be addressed by science, but was rather the domain of *dialogical* – or moral, ethical, practical reason. Finally, he brought the subjective aesthetics dimension back into the picture in his *Critique of Judgement*, thereby completing his attempt at integrating the value-spheres of art, morals, and science.

Again, the paradox of money can then be extended to a paradox of science that can be summed up as follows: science itself relies on instruments and structures found only in the interior dimension. These structures not only include cultural backgrounds, linguistic frameworks, and ethical norms, but also devices such as logic, statistical analysis, algebra, complex numbers and so forth, all of which scientists make extensive use. And then scientism claims this interior dimension does not exist in the first place. In other words, the interior dimension both partly shapes our empirical knowledge and can be inquired in its own right.

Other scholars have insisted upon integrating the three value spheres of art, morals, and science. For instance, Karl Popper points out to that, by suggesting that we divide the view of reality into three sub-realities which he calls Worlds. The first World is the physical world investigated by empirical science. The second World refers to the psychological or mental world of thoughts, feelings, perceptions. And the third World is the domain of products of the human mind: tales, stories, myths, languages, songs, paintings and sculptures. The German sociologist and philosopher Jürgen Habermas also divides reality into three worlds: the subjective world, the social world, and the objective world.

Maybe the easiest way to remember the three value-spheres is to use Plato's the Good, the True, and the Beautiful. In this case, the True refers to the objective of empirical world; the Good refers to the intersubjective space of ethical appropriateness; and the Beautiful refers to the subjective or aesthetic dimension.

So the question remains: how do we explore these interior dimensions? We've already seen that empirical science, which explores phenomena that have a simple location, is not suited to explore the intangible interior.

Wilber has identified four epistemological families that explore the interior either in its individual or collective dimension: *phenomenology*, which investigates direct experience (the insides of individual interiors); *structuralism*, which explores patterns of direct experience (the outsides of individual interiors); *hermeneutics*, which examines inter subjective understanding (the insides of collective interiors); and *cultural anthropology*, which studies patterns of mutual understanding (the outsides of collective interiors). (Esbjörn-Hargens, 2006). We'll soon examine how a domain of inquiry derived from structuralism can shed some light on the ethical development of individuals.

Level five leadership

One question that keeps intriguing the public is why do we have, at one end of the spectrum, people such as Joan Bavaria, who pioneered the whole socially responsible investment (SRI) movement and, at the opposite end, people such as Bernie Madoff who used his cognitive capacity to design one of the biggest financial fraud in history.

Joan Bavaria (1943-2008) was the founder of Trillium Asset Management, an independent investment adviser whose mission is to *Invest for a Better World* (since 1982). On the company's website, we can read some words that are employed to describe her character and actions: "humour, compassion, dedication, vision, humanity, mentor, hero; unending commitment to serving clients; a unique vision for how the capital markets intersect with society and the environment…"

When I read testimonies from people talking about Joan Bavaria's character, Jim Collins' work on leadership immediately came to my mind. In his seminal book *Good to Great*, he shares a framework that explains how elite companies were able to produce sustainable results for at least fifteen years. The first key element he describes in his book is that these exceptional companies were led by what Collins calls Level 5 Leaders. In his *Harvard Business Review* article "Level 5 Leadership," he writes that "Of 1,435 companies that appeared on the Fortune 500 since 1965, only 11 made it into our study. In those 11, all of them had Level 5 leaders in key positions, including the CEO role, at the pivotal time of transition." And, when he sums up what level 5 leaders' character is about, he uses the following terms: "Personal humility"; "Relies principally on inspired standards, not inspiring charisma, to motivate;" "Channels ambition into the company, not the self; sets up successors for even greater success in the next generation." What we read about Joan Bavaria is very close to the description Jim Collins makes of level 5 leaders. Yet he admits there is one key element he has not been able to delve into with his research, and that is what he calls the "black box" of inner development of an individual to Level 5.

The black box of inner development

Once again, Jim Collins himself has been a victim of the disaster of modernity – though by his own recognition – by focusing his research on the exterior dimensions of reality: he used empirical studies to investigate leaders and he concentrated exclusively on the financial bottom line of companies. Indeed, to investigate an individual's inner development requires making use of the appropriate method of inquiry, typically developmental psychology, which is itself influenced by structuralism. For over half a century, developmental theorists such as Jean Piaget, Jane Loevinger, Jenny Wade, Erik Erikson, Susanne Cook-Greuter,

Howard Gardner, Robert Kegan, Lawrence Kohlberg, and Carol Gilligan have investigated the interior unfolding of the human being.

Howard Gardner's work on "theory of multiple intelligences" is particularly helpful when it comes to understanding why individuals with comparable cognitive capacities may display very different ethical behaviours. He explains, "We observe daily that only one kind of talent – say, technological creativity – is being rewarded, and only one measure – say, profitability in the marketplace – is being recognised. These indices are insufficient; other parts of the human spirit merit recognition, respect, and veneration." (Gardner, 1999). While acknowledging the importance of intelligence quotient, Gardner invites us to value other important manifestations of human intelligence (interpersonal, intrapersonal, musical, spatial, and bodily-kinaesthetic). He agrees that his way of framing his theory is simply one of several legit approaches to look at the different human capacities. His and others' work in the area of developmental psychology form the backbone for a broader comprehension of human interior's unfolding referred to as "developmental streams." Taking Gardner's and his peers' work into consideration, we can point to five human aptitudes most appropriate to understand discrepancies in ethical behaviours: Cognitive aptitude – general intellectual abilities including logic, reason, linguistic, analysing, and decision-making; Emotional aptitude – ability to access one's own emotions and those of others, to derive meaning from them and to manage them; Ethical aptitude – being able to use accessible information, and to take decisions with regard to the needs and wants of others to bring about the highest good for all concerned; Physical aptitude – awareness of one's body and ability to use it in skilled ways; Spiritual aptitude – ability to gather and use wisdom in the investigation of "what matters most."

And so different people display unequal levels of "expertise" in various domains. We can illustrate these discrepancies using a "psychological equaliser."

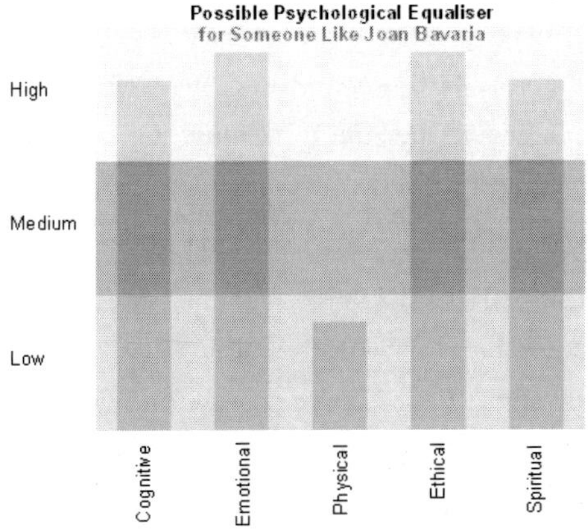

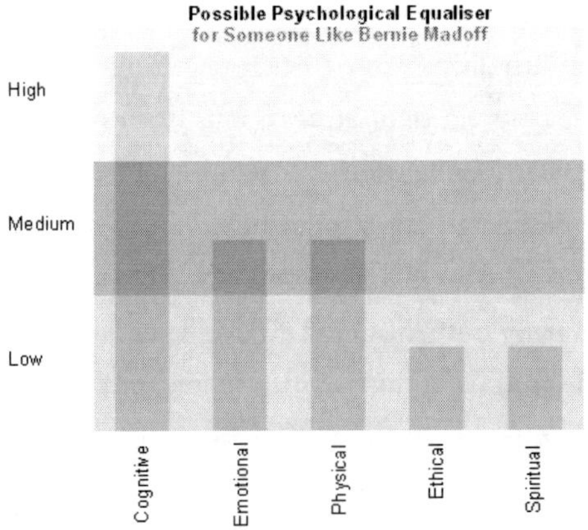

Let's dive into some *very broad* orienting generalisations around what low, medium, and high levels of ethical aptitudes might look like. We may compare people that exhibit a low – or pre-conventional (Kohlberg, 1973) – level of ethical aptitude to children who will determine the rightness or wrongness of their actions on the basis of whether they get caught or not. The main difference between adults and children with a similar ethical capacity lies in adults' cognitive capacity to design complex schemes in order to avoid getting caught. As long as they can do so, they will act with the purpose of immediate gratification without attending to the impact their behaviours might have on others.

The medium – or conventional – level of ethical aptitude is what most people equal ethics to when they think of, or use this term. At this stage, it is about behaving according to the rule of the law. Or similar to adolescents, it is also about acting in conformity with group expectations. Consequently, people won't break the rules and may even experience guilt by doing so, even if they don't get caught.

At a high – or post-conventional – level of ethical aptitude, it is not about being told how to live, or about how to give precise and definitive answers to moral questions, or about following a textbook. It's rather about holding the space for an overarching framework for thinking to emerge. Indeed, such a framework is needed to make nuanced judgements around highly ambiguous dilemmas, to make sense of people's and cultures' different ethical structures, and to take a multiplicity of perspectives into account. Post-conventional ethics focuses on one's intentions rather than one's outward behaviours: from the outside, you may observe two individual exhibiting very similar behaviours, but they may actually be moved by very different intentions. At this stage, the challenge is about becoming a truly authentic and courageous individual who stays present and centred, holding to his – world-centric rather ethnocentric or egocentric – principles in the face of difficult and complicated choices.

We have yet to examine how to foster the development of integrated professionals that display excellence in both the exterior (technical) and interior (ethical) dimensions. It is time to move now from epistemology to application.

From philosophy to action

Getting back to our main thesis, it is not by merely attempting to apply ethics as a band aid that we'll be able to heal the deep wounds produced by the excesses of finance. For us practitioners, the question is how can we weave ethical concern or the interior dimension into the very fabric of everything we do in relation to ourselves, others, and organisations. In other words, one mode of framing the concept of ethics is that being ethical is about leading oneself with the purpose of being – and staying – in alignment with one's values, thereby demonstrating personal integrity. In relation to others, ethical concern is about cultivating mutuality and engaging with others with the intention of fostering reciprocation and interdependence. Still at an organisational, inter-organisational level and beyond, ethical concern is about being compelled to act with the purpose of advancing sustainability.

One particular *practice* that can blend these three objectives is called action inquiry. "It is a way of simultaneously conducting action and inquiry as a disciplined leadership practice that increases the wider effectiveness of our actions" (Torbert, 2004). The action part refers to our behaviours – what we do, what we say. The inquiry part points to questioning and reflecting – within ourselves, or in relation to others – as we engage in anything that we do.

To ground ourselves, let's dive into the story of Steve Thompson, as he reflects on an incident with his boss, Ron Cedrick (excerpted from Torbert, 2004, pp.14-16):

> "Steve's team is laying underwater pipeline when a storm begins to blow around their (…) platform.
>
> The most critical part of this dangerous procedure is the launch and recovery of the six-man bell through the "interface" – the wave-affected first 25 feet below the ocean surface. Rough seas have separated more than one diving bell from its winch. When this happens, there is little hope of returning the divers alive.
>
> It was my first job as project manager, so it was of particular importance to me that the crew was doing an outstanding job and Cedrick was extremely pleased with our performance. (…) And, no matter how difficult, his projects always came in ahead of schedule.

The bell had just gone into the water for an anticipated 12-hour run when the wind changed direction and was coming at us from the same direction as the moderate swell, just as it does before it really blows. I alerted the shift supervisor to keep an eye on the weather and went up to the bridge for a look at the most recent forecast and facsimile, which confirmed my suspicions.

Just then, Cedrick came up to me, "I personally appreciate the fine job you and your boys are doing and I know it'll continue. I know the weather's getting up a bit, but we have to complete the flow line connection today to stay ahead, so we need to keep that bell in the water as long as we can before we let a little ole weather shut us down. I've seen the respect those boys have for you and I know they'll do what you ask."

"Yes, sir" I responded confidently. What was going on inside me at that moment sounded different though. The moment I reviewed the weather on the bridge, I became tense with fear. I was afraid I wouldn't have the strength of character to shut down the operation in the face of my overwhelming desire to succeed objectively and in Cedrick's eyes. I was also afraid I would have to deceive my people into thinking that pushing our operating limits was justified.

The outcome was all too predictable. I kept the bell in the water too long. The weather blew a gale. The recovery of the bell through 20-foot seas was perilous. I compromised the safety of the divers and set a poor precedent for the permissible operating parameters. I received no satisfaction from the major bonus Cedrick gave me for "pulling it off" – we did complete the flowline connection. Inside me, the awareness that I had manipulated and jeopardised the safety of my fellow workers galled my illusion that I was an honest, ethical man."

Now let's just replace Steve Thompson with a portfolio manager or a trader who is subject to an intense pressure coming from every corner, clients, colleagues, and his or her institution. Now let's just add the constraint that he or she has to act and take decision moment to moment. How can ethical concern be put into the equation, not only before or after the fact, but as any situation unfolds second after second?

Here are some learnings that we can derive from Steve's story:

To use a terminology borrowed tfrom systems theory, finance professionals have to engage in triple-loop learning. In other words, not only do they have to monitor their actions (single-loop) and adapt their strategy (double-loop) with the purpose of achieving some desired results, they also have to develop what Torbert calls a "super-vision" (triple-loop) that allows them to take a step back in the moment in order to, when necessary, give space for ethical concern to emerge. When recounting his experience, Steve Thompson shares how he felt tension and fear because he was facing multiple conflicts of interest as Cedrick pushed him to resume the operations: he wanted to stay true to the image his boss had of him; he wanted to perform well – who does not want to? – he wanted to attend to the well-being of his team; and he wanted to view himself as an ethical man. What he lacked during his encounter with Cedrick was a capacity to not only be aware of the incongruity that was happening in himself, but also to maintain this awareness in order for him to change his course of action.

Torbert suggests several practices to advance one's capacity to sustain inquiry in the midst of action: Noticing how we feel as we move from one activity to another, or after interactions we have with any interlocutor; keeping a journal to investigate the various territories of our experience – our achievements, our behaviours, our strategies, and our intentionality; attending to the way we speak – are we sharing our intent behind a conversation; are we elaborating on our thinking; are we inquiring into others' opinions, and so forth?

Steve's story brings out another issue, that of unilateral power. In the story, we can witness how Cedrick made use of his cognitive and interpersonal abilities to slyly put pressure on Steve. First, he relied on his primary positional authority as Steve's superior; then he used his secondary positional authority as an expert; and finally, he minimised the situation by reducing the storm to some "little ole weather." On a larger scale, we can see how such approaches resting on unilateral power – action without inquiry – can give birth to major scandals. Symmetrically, inquiry without action might lead to parapraxis – in the case of Steve Thompson, he had a glimpse of awareness that allowed him to feel some tension within himself, but not sufficiently to engage in a mutual conversation with his manager.

Moving from the personal to the institutional, we can say that the whole socially responsible investing (SRI) movement is practising a type of triple-loop learning. Strategically, it has deployed new approaches such as corporate engagement, community investing, and public policy advocacy (double-loop). The SRI movement also pioneered new methodologies to assess companies' performance by taking economic, social, and environmental aspects into account. And it has enunciated a new purpose for investing. For instance, we saw previously that Trillium Asset Management Corporation's raison d'être is to Invest for a Better World.

The SRI movement is a good indicator of how a whole domain of activities can evolve by putting ethics directly into the finance equation, by integrating the interior and exterior dimensions of any issue, and by weaving action and inquiry together. Companies are then invited to not only engage in single-loop operational changes, double-loop strategical adaptations, but also in a triple-loop reflection on their raison d'être. We can only hope for the SRI movement to spread so that corporations abandon a pursuit of profit devoid of ethics to fully embrace a triple bottom line approach full of ethical concern.

Bibliography

Esbjörn-Hargens, S., 2006. "Integral Ecology: A Post-Metaphysical Approach to Environmental Phenomena", in: *AQAL Journal of Integral Theory and Practice 1*.

Gardner, H., 1993. *Frames of Mind: The Theory of Multiple Intelligences*, New York: Basic Books.

Gardner, H., 1999. *The Disciplined Mind*, New York: Simon & Schuster.

Stagen Leadership Institute, 2004. *Human Performance*.

Torbert, B. and Associates, 2004. *Action Inquiry, The Secret of Timely and Transforming Leadership*, San Francisco: Berrett-Koehler Publishers.

Wagner, Richard B., 2006. "Integral Finance 201: The Four Dimensions of Money", in: *AQAL Journal of Integral Theory and Practice 1*.

Wilber, K., 1998. *The Marriage of Sense and Soul*, New York: Random House.

Wilber, K. *et al.*, 2008. *Integral Life Practice*, Boston and London: Integral Books.

12

FINANCIAL DERIVATIVES AND RESPONSIBILITY: HOW TO DEAL ETHICALLY WITH FINANCIAL RISK

Simone Heinemann

Every day we make decisions that involve financial and economic risks. Which investment option should we choose? What kind of car insurance should we get? Should we save money or spend it right away? Risk can create opportunities. But it can also imply a possibility of loss which should be avoided whenever possible. Many of our financial decisions which involve risk are taken individually. In many of these cases the consequences, e.g. the gains as well as the losses, only affect the risk bearer himself. But, as the sub-prime crisis 2007-8 has shown, financial risks taken by individual parties can also be associated with costs for parties other than the risk creator – outside and within the financial system. Such cases have particular ethical relevance: The creation and dispersion of financial risk can potentially harm traders as well as society as a whole.

One of the means for dispersing risk is financial derivatives. Derivatives are a particular kind of tradable contract. As the name suggests, their trade value is derived from the value of other assets, historically commodities but also corporate shares, currencies, interest rates, etc. Derivatives have often been said to have been involved in several financial debacles as the scandals of Barings Bank, Metallgesellschaft or the fall of LTCM for example. They are especially known for providing leverage. Through derivatives trading a whole range of different and complex products for managing financial risk has become available. Still, their impact on the aggregate level of risk society has to bear is unclear. This paper seeks to show that financial derivatives are an ethical matter. We have to ask ourselves which aggregate level of risk is ethically acceptable. And we have to be aware of the fact that the risks taken on the individual level can lead to the materialisation of external costs that may drastically reduce human welfare. In this paper, I will pursue a normative investigation of risk-taking and present three guidelines for dealing ethically with financial risk.

What are financial derivatives?

Four main forms of derivatives exist: futures, forwards, options and swaps. All of these instruments are traditionally defined as instruments that insure against, or transfer, risk. One of these basic types of derivatives, a forward, for example, is an agreement by two parties to engage in a financial transaction at a future (forward) point in time. An example of a forward might be an agreement for a farmer to sell ten sackfuls of potatoes to a merchant, six months from today, at a price agreed today, say 100 Euros, which is, let´s suppose for simplicity's sake, the market price of today. If the market price of the underlying commodity, potatoes, goes up during the following six months, the value of the contract decreases, since its owner, the farmer, would then have the essentially worthless right to sell his potatoes at a price lower than the market price. If the market price of potatoes decreases during the next six months, the value of the forward contract increases, since the forward would specify a higher price than the market price and the farmer could make a profit despite lower market prices. Thus, derivatives are at the same time instruments for managing, transferring and hedging against risks caused by possible fluctuations of the market value of the underlying asset: In case the market price of potatoes decreases, the farmer can sell his ten sackfuls at the agreed and higher price.

The other three basic types of derivative are similar to the forward contract just described in that they provide a means of trading risk: Futures contracts are standardised forwards, which means that they can be exchange traded. The standardisation makes it more likely that different parties can be matched up in the futures market, thereby increasing the liquidity of the market. An option gives the purchaser the option, or right, to either buy (call option) or sell (put option) the underlying asset at a specified price either at the expiry date or within a given period. Swaps, which are much more recent financial instruments, are agreements to exchange, or swap, interest payments on loans (very often a floating rate and a fixed rate loan). These basic types of derivatives can be recombined as can be seen by financial constructions such as swaptions (a combination of options and swaps) and compound options (options on options).

The immense growth of financial derivatives

Derivatives based on physical products originated in the agricultural markets, covering everything from lemons to oil. They can be said to have originated 4,000 years ago.[1] Even today derivatives based on physical products remain crucial and important markets. Yet, within the last thirty years there was a substantial growth in financial derivatives, based for example on treasury bills and bonds. They have spread in form, with new contracts being invented constantly. The invention of derivatives made it possible for participants in the global financial market, ranging from international corporations with sophisticated financial

[1] Swan, E.J., *Building the Global Market*, The Hague: Kluwer Law, 2000, 28.

operations to households with mortgages, to better cope with risk – be it the risk of changes in commodity or stock prices, exchange rates, interest rates or market liquidity. Since the 1970s the range of futures and options contracts trades around the world increased tremendously. New hedging possibilities opened up so that those who want to reduce the economic uncertainty surrounding them are allowed to do so at a market-determined price, whilst those who are better equipped and willing to bear certain risks have expanded opportunities. Today the derivatives market's notional value is estimated at over \$583 trillion[2] –about \$100,000 in derivatives contracts for every person on the planet. Such developments highlight the importance of understanding the risks inherent in derivatives as well as their effects on society.

Why they are ethically relevant

Economists in recent years have devoted an extraordinary amount of time and attention to the study of financial derivatives. Still, the symptomatology of derivatives trading reveals them to be rather an ethical, not just an economic or mathematical, problem. The article will try to illustrate the ethical problems posed by financial derivatives. The heart of the argument will be that derivatives do not simply provide a means to exchange financial risk but in fact can also create risks and future uncertainties that might be – in certain cases – ethically inacceptable. I will unfold this argument, and its implications, in two ways. First, I will tackle the question why we do and should care about derivatives. I will show that, from a social perspective, the transformation and dispersion of risk, caused intentionally by trading derivatives, might pose problems as derivatives have been involved in the current financial crisis as well as in other disastrous financial debacles. Second, I will identify three cri-

---

[2] Bank for International Settlements, "Semiannual OTC Derivatives Statistics at End-June 2010. Amounts Outstanding of Over-the-Counter (OTC) Derivatives", *www.bis.org/publ/otc_hy1011.pdf.*

teria or guidelines that are necessary when dealing with financial risk, especially when trading derivatives.

Thus far, the examination suggests that derivatives deals probably benefit traders. Derivatives make it possible to commoditise risk and hence to buy, sell, restructure and price risk. Thus, derivatives change the way corporations and banks manage their business and make decisions on risk. In addition to that, derivatives are often a cheaper alternative to investing in the underlying asset. Their significance lies in the lower transaction cost as well as in the possibility of price arbitrage. Price arbitrage refers to the ability to trade on differences between the price of the derivative and the price of the underlying asset, or between prices in different markets. Hence, up to this point, we care about derivatives in a positive way because they serve at least the functions mentioned above. But this approach doesn't seem to be sufficient. For it is still questionable whether such trades benefit society as a whole. In order to go further and to work out why everyone should care about derivatives (even non-traders) it seems important to separate the private and social benefits of financial derivatives.

Private benefits and social costs?

From a private perspective, it doesn't appear dubious at all that derivatives provide efficiency and benefit traders.[3] For individual parties, derivatives constitute a valuable means in dealing with risk. We can conclude that, within the microethical sphere[4], emphasis is placed solely on the fact that derivatives always have two sides, a long one and a short

---

[3] Efficiency, for example, through intense competition between intermediaries, providing greater transparency, liquidity and price information. It is in fact not always clear that derivatives benefit traders, see also Stout, Lynn A., "Insurance or Gambling?" in: *Brookings Review 14 (1)*, Winter 1996, 40ff.

[4] For further elaboration on the difference between microethics and macroethics and the importance of financial macroethics cp. Steigleder, Klaus, "Ethics and Global Finance. Outline of a Macroethical Approach" in: Michael Boylan (ed.), *The Morality and Global Justice Reader*. Boulder, Co: Westview Press, 2011, p. 169-184.

one : Individual traders decide which position to take and which risk to manage. A counterparty enters into a contract in order to take over the risk the first party is not willing to bear or vice versa. Both parties act on their own behalf. And, at all times, the positions even out and for every winner there is a loser. To put it another way: trading in derivatives is a zero sum game: One derivatives trader's gain is necessarily balanced by another's loss. If derivatives trading were costless, the positions would just cancel each other out. Derivatives markets would move wealth around but neither increase nor decrease total wealth. But trading derivatives is not costless. Stout estimates (conservatively) that derivatives are costing investors, as a group, tens of billions of dollars.[5] Still, ex ante, both parties experience an efficiency gain because derivatives enable them to manage risk they might otherwise have to bear. In this context, the ethical analysis of derivatives transactions focuses exclusively on the obligations or duties of people in financial contracting and fairness in market transaction, whereas ethical behavior is constituted primarily by the contractual relation in which one party agrees to assume certain duties – in return for some compensation, of course.

From a social perspective, it is not as simple as that. As the International Monetary Fund (IMF) itself recognised already in 1994, although derivatives can be used effectively to reduce the risk borne by individual agents, they cannot reduce the overall risk in the system but rather can "only transform and re-allocate" risk.[6] At first sight, the transformation and re-allocation of risk may not pose a problem. However, if we take a look at the financial crisis of 2007/08, a flood of losses has been reported by banks, corporations, funds, state and local governments. The leading cause of the crisis that spread out across the globe was the transformation and re-allocation of risk, wherein the use of derivatives played

---

[5] Stout, Lynn A., "Insurance or Gambling?" in: *Brookings Review 14 1*, Winter 1996, 41.

[6] IMF Survey, *Banks and Derivatives Markets: A Challenge For Financial Policy*, 21 February 1994.

a major role. A proliferation of further forms of derivatives took place, involving not only asset packaging but the breakdown of risk into smaller and smaller discrete units. RMBS and CMOs were designed to assemble large packages of loans and divide them into slices of obligations that are sold as having different risk and return characteristics. These instruments aimed at dispersing risk so that risk would not have to be carried by the lender who made the loan but could be traded like a bond or share of stock among different financial investors. At their heart lies a calculated analysis of risk and an attempt to divide it so that parties take the risks they want and lay off those they do not want.

Systemic risks and costs

The risks traders deal with on the micro-ethical level play a major role from a macro-ethical perspective. Individual traders try to seek security through calibrations of risk that will, one hopes, reduce their imagined losses or harms. But, if they are successful in predicting the unknown (and yet uncertain) future and make spectacular gains, they can also make spectacular losses, as various financial catastrophes illustrate. One may think, for instance, of the bond crisis in 1994. Just ahead of the crisis it was widely reported that George Soros had lost $600 million speculating with derivatives against the yen. When the bond market crashed, concerns came up as many derivatives traders (mostly hedge funds) suffered heavy losses. It was suspected that the traders could start to default on their bank loans and that they could spark a chain reaction affecting the whole financial system. From a systemic perspective, the risk transformed and transferred by individuals may threaten the whole financial infrastructure of the economy – interest rates, mortgage rates, the value of personal and corporate pensions. So called systemic risk may also heighten the possibility for large companies to go out of business. As the current financial crisis shows, even banks may not be too big to fail when confronted with systemic risk. As we have seen in the crisis of 2007/08 systemic risk can bring about a systemic shock that affects a considerable number of financial institutions or markets in a strong sense. The general well-functioning of the financial system may be impaired in the case of such an event, which means that i. a. savings may not efficiently be channelled into investments and an extreme credit rationing in the real sector (credit crunch) may result. Possible consequences of systemic risks such as the increase of the unemployment rate and with that poverty and homelessness have been in the news since the beginning of the last financial crisis. Systemic risks are threats to the system as a whole, which means that they differ from risks that menace specific households, firms, financial institutions or even markets. They can be catastrophic for an economy.

As leverage is a key component of systemic risk, derivatives may play their part in it. Derivative innovations made it possible to hedge risk but also made it possible to engage in highly leveraged speculation. In the boom preceding the financial crisis 2007/08, leverage increased massively along with the supply of illiquid high-risk derivatives.[7]

Derivatives also tend to strengthen linkages between market segments and institutions. With that, disruptions in one market are more likely to spill over to and affect other markets, which may result in a domino effect. In addition to that, banks had a strong incentive to create products so complex that they could not be sold on exchanges at all. Eighty percent of derivatives are now sold over-the-counter in non-transparent private deals.[8] Concealing the risks that traders take and disperse adds opacity to the market and poses an unseen risk to the functioning of the financial system should the traders fail. When the risk materialises it may not be possible to prevent a system collapse. Therefore we need to take over responsibility for the risk itself before it's too late – before the risk materialises.

---

[7] Crotty, James, *Structural Causes of the Global Financial Crisis: A Critical Assessment of the 'New Financial Architecture'*. Working Paper 2008-14. University of Massachusetts Amherst, August 2008, 1-61, see 47 f.
[8] Ibid, 25.

Risk, the unknown unknown

It can be concluded that, on financial markets, risk has become a commodity that can be bought and sold according to mutual agreement and that seems to be even more flexible than any other product. Here, the term "risk" refers to both possible (negative) events to which probabilities can be assigned as well as to possible (negative) events to which no probabilities can be assigned. Whereas the former definition describes risk in a narrow sense, the latter definition corresponds to what we call uncertainty. To the economist, risk is a term of art that means variation in outcome, chances of gains as well as losses. Consider someone who offers his friend the choice of either receiving a euro or flipping the euro and getting two euros if it comes up heads, and nothing if it comes up tails. A 50 percent chance of receiving two euros is, statistically speaking, worth one euro. Flipping the coin is riskier, however, because two euros or nothing is a more variable outcome than one euro with certainty.

In the financial world, very few problems are akin to coin-tossing problems. In coin-tossing situations we are faced with sharp and objective probabilities which our decisions can be guided by. A typical coin toss is not uncertain, because we know with surety that the probability of either event is 50 percent. Financial decisions are often influenced by much more complex and nuanced conditions. With regard to derivatives, we can assert that their value changes over time and depends on the future behavior of the underlying financial commodity (prices, interest rates etc.) from which the derivative is derived. This behavior is, as of today, unknown. Depending on the unknown future, the risk associated with derivatives is therefore much more difficult to assess. In dealing with derivatives, we cannot know the risks we face, neither now nor in the future, but we must act as if we did, when we strike a deal.

Risk and ethics

As a matter of fact, risk is inherent in all business activities regardless of the economic order. The critical concern, therefore, is not whether the element of risk is present in a certain business activity. (For risk creates opportunities for economic activity, investment and commerce that contribute to a well-functioning and productive economy.) It is rather the impact of a given transaction on the aggregate level of risk the community has to bear. On the level of the individual trader, risk can be reduced or remains the same by being transformed and transferred. But this is not the case on the systemic level. If a derivative transaction resulted in an increase of the aggregate level of risk, it might negatively affect economic activity and burden those who are not primarily involved in the transaction. From an ethical perspective, derivative transactions have to be considered as social situations of risk as risks may have to be borne by individuals or groups who have not created the risk. Thus, derivatives have social externalities. Even if the damage or the loss incurred is only potential, as decisions are made under the conditions of uncertainty, they are of ethical relevance.

Ethical problems while dealing with risk arise when – in the event of the materialisation of the risk – those bearing the risk suffer a loss of welfare that infringes their rights to individual goods such as physical integrity, well-being and the right to pursue their projects. A systemic financial crisis can involve a massive infringement of rights as it is no more assured that the rights of individual agents are protected. Due to the fact that the breakdown of financial markets can result in extremely adverse effects, institutions both governmental and non-governmental, may be prevented from securing the conditions needed to insure common and public goods. As a matter of fact, there is usually no compensation paid to the ones actually harmed. The process of carrying out the payments and ascertaining the appropriate compensation would involve enormous transaction costs. Besides, often it is impossible to identify the risk imposer as we are dealing with cumulative and multidimensional risks. A well-functioning financial market is therefore morally relevant as it is an indispensable element for the protection of rights. With reference to derivatives, we have to make sure that there are certain negative events that must not be risked and ought to be prevented if possible even if the probability of their occurrence is low. We need detailed considerations and analyses, especially on the impact of derivatives on systemic risk. This is also important as the financial crisis 2007/08 made obvious some upsetting deficits in risk management. Systemic risks caused by financial innovations were neglected. In addition to that, the assumptions in the estimations and calculations of risk were in many cases unwarranted as they portrayed the illusion of being able to make reliable estimations and calculations of probability. The problems cannot always be traced to the derivatives as such. Often, ultimate failures of the top management, who do not see through complicated derivatives transactions, lead to financial catastrophes, as the Barings case illustrates. In order to deal responsibly with financial risk we need to be aware of the fact that the creation and dispersion of risk is ethically relevant, even before a financial catastrophe occurs.

Three guidelines for dealing ethically with financial risk

Risk is absolutely central to derivative instruments as well as to the handling of them. The reason we need to care about derivatives lies in their ability to provide tools for the management of risk, as well as in their power to fuel the individual and – most importantly – the systemic dispersion of risk. Systemic risk can be catastrophic for an economy as it may lead to a system collapse and the violation of fundamental human rights. We need guidelines that help prevent systemic crises, providing precautionary methods both for the micro- and the macroethical level:

1. Avoidance of systemic risk
2. Distinguishing risk-generating from risk-dispersing instruments

3. Transparency through oversight

The avoidance of systemic risk

First, we need macroprudential insight that should focus on the financial system as a whole and that seeks to avoid and at least to minimise system-wide distress. We need to understand that risk is endogenously created and transported through the system. Surveillance needs to be accomplished internationally as market participants act on a global level. As far as derivatives are concerned, their impact on the systemic level of risk is still unclear. Further research is required by scientists as well as finance practitioners and professionals in order to bring to light which derivative transactions on the microethical level pose a cumulative risk to the well-functioning of the entire system. By integrating the concept of systemic risk avoidance into theory and practice, calibrations and models of risk would have to be adjusted.

Distinguishing risk-generating from risk-dispersing instruments

Second, we need to develop methods to distinguish risk-generating from risk-dispersing derivative instruments. Whereas carefully chosen derivative deals may reduce the risk inherent in doing business, there are transactions that can provide powerful leverage mechanisms for creating risk with a negative influence on economic stability. More risk can be created for example when by hedging some risks, individual investors gain exposure to another risk. In addition to that, derivatives can also be risk-generating when the risk involved in the transaction is concentrated not among those most capable of bearing it, but among those most willing to take it. Individual traders and institutions may be too confident to bear massive risk jeopardising the welfare of the system.

The second guideline focuses mainly on connecting the micro-ethical and the macro-ethical sphere: With derivatives, individual traders can place enormous volumes of bets on the movement of market variables. Especially those derivative transactions involving short-selling, credit default swaps or the speculation on food prices have often been said to be risk-generating, market-destabilising and welfare-reducing. Also, it is often assumed that speculative derivatives trading used for gambling purposes may increase the risk-bearing of both contract parties, just as gamblers increase their risk by betting. There is empirical evidence that this is likely to result in increased market risk, reduced investor returns, price distortions and bubbles that diminish social welfare. Definitely, more research is needed on the risk-structure of different derivative forms and critical concerns have to be checked closely.

Although the second guideline addresses in particular the behavior of market participants, it seems unrealistic for individual parties to be able to assess which derivative strategy might be risk-generating and which might be risk-dispersing because they only play a small part in the global system of risk. Institutional regulation is needed to make sure that traders only take over the risks they are able to bear. This can be achieved by demanding risk-adequate collateral such as margin deposits, on exchanges as well as and most importantly on OTC-markets.

Transparency through oversight

Third, we need to establish transparency through regulatory oversight. In general the writer of the derivative contract doesn't know the identity of the current owner of the contract. In addition to that, the regulator or the state agency, typically the central bank, that is in charge of macro-prudential supervision doesn't know it either. Subsequently, it is impossible at this point to determine whether the current distribution of risk inherent in the derivative contracts is systemically stabilising or destabilising and whether the owners of the contracts are too interconnected or too big to fail. Very often, it is argued that it is useless to regulate derivatives any further, as traders always find a way to circumvent regulatory acts. Furthermore, it may seem questionable whether regulatory institutions charged to oversee transactions and to foresee systemic risk can realistically accomplish their task as even institutional investors and rating agencies failed to do so prior to the crisis of 2007/08. It is self-evident that systemic risk cannot be completely prevented from occurring, neither by securities regulators nor by financial market authorities. Transparency, expertise and resources are needed to analyse and to determine which risks are ethically acceptable and which are not. Still, this must not prevent us from trying. There is an ethical imperative to gather and share information and to set up regulatory institutions to monitor systemic risks created or dispersed by financial instruments and to alert market participants if a buildup of systemic risk is likely to occur.

Conclusion

Derivatives may improve the allocation of risk, but there is no guarantee that they will. There are certain negative events such as a financial crisis or catastrophe that must not be risked and ought to be prevented.

Up to now, a qualified ethical analysis of the acceptability of aggregate risk generated on financial markets is still lacking. This is probably one of the major reasons why so many mistakes have been made in the management of financial risk. Further research is required by scientists as well as finance practitioners and professionals in order to find out which financial transactions on the microethical level pose a cumulative risk to the well-functioning of the entire system.

The guidelines presented above (1. Avoidance of systemic risk, 2. Distinguishing risk-generating from risk-dispersing instruments, 3. Transparency through oversight) do not claim to be complete. The aim was to clarify the importance of the tasks and to show that solutions are urgently required. Integrating these guidelines into theory and practice would help market participants understand that financial risk can pose massive threats to the welfare of the system and of society as a whole. Taking risks responsibly is part of a necessary framework for promoting ethics and integrity in finance.

13

INTERNATIONALISM, INSTITUTIONS AND INDIVIDUALS: SYSTEMIC CHANGES FOR A SYSTEMIC ETHICAL CRISIS

Geoffrey See

It was 2006, when the world still celebrated the heady days of ever-rising property values, ever-rising equity values, and ever-rising bonuses for the investment bankers, hedge fund managers and private equity captains who made the good times happen. The head of McKinsey's Corporate Performance Center in New York was in the Wharton School giving a presentation on "The Tao of Finance". There was a reverent hush as the students eagerly took notes on valuing companies. No one would have imagined then that the good times would roll to an end just one year later.

What is the way of finance?

I found it interesting that he chose the Chinese word "Tao". In modern Chinese, the character translates as "way" or "path". Perhaps the current financial crisis could have been averted if the hordes of business school students eager to find their place on Wall Street had had a different conception of "The Tao of Finance": The fundamentals of finance should be founded on ethics, and not just on *Corporate Valuation 101*.

Finance is built on a complex social system facilitating the exchange of goods and services that are often abstract and intangible. Wealth in such a system is built on the interplay of trust and ethics. As such, ethics is as important in establishing the modern financial system as CAPM (Capital Asset Pricing Model), DCF (Discounted Cash Flows), or any other modern valuation techniques so emphasised in business school. They are like the Yin and Yang of the financial world, both are essential for harmony to exist.

The enormity of the current global credit crisis reveals something fundamentally wrong with the financial system. For a field meant to create wealth and that succeeded at doing just that for so many years, it has suddenly given way to a rapid and massive destruction of wealth. And this impact is being felt not just on Wall Street, but also on Main Street, which now faces massive retrenchment after years of heady growth.

The current financial crisis is a major challenge, and to be fair, the crisis is not just the fault of the financial industry, even if at the World Economic Forum's "Summer Davos" in China, I watched Morgan Stanley's renowned Asia Economist, Stephen Roach criticise poor regulatory policies, such as the Fed's low interest rates, as a cause of the current mess. While astute in his analysis, he misses the point of the public's outrage: people want to know that we can trust the financial industry and the financial elite to act in the public's interest, instead of requiring an adversarial government watchdog to make them behave.

Systemic and widespread ethical failure

Banking has undergone incredible changes in the last 30 years. Investment banking, a segment of the financial system, exemplifies this transformation. In 2006, I met Joseph R. Perella, a former Morgan Stanley investment banker and an industry legend, just as he was setting up a new investment banking boutique. He claimed that relationships between investment bankers and their clients have changed from one built on trust to one that is commoditised, arms-length, and ruled by caveat emptor.

More broadly, investment banks themselves have became giant trading machines, piling on layer upon layer of complexity on an already opaque system, making the role of ethics all the more important in a system increasingly reliant on self-policing.

The current crisis reveals that the financial industry has failed this ethics test. The collapse of Madoff's $50 billion Ponzi scheme is an extreme example of a broader abrogation of corporate responsibility in the financial sector. UBS's alleged role in helping its US clients to evade taxes reveals a company that aggressively chases profits at the boundaries of the law. Most pertinent to today's financial crisis is the aggressive selling of collaterised debt obligations (CDOs) that placed sub-prime mortgages in the hands of investors who are ill-equipped to monitor and evaluate the actual risks of their investments.

Some people in the financial industry argue that such relationships come with *caveat emptor*, "let the buyer beware". While such arguments might hold sway in a court of law, they offend the general public who trust the financial system, and expect this system to have a certain level of ethics and responsibility. Profit seeking has to happen within the bounds of corporate responsibility. Firms exist because they have a mandate from society to steward society's wealth. In return, they is responsible to society, in ways that go beyond simply obeying the law.

Multi-level solutions

The widespread ethical failures of the financial industry call for equally broad-reaching changes to the industry. In looking at Madoff, we witness an individual at the epicenter of a financial fraud. In examining the sub-prime mess, we witness institutions who fail at putting their clients first. In studying UBS, we witness an international clash over the meaning of banking secrecy.

The ethical problems in finance are multi-dimensional, with causes situated at different levels of corporate organisation. This means that the comprehensive solution we need should comprise three levels: the individual, institutional and international. Each of these levels exerts a different set of pressures on ethical decision-making. The following analysis defines how the organisation and composition of the financial industry at each of these levels poses systemic challenges to ethical decision-making. It then outlines solutions to ethical challenges at each level, with the aim of creating an interlocking system that reinforces ethical decisions made by individuals, firms and the entire financial industry.

The internationalism of financial firms

The rise of international firms, whether pursuing a multi-domestic or transnational strategy, resulted in firm assets that are embedded in different locations. In turn, these assets are embedded in the local legislative and cultural context (Yip, 1989).

Financial firms in particular are some of the world's most globally oriented firms as they deal with footloose capital – even under present circumstances, capital is an incredibly mobile asset.

	Internal	**External**
Internationalism	Differences in culture across business units	Differences in ethical and legislative context across countries
Internal and external challenges exacerbated by international competition		

Figure 1: Internationalism's impact on ethical performance

The internationalism of financial firms poses major challenges for their ability to behave ethically. Two specific challenges arise out of this situation (see Figure 1). The first challenge arises from the embeddedness of firms in the local legislative and cultural context. Operating in different regimes raises the complexity of ethical issues a financial firm faces. Differing conceptions of ethics in the different cultural contexts and the different laws that govern firm behavior prevent the firm from defining a global ethical standard. Without a common definition of ethics, actions in one part of the firm can be excoriated by its critics in another part of the world, often with just cause.

The other challenge arises internally. Culture across a transnational firm is far from uniform, frequently patchy and often inconsistent, thus leading to blind spots in detecting internal corporate practices that lead to unethical behavior. Business units in different parts of the world could adopt different practices making it difficult to ensure ethical decision-making. The differences in managerial structures under this international setting pose problems for firms trying to pursue one-dimensional solutions that assume compliance across the board. Instead, financial firms need to pursue solutions that address this international dimension of ethical behavior. An example of this internal inconsistency in structures is exemplified by a study of Japanese brokerages with operations in both New York City and Tokyo. Although they belonged to the same company, many firms ended up adopting different reward systems in their different locations: New York branches had a market-oriented reward system while the Tokyo branches had a hierarchal-oriented reward system (Zaheer, 1995).

These two problems are exacerbated by one last aspect of internationalism. Competitive pressure from outside a country can erode the stability of agreed-upon codes of conduct within the financial industry in a country. As ethical codes for an industry are developed largely on a national level, based on a common cultural context and over time, the entrance of a foreign competitor or the desire to overtake a competitor abroad can erode codes of conduct at the national level.

Financial firms have gone international and their internationalism is here to stay. Thus, it is imperative that we develop measures to address both the external challenge and the internal challenge to ethics posed by internationalism.

A demand for a global ethical standard

Ethicists have proposed various solutions to the external challenge of differing ethical demands and context caused by firms' embeddedness in different country contexts. Relativists believe that firms should tailor local policies and operations to the ethical demands in each country. However, such an approach is inappropriate for financial firms as it clashes with the cross-border realities of the financial industry. UBS's problems juggling tax secrecy laws in Switzerland, where it is headquartered, and its alleged attempts to aid tax evasion elsewhere in the world, is an example of how inter-connected markets demands a global ethical standard.

In a world of inter-connected markets, firm operations between different countries are linked even in the most localised of firms. Business units in a firm share common resources that make units of a firm in one part of the world ethically culpable for actions in another part of the world. For example, the capital flow across borders that takes advantage of arbitrage opportunities links business units across countries. HSBC, which claims to be the world's local bank, sells a common brand across countries that would be tarnished by inappropriate actions taken in any part of the world. These interconnections demand a global ethical standard.

The important integration of all cultures

Ethical imperialists argue the opposite: instead of the endless conflict between localised ethics, firms should adopt a single and effective firm-wide code of ethics. Underlying this approach is the belief that a fundamental set of ethical obligations is relevant to all cultures and to all companies. In particular, a globalised financial industry should be most receptive to such an approach.

Such a rigid code is easily criticised as cultural imperialism. Critics have observed that a universal ethical code is often based on Western standards. Differences in interpreting ethics exist between different societies, and financial firms need to be able to adapt some of their processes and procedures to these differences.

Perhaps gift-giving for the purpose of cultivating business ties is frowned upon within Anglo-Saxon circles, but should such an action be as intolerable from an ethical viewpoint in China or Japan? For investment bankers in China, gift-giving is often fundamental to building the *guanxi* necessary for long-term business relationships, although such actions can easily become a slippery slope. For their counterparts in Japan, friendships are often built on the exchange of gifts. In these countries, gifts do not necessarily have the same connotations of direct bribery as in the West but instead fall into an ambiguous grey area. New approaches are needed to address these problems.

Consensus can exist

Some ethicists and philosophers have argued for a third way that attempt to find common ethical ground in the major cultures of the world. The late philosopher of business ethics, Thomas W. Dunfee (Dunfee and Donaldson, 1999) argues that an Integrated Social Contract underlies ethical business behavior. Hypernorms, norms common to most if not all of the world's major cultures, form the ethical standards firms should conform to. In each society, micro-social contracts exists that business units in these countries can then obey separately. While Dunfee does not specifically identify what these norms would be, he argues that they can be identified for relevant industries and communities. Perhaps this allows financial firms to escape the external challenge of internationalism by binding them to a world-wide code of conduct on ethical issues where consensus exists, while allowing them the flexibility to adapt their operations elsewhere.

Agreeing on this global code of conduct should be an urgent task for the financial industry. This can help ensure that ethical behavior crosses borders. In addition, financial firms need to be constantly aware of the *external challenge* as ethical standards are evolving and changing. De Bettignies argues that a new mindset will develop in China that espouses the traditional and the western simultaneously in ways that are neither Western nor traditional Chinese (see *www.emeraldinsight.com/learning/management_thinking/interviews/pdf/bettignies.pdf*). The fusion of thoughts in various countries around the world will lead to a different set of ethical demands in the future. Financial firms have to adapt their operations to these changes to conform to changing ethical standards.

An ethics audit system to face internal challenge

Unlike the external challenge, the internal challenge arises not from incongruence between the firm's behavior with its environment's demands, but from the difficulties of managing the modern financial firm. The modern financial firm is a complex international entity. Many banks have operations spread across the globe. This internationalism poses a practical challenge: ensuring compliance with codes of ethics for an entire firm, across the world, is incredibly difficult, especially since business units' attitudes towards ethics in different parts of the world might differ. A headquarters-imposed ethics requirement might be ignored by operations at the country-level.

The challenge is to make monitoring and enforcement of codes of ethics more effective for transnational financial firms. Audit systems play a major role in monitoring country or regional level performance, and perhaps a similar audit system can play a role in ensuring ethical performance. For an ethics audit system to work, the audit team needs to have an explicit focus on "accounting for ethics". The current accounting system fails to uncover ethical failures effectively as such failures, when they do not directly influence balance sheet results, often fall outside of the system's purview. Furthermore, when an ethics audit team exists and has an explicit goal of uncovering ethical failures, their awareness of what they are looking for can greatly increase the chances of detecting ethical failures.

Such ethical audit teams need to be hired and managed out of headquarters if they are to be effective. Conflicts of interests are prevalent in the accounting industry. If the company desires to crack down on ethical violations, its ethical audit teams must be free of such conflicts of interests to be effective. This is possible if they are hired externally and are responsible to senior level management instead of local operations.

Isomorphic pressures at the institutional dimension

At the institutional level, isomorphic pressures restrict the domain of ethical options faced by individuals. Organisations adopt similar processes or structures when facing similar environmental constraints. Organisational behaviorists call this institutional isomorphism. Isomorphic pressures influence the structure and culture of an organisation, shaping the ethical choices of a firm at the institutional level.

Different forms of isomorphism exist. Financial firms adopt similar reporting measures of assets to seek legitimacy in the eyes of external stakeholders (coercive isomorphism). Professionalisation leads to similar behaviors between different financial firms, made all the more apparent by the constant flow of talent between firms on Wall Street (normative isomorphism). Under uncertainty, Wall Street firms also engineer similar financial products and pursue similar trading strategies, consoling themselves by noting how their competitors are doing the same (mimetic isomorphism). We can make financial firms more responsible by shaping these isomorphic pressures to influence firm behavior.

Changing the underlying isomorphic pressures in the industry to reinforce firm-level ethical decisions is about changing the fundamental behavioral drivers in the industry. Current ad-hoc measures introduced to ensure ethical behaviors are often relegated to superficial box-ticking that can be easily circumvented by the talented people that work in the financial industry. This is because such measures fail to truly change the institutional structure of financial firms in any meaningful way.

A common story that reflects this problem emerges from risk control departments at investment banks. In theory, traders are supposed to be answerable to the risk control department for their trades. In reality, highly profitable traders perch at the top of the corporate hierarchy and employ a range of strategies to delay or avoid compliance with risk controls. Requests for information can be brushed aside, risky trades are explained as being sophisticated, and evasive answers buy time. Isomorphism has resulted in a common industry structure where revenue centers are prioritised in decision-making processes over cost and control centers, leading to ethical lapses.

What can be done?

The firm is embedded in a network of social institutions that control and shape its behavior. To achieve the deep-rooted ethical changes in the financial industry we are arguing for, we need to shape isomorphic pressures to lock in desirable institutional characteristics.

The relatively free flow of talent between financial firms poses a critical challenge. The constant inflow of personnel shaped by the cultures of other firms dilutes measures taken by any firm to ensure ethical behavior. As soon as Lehman Brothers collapsed, top executives at the failed firm were recruited by other Wall Street firms. Thus, measures promoting ethics have to influence the industry as a whole, instead of being atomised actions taken by individual firms – brave actions that will unfortunately by weakened by the constant inflow of personnel.

The professionalisation of finance

Professionalisation of the financial industry would be a bold step forward in building a common ethical culture for financial professionals. Parts of the financial industry that deals with complex financial instruments are remarkably similar to professions such as law or medicine. The practitioners have a consensus on a body of knowledge surrounding their work, and are asymmetrically equipped with this knowledge vis-à-vis their customers. Professionals in finance also have relatively homogenous backgrounds – coming from a small set of universities or business schools. Given the importance of finance for the modern economy and the shared backgrounds of practitioners, the industry is ripe for professionalisation.

Professionalisation of finance is meant to allow the industry to develop a common set of ethics and sense of responsibility to society. By having financial professionals uphold industry-specific ethical standards, we force them to confront the responsibilities their importance to society entails, and become more conscious of the impact of their decisions. By socialising them to an industry-standard for ethics, we enable these professionals to understand how their profession as a whole should approach ethical dilemmas. Such a professional body also allows firms to overcome the problem of atomised socialisation to codes of conducts: by having an industry code of conduct, the flow of professionals between firms poses less of a challenge in maintaining an ethical culture.

Full professionalisation of finance can take place by developing a national or regional body to build consensus on financial issues. Given that many financial professionals are trained in business schools, such training grounds have to be included in the professionalisation process. A business degree (or programme) should be a prerequisite in the industry, and much thought should be given to how individuals are socialised through this programme. The next section looks at this in greater detail, but with a focus on how ethics in general is affected by the current business school process, which I argue is flawed and self-destructive.

Room for individual decision-making

While the international structure of firms and the institutional isomorphism of firms influence ethical outcomes, we cannot ignore the role individuals play at all levels of the firm in ensuring ethical behavior. While I argued that a set of forces circumscribe the domain of possible choices individuals can make, they do so in ways that still leave considerable room for individual decision-making. The ethical compasses of individuals still influence how they choose over their remaining options.

I recommend an approach to reshaping ethics in individuals in the financial industry by focusing on the main socialisation process for such individuals. A large proportion of financial elites in the commanding heights of the financial industry (i.e. those who work in the top investment banks, private equity firms and hedge funds) come from a small set of business schools. Business schools (both at the undergraduate and graduate level) play a significant role as a gatekeeper for the financial industry, socialising individuals who go on to wield influence in finance. But this system is broken.

It is essential that we reform the process by which financial talents are trained. In addition to developing *professional ethics* in support of the professionalisation of the industry, business schools need to work with companies to ensure that ethics become an integral and useful means of selecting potential employees. This has to go beyond simply having more ethics classes or mandatory ethics components. Instead, we need a reform in the overall environment of many business schools. The current environment creates unhealthy social pressures that retard student ethics. Some schools have taken the lead in changing this environment, but more has to be done.

Business Schools: Ethics as secondary to success

My personal experiences studying at a business school made me realise the need for reform in the business school environment. In an incident at business school, a friend approached me to edit his resume. Instead of stating his actual role collecting data for a professor, the resume implied that my friend had a forthcoming academic publication. Who could blame him? After all, this is part and parcel of the hyper-competitive race for the most prestigious Wall Street jobs or consulting gigs. He eventually got his dream job at a top firm.

In another incident, a friend was awarded a prestigious award from a top investment bank for his leadership in society. His biography for the award talked about how he worked on a social entrepreneurial project using cutting edge technologies to deliver education to underprivileged students. His friends mentioned that all he did was to teach English to students over the Internet for a private tutoring company. Who could blame him? After all, business schools too often focus on packaging its students in ways that clash with reality.

In pointing out these examples, I am not trying to assign blame to these individuals, but to draw attention to the environment which compels individuals to act in unethical ways. Such actions are by no means rare in a business school. While administrators at business schools are genuinely concerned about the ethical conduct of their students, the overall culture at such schools is one where ethics is considered secondary to "success" – usually a well-paying job in the finance or consulting industry. It is an environment where students feel that they have to "do whatever it takes" to get the job done.

Business schools that fail to create a culture of ethics fail to develop business leaders capable of questioning unethical practices in finance and other industries. Creating such leaders is important, as the rapid pace of decision-making in the financial industry and broad impact of those decisions make such decisions particularly complex. This complexity renders the tradition of box-ticking as a means of fulfilling ethical mandates irresponsible if not dangerous. For the investors who invested in Madoff and helped him solicit investment funds, perhaps it should have crossed their minds that reaping these outsized returns might involve some ethical breaches? Then again, who can fault them when ethics has been confined to a box to fill rather than a crucial consideration throughout the investment process?

What kind of business leadership is wanted?

By targeting business schools for change, we can focus our effort on a major pipeline socialising individuals into the finance industry. Furthermore, the current financial crisis provides additional impetus for business schools to do some soul-searching on how their alumni have contributed to the current mess, and how they can ensure that the next generation of business leaders to emerge from their schools can change this system. For too long, business schools have focused on helping their students succeed within the existing corporate system, rather than helping their students shape it.

This debate, at its fundamental level, is about what business leadership should be and could be. Is leadership defined as having alumni who go on to become the Presidents and CEOs of Morgan Stanley, Goldman Sachs, or Blackstone? Or is it about alumni who through their positions in these companies (or outside of corporate circles) help shape business responsibility? It is a fundamental question about position versus impact. Business schools have tilted too much towards the former and they increasingly must address the latter.

Such a revolution in thinking is slowly taking place: in the US, Harvard Business School in its centennial celebration last year, asked itself what impact it wanted its students to have on society. In the Wharton School, newly elected dean Thomas Robertson declares a vision of business as a force for good. Internationally, INSEAD has a long history of promoting the idea of sustainability and corporate responsibility, setting up important centers and programmes in this area.

By changing the philosophy on which business schools are built, schools will be able to provide an environment more conducive to developing ethical leaders. By changing the purpose and approach of business schools, we can provide an environment for nurturing leaders who want to make an impact on the corporate world, instead of students who simply want success – defined as a top position at a top firm. This requires a thorough change in the culture and purpose of business schools instead of piecemeal programmes that struggle against an entrenched culture.

This change will require bold visionaries to implement. Successful alternatives to the current business school model do not exist. Tried and tested actions are hard to specify, given the diversity of paths in making the change. There are no easy solutions here. Schools will have to make the leap of faith, and some might fail along the way. But the greater threat to creating an ethical financial system is for schools to fail to try.

From top to bottom

The ethical crisis in finance has deep roots at all levels of the industry, from its international nature, to the institutions that define the industry, down to its individual employees. Bringing ethical behavior back into the industry requires us to comprehensively tackle the problem at the different levels at which it exists.

At the international level, ethics have to be effective across the firm, with stronger emphasis on monitoring. Corporate behavior has to be aligned with an evolving external definition of ethics. At the institutional level, professionalisation of the finance profession can aid in defining ethical standards at the industry level, thus preventing the flow of individuals between firms from eroding the effectiveness of company-level ethical codes. At the individual level, we can target the key pipeline into the financial industry – the business school – for reform, in order to nurture leaders who want to use their positions in the financial world to pursue corporate responsibility.

An ethical financial system is essential to the healthy functioning of the entire economy. Making these changes should be an essential part of the rehabilitating the financial system from this age of excesses.

Bibliography

Dunfee, T./ Donaldson, T., 1999. *Ties that Bind*, Harvard: Harvard Business School Press.

Yip, G., 1989. “Global Strategy… In a World Of Nations?”, in: *Sloan Management Review 31 (1)*, 29-41.

Zaheer, S., 1995. “Overcoming the Liability of Foreignness”, in: *Academy of Management Journal 38 (2)*, 341-363.

14

ACCOUNTABILITY AND THE SECOND LINE OF DEFENCE

Immaculate Dadiso Motsi-Omoijiada

> "There are two superpowers in the world today in my opinion. There's the United States and there's Moody's Bond Rating Service. The United States can destroy you by dropping bombs, and Moody's can destroy you by downgrading your bonds. And believe me, it's not clear sometimes who's more powerful."
>
> Thomas Friedman

It has been argued that the current global financial turmoil, touted as the worst since the Great Depression, is taking place because regulatory lines of defence failed to hold and prevent the crisis. Sequentially, risk management at firms, then market and official analysts and finally established regulatory bodies each failed to halt the financial meltdown that has pushed most major economies around the world to the brink of recession and caused significant slowdown and failure of some emerging market economies.

The focus of this paper is on the second line of defence in general and Credit Rating Agencies (CRAs) in particular. This is in recognition of the vital and indispensible role that the CRAs play in the global financial system and, as demonstrated by recent events, the great impact of their failure to effectively fulfil their mandates on global financial stability.

With this in mind, this paper is divided into seven sections. (1) An overview of CRAs; (2) The role of CRAs in the current financial crisis; (3) Key issues to address; (4) Recent regulatory developments; (5) Proposed regulatory options; (6) Options Analysis and; (7) Recommendations.

Overview of CRAs

Origins

CRAs trace their roots to more than a century ago when investment in railroad began. [1]In the late 1860s Henry Poor published a manual that provided information for investors – a lucrative business that John Moody also established in 1910 by publishing a book analysing railroads and their outstanding securities and assigning ratings to them. By the 1930s, investment policies requiring that bonds be rated were instituted. Today, there are three main international CRAs and a plethora of national and regional CRAs around the world.

Function

Henry Poor and John Moody started analysing and rating railroads after realising that investors often lack the information to determine the soundness of their investment. In the same way, today, rating agencies deal with principal-agent problems and asymmetric information.[2] Here, the ratings reflect the CRA's estimate of the probability of default over a given period. CRAs therefore fall under the second line of defence since,

---

[1] Perkins, Tara, 2007, "Misguided or Misunderstood?" Globe & Mail, 7 September 2007.

[2] Portes, Richard, 2008, "Rating Agency Reform", *www.voxeu.com?q=node/887*

like auditors, investment analysts and journalists, they act as gatekeepers of investment-related transactions between market participants. In this way, CRAs play a critical informational, regulatory and transactional role in the global financial system.

Modus operandi

A credit rating is defined as an "opinion forecasting the creditworthiness of an entity, a credit commitment, a debt of debt-like security or an issuer of such obligations, expressed using an established and defined rating system".[3] A rating agency derives its rating from both publicly available information and private information provided by firms and analysts. This information then goes through the rating agency's credit model to produce a rating.[4] These ratings signify financial soundness and regularity in interest and principal payments. They range from AAA for the highest quality bond instruments to D for instruments in default.

Role of agencies in the current financial crisis

Although there are several ways to explain the evolution of the current financial crisis, the one that best explains the role of CRAs is the one that sees the current financial crisis, like most financial crises before it, as being triggered by the emergence of innovation. This time, instead of the steam engine or the radio, the crisis emerged from the development of a "new tool of financial engineering" which, as in previous crises, investors were wary of at first before rushing in upon seeing the extraordinary returns, which lead to upward surges in asset prices that eventually burst and petered out.[5]

---

[3] Champsaur, Amelie, 2005. "The regulation of credit rating agencies in the US, and in the EU: Recent initiatives and Proposals". *www.law.harvard.edu/programs/pifs/pdfs/amelie_champasaur.pdf*

[4] Portes 2008.

[5] Reinhart, Carmen, 2008, "Reflections on the International Dimensions and Policy Lessons of the US Sub-prime Crisis". *www.voxeu.com?q=node/988*

More specifically, complex financially structured products came into the market when banks started using an "originate and transfer" approach to housing loans. These loans, a large proportion of which were sub-prime, were then securitised by investment companies who shopped around for higher ratings before selling the instruments to investors.

In this scenario, even the more sophisticated risk-hungry investors did not know how to value these new assets, and so had to rely on and trust the ratings provided by the CRA involved in the securitisation.[6] The CRAs, encouraged by their own incentives heeded underwriters' assurances of the power of pooling to decrease the probability of default and their ability to predict despite a limited track record. As these structured products did not trade, and were sold only over the counter, their price transparency and market liquidity was low.[7]

Because of this, it is widely believed that the CRAs failure to provide correct ratings on these high risk products and hold the second line of defence played a crucial role in the current financial crisis. This lead the US Congress House Oversight and Government Policy Committee to recently hold a hearing that concluded that the top three CRAs "were aware of serious problems but continued company practices which benefited the bond issuers while disregarding the interests of the investors who relied on S&P, Moody's and Fitch ratings".[8]

Key issues to address

There are several problems associated with the CRAs that prevent them from performing their role more effectively. These are linked to key issues that need to be addressed in order to more fully understand the areas in need of reform.

---

[6] Guillermo de la Dehesa, 2007, "How to Avoid further Credit and Liquidity Confidence Crises". *www.voxeu.com?q=node/657*

[7] Ibid.

[8] US Congress, 2008. *Transcript: House Oversight and Government Policy Committee, oversight.house.gov/story.asp?ID=2250.* 22 October 2008

No competition

Firstly, it has been observed that there are some natural monopoly characteristics in the credit rating industry because of network effects[9]. Network effects here refer to how investors want consistency of ratings across issuers. The natural monopoly also stems from the barriers to entry created by regulators who rely on ratings and as such use stringent criterion to determine whether or not an agency holds this regulatory license. CRAs also require highly qualified analysts, as well as high tech and sophisticated rating methodologies that are proprietary.[10] In this way, the credit rating industry displays the same quality deficiencies (in terms of accuracy, lack of rigor and innovation) evident in any monopolistic market.

Conflict of Interest

Secondly, and this is the most expansive critique of CRAs, there is an apparent conflict of interest in the business models of CRAs, which allow them to first advise on how the construction of a security would affect its rating and then issue a rating that confirms its advice – earning two separate fees in the process (Figure 1, opposite). For example, 44% of Moody's revenues in 2006 came from its structured finance activities.[11] This conflict of interest potentially reduces the objectivity of the ratings provided by CRAs and leads to the problem of perverse incentives in the rating process.

Incentives

Thirdly, as is evident from what was alluded to above, there is an apparent incentives compatibility issue with CRAs. In the first instance, CRAs have an incentive to give high ratings in a situation where because the issuer pays for the ratings, he may also shop around for the

---

[9] Portes, 2008.
[10] Champsaur, 2005.
[11] Richards, 2008.

most favorable rating (the best deal). In the second instance, due to the same dual business model, CRAs also have incentives to ensure that securitisation takes place as this generates more business to them by providing more products to rate. To illustrate this, Figure 2 below shows how the revenue of the three big CRAs increased during the time leading up to the current implosion of the global financial system.

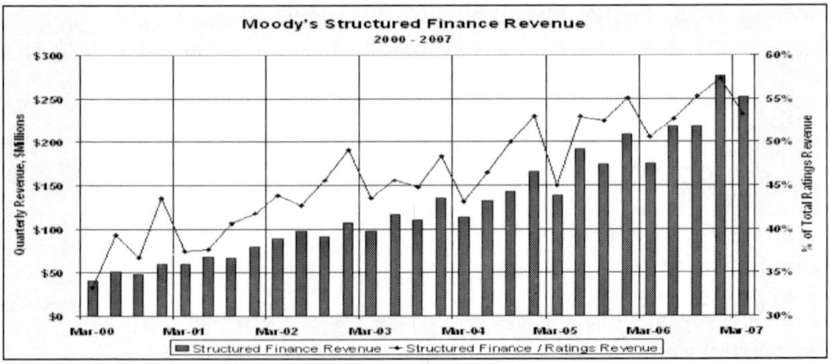

Figure: 1 Moody's Structured Finance Revenue
Source: *www.lewrockwell.com*

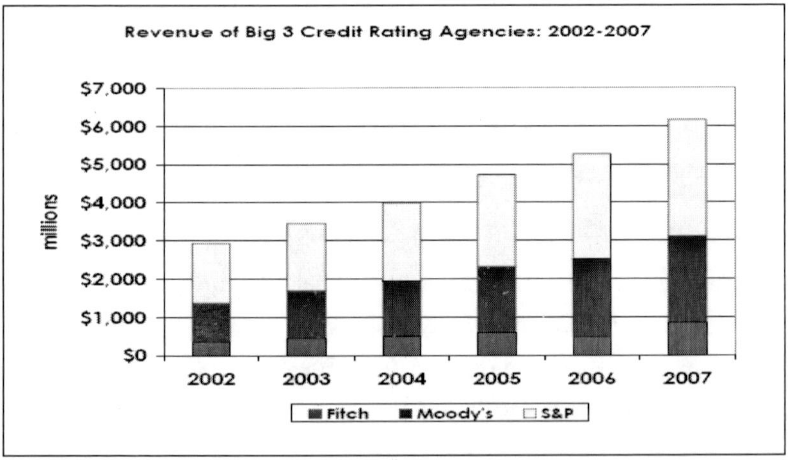

Figure 2: Revenue of Big 3 CRAs (2002-2007)
Source: *www.lewrockwell.com*

Accuracy and Pro-Cyclicality

Fourthly, the accuracy of CRAs has been questioned. Agencies are blamed for reacting ex post rather than anticipating defaults. In this way, the ratings are not only lagging indicators[12] but also *pro-cyclical* creating the herding effects, and magnifying instability as they did during the Asian Financial Crisis. In this crisis, as in the current crisis rating agencies, following their pro-cyclical tendencies, overreacted in their effort to distract the investing public from their laxness of the past few years by strict standards going forward[13] creating the de-stabilising herding effects mentioned here. Furthermore, critics have highlighted how the agencies' data and their models are suspect. For example, in rating the securities involving sub-prime mortgages, the agencies are said to have used data from an extended period of rising house prices, during which doubtful mortgages had been validated as householders' equity grew.[14] This led, in part to the inaccuracy of the ratings they provided for these products. With regards to the models' simulations CRAs used, it was noted that these may not be helpful when markets become so disorderly that they exceed the models' parameters and tail risk occurs. This is exacerbated by the questionable used of the same metric to evaluate sovereign risk, corporate bond risk, and complex instruments like collateralised debt obligations.[15] It is because of these and other accuracy issues that, some literature points to the fact that rating agencies do not add value. This is because the quality of information they provide is believed to be no better than what a good analyst could extract from publicly available data. The questionable accuracy has prompted several detailed studies casting doubt on their ability to assess credit quality better than measures based on market spreads or to predict major changes.[16]

---

[12] Ibid.
[13] Reinhart, 2008.
[14] Ibid.
[15] Ibid.
[16] Levich *et al.*, 2007. *Credit Rating Agencies and the Global Financial System.*

Regulatory dependence of CRAs

The final key issue to consider is the dependence of regulators on rating agencies. This extends the scope that stakeholders with vested interests should consider when addressing CRA-related regulatory issues and reflects the effects of poor ratings on financial stability. A case in point here is the dependence of Basel II's capital adequacy standards for banks on ratings. This is particularly problematic in a scenario in which credit ratings do not adequately reflect credit risk. Here, "the banks' capital structure might give the illusory impression that it constitutes a sufficient cushion against risk, which could threaten the safety and soundness of the banking system".[17]The same is true for the US National Recognised Statistical Rating Organisation status, whereby a wide range of investors are required not to hold securities whose ratings are below "investment grade", and ratings affect the risk weightings of banks' assets in calculating capital adequacy ratios.[18]

Recent regulatory developments

Appendix 1 shows the current regulatory framework for CRAs. As this is beyond the scope of this study, IOSCO, the main regulatory tool, as well as recent regulatory developments in the European Union and in the United States will be briefly highlighted.

IOSCO

The International Organisation of Securities Commissions published its Code of Conduct Fundamentals for Credit Rating Agencies in 2004. This code focuses on voluntary "corporate governance rules designed to (1) ensure quality and integrity of the rating process; (2) remain independent and avoid conflicts of interest; (3) assume their responsibility to market participants through greater methodology transparency and ade-

---

[17] Champsaur, 2005.
[18] Portes, 2008.

quate treatment of confidential information provided by issuers".[19] The key shortcoming of these provisions is that IOSCO does not address the issue of the enforcement of the code. Instead, it leaves enforcement to either national regulators or market mechanisms[20] that, in light of the current crisis, have been ineffective.

European Union

October this year saw the drafting of a law designed to prevent conflicts of interests between CRAs and their clients in the EU The legislation aims to forces CRAs to disclose their working methods and to encourage the emergence of new agencies. Under the draft proposal, CRAs will not be allowed to combine their work with consultancy and specific rules are given on how staff members are paid and how long they can work with clients. These are that (a) pay should be determined primarily by the quality, accuracy, thoroughness and integrity of their work; (b) for companies with more than 50 staff members, a four-year time limit would be placed on work with individual clients to prevent relationships from becoming too close and; (c) there would then have to be a two-year break before the individual worked with the same client.[21]

United States

In the US, preliminary steps to address the issue of CRAs in light of their role in the current financial crisis were taken in the form of a hearing by the House Oversight and Government Policy Committee. Here, the current heads of S&P, Moody's and Fitch were issued with firm statements after testifying with US legislators announcing clear intentions to hold CRAs accountable for their actions.[22] This may be impetus for future EU-like regulatory procedures to be taken in the near future.

---

[19] *www.iosco.org/pubdocs/pdfIOSCOPDI151.pdf*
[20] Ibid.
[21] Castle, Stephen, 2008. "EU prepares tight rules on credit rating agencies", *International Herald Tribune*, 29 October 2008.
[22] US Congress, 22 October 2008.

Proposed regulatory options

With these key issues in mind, several regulatory options can and have been proposed. Apart from their role in the current financial crisis, reasons behind calls for regulation stem from studies that have refuted the claims that reputational concerns lead to reliable ratings by CRAs. Here, it was previously argued that CRAs provide accurate information to market participants in order to safeguard their reputation of ensuring reliable ratings. However, it has been noted that "worrying about reputation is not the same as worrying about providing reliable ratings".[23] This is because CRAs can be too conformist, too conservative or too bold precisely because they worry about their reputation.[24] It is for all the reasons mentioned here and above that various proposals for the regulation of CRAs have been put forward. A brief description and discussion of each option shall be given before their respective merits are analysed.

Status quo

This will entail leaving the current status quo as it is, since market participants will lobby against anything stronger. Moreover, the French Autorité des Marchés Financiers believes that the voluntary code has been implemented in a "globally satisfactory manner".[25] The main problem with this proposal is that it does and cannot solve the incentives problems mentioned above.

Nationalising the agencies

The first proposal to be considered is the nationalisation of the CRAs. This comes from the classification of ratings as public goods which should therefore have public funding as they are essential in ensuring that the global financial plumbing operates smoothly. Some have

---

[23] Mariano, Beatriz, 2008. "Do reputational concerns lead to reliable ratings?" 12 July 2008, *www. voxeu.com ?q=node/1397*
[24] Ibid.
[25] Ibid.

taken this proposal even further by calling on governments to set up a public rating agency (PRA).[26] The key feature of such a PRA is that it would not aim to make profit and would not have an interest in providing overly generous rating thus avoiding the incentives and conflict of interest problems mentioned above. It is proposed that such a PRA be funded with taxpayers' money, that it should be organised at the European level and combined with the European Financial Services Authority (EFSA) in the EU The main problem with this proposal is overcoming the lack of political will combined with the powerful lobby that is sure to be presented by the CRAs.

Abolish official recognition of CRAs' ratings

This proposal would involve eliminating the regulatory license of CRAs by removing the NRSRO designation and merely requiring agencies to register with the regulators. Intuitively, it can be seen that awarding CRA ratings with official recognitions places the ratings above suspicion by investors who then fail to conduct their own risk assessment before making investment decisions. No official recognition will force investors to see ratings as one of many tools that can be used to inform investment decisions, and thus allow them to gauge risk more accurately. For CRAs the barriers to entry and almost "god-like" status will be removed. The main problems with this proposal are that such a move will increase the regulatory burden on the regulators and would suppress the role of CRAs in Basle II, which, after all the effort put into crafting it, is likely to encounter great opposition.[27]

---

[26] Beetsma, Roel, 2008. "The Case for Public Sector Credit Rating Agencies". *www.economonitor.com/blog/2008/10/the-case-for-public-sector-credit-rating-agencies*. 27 October 2008.
[27] Portes, 2008.

Reviving subscriptions

Prior to the 1970s, the CRAs revenue came from a levy on the investors who used their ratings. At this time, the CRAs were not "tied up in the system" as they are today.[28] This would reduce the incentives and free rider problems mentioned above. The main problem with this proposal is that it is linked to the public good aspect as described by Portes who notes that there will be free rider problems and payment by the user of the information will be either suboptimal or unenforceable, which is the reason why the CRAs stopped this practice in the 1970s.

Providing additional information apart from ratings

This would address the accuracy problems highlighted above. This should include details such as assessment of the liquidity characteristics of the instruments and of likely volatility of its market price. In addition to this, it has been suggested that agencies provide a range of risk for each instrument rather than a point estimate[29] and develop a distinct rating scale for structured finance products.[30] The main problem with this proposal is that the agencies do not seem well equipped to do that as these kinds of risk are almost impossible to measure quantitatively. The CRAs are likely to lobby strongly against such an expansion of the depth of their work.

Introducing explicit legal liability for negligence and malfeasance

At the moment, CRAs successfully maintain legal immunity from malfeasance claims on the ground that they are only financial journalists publishing their opinions, which are protected by free speech, although, as pointed out by Portes, Moody's is much more profitable than the Financial Times, suggesting that they are earning some rents (their "reputational capital" and the regulatory license conferred by their role in the

---

[28] Perking, 2007.
[29] Portes, 2008.
[30] Ferguson et al, 2007.

financial system.[31]. Apart from the evident shortcomings of the free speech argument, being able to hold them more legally accountable will be a way to ensure that they take full responsibility for their ratings, and as such, be more thorough and meticulous in the provision of these ratings. However, the main problem with this proposal is that quite simply, CRAs will be sued out of business should such legal liability be in place as every investor who makes losses on a AAA rated product will demand redress.

Separating rating from consultancy and advisory functions

This will need to go beyond Chinese walls[32] and will entail ensuring the CRAs do not engage in consultancy work and that their structured finance business is stopped. This will eliminate the conflict of interest problems mentioned above. The main problem with this proposal is that the CRAs are likely to put up great resistance to giving up a highly remunerative line of work and to accept a dramatic decrease in their revenue stream.

Decrease barriers of entry

The rationale for this is that it would allow more CRAs into the market and create competition that will improve the performance of CRAs. However, the main problem with this proposals is the natural monopoly tendencies of the industry alluded to above as well as the possibility that more players will exacerbate the incentives problems and there will be more competition to gain issuers business, which may be done by providing the highest rankings.

---

[31] Portes, 2008.
[32] Ibid.

Options analysis

Table 1 looks at the extent to which the policy proposal addresses the problem category as highlighted above. Here, "yes", "no" and "maybe" are used to indicate whether or not the proposal addresses the problem.

PROBLEM CATEGORY → POLICY PROPOSALS ↓	Incentives	Conflict of Interest	Accuracy	Pro-Cyclicality	Competition
Nationalisation	YES	YES	MAYBE	YES	NO
No official recognition of CRA ratings	YES	YES	NO	NO	YES
Status Quo – Voluntary Code of Conduct	NO	NO	NO	NO	NO
Reviving Subscriptions	YES	YES	NO	NO	NO
Additional Information	NO	NO	YES	YES	NO
Legal Liability	YES	MAYBE	YES	YES	NO
Separating functions	YES	YES	NO	MAYBE	NO
Decrease Barriers to Entry	NO	NO	MAYBE	YES	YES

Table 1: Which problem category does each policy proposal address?

This exercise shows that no one solution can address all the problems relating to CRAs. This means that a policy package comprising key suggestions from each proposal will be needed.

The elements to be included in such a policy package should depend on the feasibility level of the implementation of that policy. Feasibility here refers to the political, lobbying and other practical obstacles that can potentially be leveled against the proposal by key market participants. Table 2 shows the relative feasibility options of each proposal on a scale of 1 (high feasibility) to 5 (low feasibility).

Here, it can be seen that introducing legal liability and nationalisation will most probably encounter the greatest political and lobbying obstacles as it threatens the very existence of CRAs. This is followed by no official recognition, reviving subscriptions and separating rating from consultancy and advisory functions. This category threatens the revenue stream of CRAs. Compared to these options, asking CRAs to provide information is less threatening and allowing more CRAs into the market even less so as the major CRAs have already established their market dominance.

FEASIBILITY (1 = high, 5= low) → POLICY PROPOSAL ↓	1	2	3	4	5
Nationalisation					*
No recognition of CRAs ratings				*	
Status Quo – Voluntary Code of Conduct	*				
Reviving Subscriptions				*	
Additional information			*		
Legal Liability					*
Separating rating from consultancy and advisory functions				*	
Decrease Barriers to Entry		*			

Table 2: What is the relative feasibility of each option?

Recommendations

In light of the above analysis, several recommendations can be made. These shall be based on the identification of the core problem with the current role of CRAs in the global financial system seems to be related to dealing with innovation, in terms of the valuation of new and complex instruments. Here, the models used by the CRAs, which fail to factor in tail events and the limited amount of information provided by CRAs, are particularly problematic. Linked to this is the fact that the god-like stature of CRAs blind investors to the inherent uncertainty associated with ratings which are treated as indicators of guaranteed returns on investments instead of probabilities. This is particularly true in the case of rating new and complex instruments as was seen in the current financial crisis.

With this in mind, I would propose nationalising the ratings function (ratings as public goods) of CRA through the setting up of a public sector rating agency as proposed by Beetsma. Here, I would propose giving CRAs two options (1) Delegate their rating function to the public sector rating agency whilst continuing with the structured finance and consultancy arm of their business or (2) Cease their structured finance and consultancy activities and focus only on providing ratings.

Should the CRA choose the second option, I would propose that ratings be paid for by subscription by investors, because, although the conflict of interest problem will be addressed, the question of incentives will not. With the growth of capital markets around the world, and the need investors have of ratings to inform their decision, the problem of insufficient revenue faced by CRAs in the 1970s should not be an issue today. The only change will be that instead of making obscenely large profits, CRAs' profits will fall within the normal range of other financial services providers.

The second caveat that will come with choosing option 2 is that the CRAs' performance will be monitored by regulators to ensure the quality of ratings. Should CRAs be seen to fall below par based on a predetermined list of key performance indicators, they will be either nationalised or have their official recognition revoked.

In addition to this, it must be ensured that ratings be accompanied by additional information beyond point-estimates as highlighted above and that CRAs' models be shown to take into account events beyond normal distributions with different instruments having different rating scales.

Basle 2, and other regulatory structures that rely on ratings, must then insist on the use of an aggregated rating of each of the main accredited agencies to increase accuracy, minimise potential errors. Here, it must be noted that the weighting of different factors by different CRAs may vary according to a set of different conditions and variables thus making certain aspects of the each CRA's rating process essentially subjective.[33] Moreover, aggregation will also potentially mitigate the effects to the high correlation and interdependence of all the lines of defense. Ideally, each has to be independent and strong. However, strengthening the second pillar in the current environment will invariably lead to the strengthening of the third pillar as well.

Finally, to prevent this particular failure in the future, whenever innovation occurs, there must be a freezing of ratings for new instruments for six months from the time the product is introduced onto the market. Here, it should be rated U as in unknown, and all known information about the product should be provided to investors. This will force investors to make their own investment decision based on their risk sensitivity levels.

Bibliography

Beetsma, R., 2007. "The Case for Public Sector Credit Rating Agencies". *www.economonitor.com/blog/2008/10/the-case-for-public-sector-credit-rating-agencies/.*

Castle, S., 2008. "EU prepares tight rules on credit rating agencies", *New York Times*, 29 October 2008. *www.nytimes.com/2008/10/29/ business/worldbusiness/29iht-rating.4.17356324.html.*

Champasaur, Amelie, 2005. "The regulation of credit rating agencies in the US, and in the EU: Recent initiatives and Proposals": *www.law.harvard.edu/programmes/pifs/pdfs/amelie_champasaur.pdf.*

De la Dehasa, G., 2008. "How to avoid further credit and liquidity conference crises", in: *The First Global Financial Crisis of the 21st Century*. A VoxEU.org Publication. London: Centre for Economic Policy Research, 2008, 151-154.

Ferguson, Roger W. *et al.*, 2007. *International Financial Stability*. Geneva Reports on the World Economy 9, Geneva and London: ICMB and CEPR.

Levich, Richard M. *et al.* 2002. *Ratings, Rating Agencies and the Global Financial System,* Washington: Springer.

Mariano, B., 2008. "Do reputational concerns lead to reliable ratings?" See *www. voxeu.com.*

Perkings, T., 2007. "Misguided or Misunderstood?" Globe and Mail. 7 September 2007. *www.theglobeandmail.com/report-on-business/article780146.ece*

Portes, R., 2008. "Rating Agency Reform". See *www.voxeu.org/index.php?q=node/887.*

Reinhart, C., 2008. "Reflections on the international dimensions and policy lessons of the US sub-prime crisis". See *www.voxeu.org/index.php?q=node/988.*

[33] Champsaur. 2005.

US Congress, 2008. Transcript: House Oversight and Government Policy Committee. 22 October 2008. *oversight.house.gov/story.asp?ID=2250.*

Appendix: Current Regulatory Framework for CRAs (EU and US)

	U.S.	E.U.
Main regulator	SEC	Bank supervisors
Regulatory tools	No registration of CRAs, but recognition by SEC as NRSRO for regulatory purposes	No registration of CRAs, but recognition by bank regulators for regulatory purposes
IOSCO Code	SEC does not recommend adoption by CRAs of IOSCO Code, but the NRSRO recognition criteria relating to conduct of business rules seem likely to be achieved by implementing the Code.	CESR recommends adoption by the CRAs of the IOSCO Code. There is no enforcement mechanism (CESR relies on market enforcement)
Recognition criteria	- Published ratings - Market acceptance of CRAs - Conduct of business rules	- Integrity of methodologies - Credibility of ratings - Conduct of business rules
Recognition goals	Efficiency of securities markets	- Efficiency of securities market (IOSCO Code) - Adequacy of capital requirements
Ongoing supervision	Limited (SEC reserves the right to reexamine conditions on which granted NRSRO status)	Permanent (as required by the CRD)
Recognition procedure	SEC discretion, although criteria are more precise under the Proposed Rule	Bank regulators are bound by the CRD rules and further details
Civil liability	No (First Amendment protection)	Never established but possible
Securities laws	Exemption under Regulation FD	No exemption under the Market Abuse Directive
Competition	The SEC believes that more precise NRSRO designation criteria will foster competition and that competition is a means of regulating CRA performance	CESR believes that competition issues should not be taken into account in establishing CRA rules and should be left to antitrust authorities.

Source: *www.law.harvard.edu/programmes/pifs/pdfs/amelie_champasaur.pdf*

15

REDEFINING CAPITALISM: AN ETHICAL RATING AND ITS CONTRIBUTION TO DEVELOPMENT

Jaime Pozuelo-Monfort

Today's world is a world of increasing differences. There are objections to the previous statement, but the World Bank's figures are self-explanatory. They point to a scenario whereby extreme poverty of the world's poorest would have dramatically increased in the past 20 years in Sub-Saharan Africa, whereas South and East Asia have benefited from the phenomenal growth of China and India.

There is overconfidence and a lack of realism in the first world as to how to tackle the situation that worsens day by day. Many individuals in the rich world, who are not directly involved with the difficulties faced by emerging economies, do not realise the depth and severity of the problems the poor encounter, or the degree to which the latter affect the daily lives of millions of people.

No easy solution seems feasible or applicable. There have been, and there are interesting initiatives that, provided their success, could bring first and third world closer together in terms of income, growth opportunities and share of the pie. However although apparently straightforward, these proposals remain simplistic and hard to implement within the present regulatory framework, even if this may be possible on the long run. This situation is exacerbated by the fact that the individual is greedy by definition.

The role of financial economics

Finance drives the economy in the developed world. The economic policies of rich economies determine the fate of emerging countries. It seems plausible to find alternatives that can be implemented through regulation in the financial markets of the developed countries, and to change some of the basics that permit their existence and operation. Capitalism has always been revisited after major crisis or crashes. The Great Depression in the 1930s, the crash of the stock market in 1987, the burst of the Internet bubble in the late 1990s, or the financial fiasco of Enron, Worldcom and Arthur Andersen in the early years of the twenty-first century, are all examples of situations in which the major players of the game redefined their roles and repositioned themselves. Many people in the first world may not see a crisis in the current environment. Many may be too optimistic, overconfident, true believers in a process we all label globalisation that brings good to everyone we know, to all around us. Some people could have misunderstood what globalisation really brings to many, wrongly taking for granted that those living in the developing world can access the same sort of opportunities and resources as those of us who live in the rich world.

As in the past, capitalism may need to be revisited. The current trend does not serve the goals set by the UN, which, given the current state of the world, are unlikely to be accomplished by the year 2015.

Jeffrey Sachs, who currently heads the Commission in charge of UN's Millennium Development Goals, points out: "We can realistically envision a world without extreme poverty by the year 2025 because technological progress enables us to meet basic human needs on a global scale and to achieve a margin above basic needs unprecedented in history." Jeffrey Sachs is right in the end but he may not have pinpointed the correct means. Vandana Shiva, a writer connected with the participatory economics movement, led by Michael Albert, makes an interesting argument: "To make poverty history, we first need to elaborate a real history of poverty. And Sachs has totally misunderstood it."

The present trend of capitalism will be that of increasing differences. Inequality tends to increase not only at global level, but also within developed nations. The system is heading in the wrong direction, but still has the virtue to redefine itself. However this will not happen automatically.

Redefining capitalism

The strong connection between financial markets and the opportunities available to emerging economies plays a key role in the search for practical ideas to redefine current capitalism, and manifests the importance of financial economics in the development of this approach. As previously stated, finance is viewed as the main driver of the first world's economies. Finance has a daily impact on the stability and growth of an economy.

There is already regulation in the financial markets that, through taxation, raises public funds for public spending. If corporations were given an option whether or not to pay corporate or dividend tax, they would definitely choose not to, based on the maximisation of the present value of their future cash flows. Or equivalently, they would adopt the one strategy that most benefits their shareholders, the one that maximises their equity.

Similarly, corporations in today's world tend to respect current regulations, but are able to skip ethical codes of conduct, always aiming at maximising their profits.

One of the key strengths of current financial markets is the financial possibilities it opens to public corporations through the issuance of stock or corporate debt.

The concept of financial rating is key to a public corporation, because it determines the cost of capital it will incur on whatever funds are borrowed from investors. The rating agencies impose strict constraints in determining certain ratings that are indicative of the financial strength of a corporation, or alternatively viewed, the established financial policies. Additionally, auditors make sure a public corporation's financial statements meet international standards and are trustworthy.

Hence there is a system in place with which the modern corporation has to comply. This system has undergone much evolution over the years, without reaching perfection. A corporation's only approach is to adapt to the regulation and the set of rules established by regulators and rating agencies. Top executives in large corporations work hard to be transparent, to not use confidential information to their own advantage, to immediately communicate whatever news may arise, either good or bad, to the financial community.

There is a growing trend in the corporate world to adopt a code of ethical conduct that includes respect for the environment, flexible working conditions, trade-offs between work and family, etc. However a firm is absolutely free to adopt such codes or not, as these have no repercussions from a financial point of view. Briefly stated, a firm's financial rating will not change whether or not the company is ethically responsible. Today's financial markets only reward the financial manners of a corporation, with the ethical dimension being considered as irrelevant.

The need for an ethical rating

We cannot live in a world governed by multinational corporations that do not have strong codes of conduct, that invest and divest huge amounts of funds as they wish, that outsource the majority of operations to third-world economies where deplorable working conditions reign, and that have no strong established ethical regulations. The rich world has succeeded in building a system that works for the first world, but that does not work globally. The system needs to be revisited, and this time the ethical component needs to be addressed.

Alongside the financial rating, companies should have an ethical rating of similar nature that would affect their financing and success in the consumer market, as much as the financial rating does in the financial markets.

Rating agencies would determine the ethical actions of a corporation, whether or not it outsources, how it invests its money, the working conditions of its employees, whether its operating policies respect the environment, what part of its corporate tax is devoted to social action and so on. And there would be (ethical) auditors that confirm whether the corporation complies with the set of ethical criteria established. A globalised economy characterised by the immediate communication of information should not tolerate unethical policies on behalf of corporations.

The statements are strong, since they touch every potential corporation that participates in the financial markets. But if a corporation currently does its homework financially speaking, simply because this is the way to operate within the system, a corporation will similarly do its homework from an ethical point of view, if this is a requirement to remain in the system.

Every potential investor looks at a corporation's financial rating prior to purchasing stock, corporate debt or derivatives that have the corporation's stock as underlying asset. The financial rating has become a guarantee for an investor because it is a definite indicator of the firm's probability of default. The ethical rating would play the same role for the consumer. Investor versus consumer is the key in this argumentation.

The consumer as actor

Products and services would be labelled with a company's ethical rating. The consumer could therefore know at any given moment whether a company is ethically responsible, and ultimately, consumers would reward or penalise a firm for not complying with the rules of the system. There is research available that links a consumer's ethical values to his or her consumption habits. Therefore and provided that a consumer does have ethical values, he or she would likely purchase products or services that align with his or her values, ethically speaking. This is why the proposed system is sustainable. In order to be successful in the marketplace a firm would have to be ethically responsible. The better the ethical rating, the better opinion a consumer would have of the corporation, and the more likely he or she will be to purchase a certain product or service.

Multinational corporations would not determine a consumer's choice. Consumers will rather determine a corporation's set of operating policies. It's about reversing the rules of the game. It's about giving the consumer the power to believe that his or her actions truly affect the state of the world. It's about only allowing those players that respect the rules to participate in the game. It's about consumers pushing those corporations that are not ethically responsible out of the market.

There is a success story in certain European savings banks that are required by regulation to devote a high percentage of their net income to social action. And these banks do so because they have to, in order to comply with the regulation. And the effects of their social policies are noticed locally.

Contribution to a development fund

On these lines, and in order to reach the maximum ethical rating, a corporation would have to give away a certain percentage of its net income, funds that would end up in a development fund. A company may choose not to do so, although by doing so it may obtain the maximum ethical rating and the corresponding consumer reward. It is a trade-off, since what a firm loses by giving away part of its funds is earned through consumer reward.

The money accumulated in the development fund would be managed by a public entity that would only invest in companies that are ethically responsible. Companies that are ethically sound, besides being financially driven, would see their financing opportunities increased. This idea follows from the ethical ratings presented above.

It is possible to picture a world with strong multinational corporations that are ethically responsible. It is feasible to imagine a development fund converted into the largest fund of human history, that only invests in companies with strong ethical codes of conduct, that devotes the rates of return of its investment strategies to development aid, and by doing so fosters ethical operating policies within corporations.

Towards a global sense of justice

Going one step further, let's suppose that by regulation, the wealthiest are required to devote a tenth of their wealth to a development fund. If this fund's principal were to be compared with other large funds, it would be the largest of any funds in the history of financial markets.

Personal wealth over a certain amount should be taxed. The current regulation taxes income and gains on assets, but does not tax personal wealth. Ultimately, nobody should be eligible to possess more than a certain amount of money without being taxed for the monetary resources held. In terms of a global sense of justice, it is simply not sustainable. And this can and should be accomplished through regulation, with changes to the tax code.

Corporations would be entitled to invest 10% of their net income in a development fund over a certain time horizon, say 5 years. After this period expires, the corporation would get the invested money back, and this would be done on an annual basis. The fund would keep the profits linked to the investment strategies, and devote them to development aid.

Rich economies would issue as much as the equivalent of 10% of their GDP in public debt and devote this money to the investment fund. Again, only the profits from the investment strategies would be used as development aid. Therefore the fund would have a principal to invest in securities that would not decrease over time.

Surplus of rich economies of the world would feed the development fund, whose rate of return would become development aid for third-world economies. Personal wealth over $1 billion would be initially asked to contribute 10% to the development fund.

And last but not least, individual investors would be welcome to allocate part of their savings to the fund over a certain time horizon, after which they would get the principal invested back.

Many of today's individual investors with certain savings on their accounts, either do not invest them and hence keep them in a checking account with either no return or very low return, or invest them in funds that yield small returns that are mostly kept by the investment managers for actively managing the funds (management fees).

These individuals could alternatively invest their savings in the development fund that could have indexed investment strategies in exchange, and would not charge management fees. The individuals would get back the principal invested after the time horizon they chose, the rates of return being kept by the fund, and devoted to development aid.

From the rich to the poor

The fund would become a redistribution instrument, from the rich to the poor. With an annual budget equal to the profits of its investment strategies, the fund would distribute the profits competitively among projects proposed to a central committee. The committee would be in charge of allocating the funds. Proposals would be submitted and analysed by the committee year round. In an annual summit, the committee would announce which proposals have qualified for funding. The projects that get funded would be monitored and audited by the development fund's auditors, who would travel to emerging countries to follow up the development of a project.

The above process guarantees that the development aid is used as efficiently as possible, that through submission, only strong proposals get funding. Furthermore, the audits would also ensure that an organisation does not receive funding again if it has previously been declared corrupt by auditors.

This global mechanism departs from the accumulation of resources through the introduction of a development fund. The mechanism does not only raise the required funds, it also allocates the money from a global perspective of fairness. The process is transparent, and all projects are given an equal chance to get funding. Projects are not only funded, but a follow-up audit makes sure the money allocated is properly used for the purpose in hand.

Within a time frame of five years from inception, the development fund would represent annual funds exceeding the aggregate budget of four of the most representative non-profit organisations worldwide, such as Unicef or the American Red Cross. If, as previously claimed, we assume that the 500 wealthiest individuals devote 10% of their wealth to the fund, total annual profits of the investment strategies would yield $20 billion per annum.

Similarly, let's consider a national economy like that of Spain, issuing the equivalent of 10% of its GDP in public debt. Spain's economy has a current public debt level as a percentage of GDP of 44% and a GDP (2004) of roughly $891 billion. The principal of the development fund would accordingly increase by $89 billion and the profits from the investment strategies devoted to development aid would rise by approximately \$13 billion if we apply two basic investment strategies.

A virtuous circle

Ethical ratings would affect a corporation's financial status, from the sales figures to the market share, mainly because ethical ratings would have a direct impact on consumer behaviour and the choices made when purchasing products and services. By adapting to a set of ethical constraints a firm could directly or indirectly influence third world economies where the firm or one of its suppliers may conduct operations. This in turn would affect, among others, a poor country's workforce and its quality of life. Furthermore it would encourage policies that promote the stability of poor countries' economies, including the fight against money laundering and illegal money transfers.

A development fund, conceived as presented above, would substantially increase the amount of funding available for development aid in third world countries and therefore have a direct influence on the causes of poverty.

Wealth redistribution has enabled modern economic societies of the twentieth and twenty-first centuries to reach a quality of life that would have been unimaginable after the two world wars. The progressive nature of the tax code is certainly something that those who earn most dislike. A wealthy individual would be better off managing that part of his or her wealth on his or her own. The progressivity of the tax code benefits many low-income households to the detriment of a lesser number of higher incomes. This represents the concept of solidarity in countries with established advanced economic systems.

Globalisation cannot serve one goal and deny others. Globalisation is not only about destroying trade barriers to sell internationally. It is also about redistribution from the rich to the poor. And if we think of the world as a common and integrated economic system where everybody is interconnected, there should be income redistribution from the rich to the poor globally, just as there is at a national level.

Susan George makes an interesting remark regarding the allocation of the funds raised through her taxation proposal: "Suppose that international taxation of international transactions, corporate mergers and acquisitions and industrial pollution is accepted; that genuine debt relief is granted and a pool of fresh funds is thereby constituted. Is that the end of the story? The most important part remains to be invented and it concerns managing and using the money. [...] Probably the best option would be a new, small UN body made up of personnel chosen from the UN specialised agencies plus a corps of roving auditors. [...] After forty-plus years of largely unsatisfactory development aid, we've had an opportunity to learn at least one thing: you can't just hand over funds to a government and hope for the best."

16

WHEN SMALL COMPANIES DABBLE IN DISINFORMATION

Saif Ullah

Companies may contract investor-relations' firms (Promoters) to increase investor interest in their securities. These promoters do not disclose their association with the companies and issue positive recommendations. A review of such cases shows that the price of the firm increases for a short period of time. In all of these, the Securities and Exchange Commission (SEC) and National Association of Securities Dealers (NASD) have been taking legal action against the investor-relations' firms, although only a handful of firms have actually been charged under Section 17(B) of the Securities Act 1934. Event day (the day that these authorities started legal proceedings) returns for the hiring firms are negative and significant. In addition, the firm's characteristics could help to identify the kind of firms that might hire these promoters. Indeed, smaller firms with free cash flow and higher capital expenditure are more likely to resort to such means. The managers of these firms are concerned about agency problems and try to increase disclosure to reduce the severity of this problem.

Internet and the trading volume

The advent of Internet has made the generation of information inexpensive and its distribution instantaneous. This fact has not been lost on managers: managers of new and small firms spent a lot of time and effort reaching out to the investing public. H. Hong and M. Huang (2005) conjecture that CEOs of these firms might spend as much as 25% of their time on investor relations. Using agencies that specialise in investor relations might reduce the cost of these activities and might enhance their effectiveness. According to D. Deller *et al.* (1999), the use of Internet as a medium to conduct investor relations is more widespread in the United States of America as compared with the United Kingdom or Germany. B. Barber and T Odean (2001) look at the impact of Internet on investors' trading behaviour specifically with regard to online trading. They argue that although disintermediation of brokerage houses is a boon for investors, the downside is the loss of advice that the investors were getting from them. P. Wysocki (1998) looks at the impact of message board volume on Yahoo! Message Board on price and trading volume of the underlying stocks. He finds that overnight trading volume is able to predict the trading volume and returns on stocks on next day. W. Antweiler and M. Frank (2004) look at the posting volume on Yahoo! and Raging Bull message boards on 45 Dow Jones Industrial Average companies. Their findings pointed out that these messages are good predictors of volatility, and have a statistically significant impact on returns. We can thus conclude from the recent studies that the spread of information via Internet seems to affect the trading volume and price of the stocks.

The "third-party" information provider

The importance of this has not been lost on some unscrupulous operators. According to a news item on British Broadcasting

Corporation (BBC) online, some spammers are contacting firms and offering them their services, promising share price increases of up to 250% in a matter of weeks. These firms usually target small investors and small firms.

Data and methodology

We collected information about Investor Relations' Specialists (Promoters) charged by Securities and Exchange Commission (SEC) from the Website of SEC (**www.sec.gov**). Litigation Releases from 1995-2006 were included. NASD website was used to find identical cases. Besides these resources, FACTIVA served to collect detailed information about these events. In all the cases, we collected the data on which promoters started promoting these stocks as well as the date on which SEC or NASD filed their complaint against the promoters. Compustat was used to collect accounting data about these firms. DataStream was a source of information on market price and trading volume data about our sample. In all, 169 firms were found that had Datastream codes available. Of these firms, 116 were used for event study around the promotion date. The reduced number of firms is due to the fact that some of these did not have enough data available for the estimation period. Ownership data from Securities and Exchange Commission files provided by EdgarOnline were also reviewed. Some of these promoters had their own websites and charged subscribers for their "independent" services. Some had their own TV programmes on which they promoted these companies without disclosing their relationship with them. In other cases, spam or discussion forums were used to promote the companies. The mean market value of the firms during the estimation period is USD 70 Million. 40 firms were listed on OTC, 4 firms on New York Exchange, 74 on Non Nasdaq OTC, 25 on Nasdaq Non National, 4 on Nasdaq and 7 on Amex. 156 firms in different studies are used in this paper. Of these, 125 firms are still active in the securities market, 2 were suspended and 29 have gone out of business.

Logistic regression was used to see if there are some definite specific characteristics that make a firm more likely to use this specific kind of investor-relations specialist. Sample firms were matched to other firms based on four criteria: (i) Four digit SIC code; (ii) Equity Market for the security; (iii) Fiscal year before event and (iv) Age of the firm. There was however no sample match against market value. B. Bushee *et al.* (2005) argue that market values for pink sheet and OTCBB firms are often unreliable.

Although the motives behind hiring investor-relations specialists might vary from firm to firm, there seems to be a general consensus that the effects will be an increase in price and liquidity. The existing studies do not look at the effect of information emanating from a third party employed by the firm on stock price and liquidity. This third party is required to disclose its affiliation with the hiring firm. However, in the data studied above (Box 1), it failed to do so, and was charged by the Securities and Exchange Commission. In the sample, the quality of information seems credible and trustworthy at first sight. However, the non-disclosure of a relationship between investor-relations' firms and hiring firms might lead to more severe information asymmetry and less credibility of firm's information in the long run. It is worth determining if these third parties are able to produce the same results that conventional investor-relations firms produce. This has important implications for credibility of source literature.

Significant but somewhat puzzling findings

Using an event study approach is a good way to look at the impact on price of promotion by investor-relations' specialists. A market model with value and equally weighed index is used to look at the impact of promotion on the stock price. Promotion or event date is defined as the date on which the Securities and Exchange Commission said that these promoters started promoting the stocks. In those cases where the Securities and Exchange Commission did not specify an exact date, information was collected from Factiva or searched for on the World Wide Web. The earliest date as the event date was taken into consideration in all cases. The reutilisation of the same firm if the promoter continued promoting the stock over a number of weeks was avoided.

There is evidence of a surge in stock price on the event date. Average Abnormal Returns of 3.05% on the event date are economically and statistically significant at a 1% level of significance. Cumulative Average Abnormal Returns (CAAR) remain positive and significant for fifteen days. This finding indicates that investor relations seem to have an effect on the stock price of the contracting firms. However, there is a wide dispersion in the abnormal returns within the sample and that needs to be explained. Precision weighted cumulative abnormal returns remain above 5% for the first twelve days and then drop to 4% by the fifteenth day after the event. Nevertheless, they still remain statistically and economically significant.

Looking next at the impact of legal action by the SEC or NASD on stock prices of contracting firms, there is a statistically significant negative effect on the Average Abnormal Returns of these firms on the days that legal action commenced. This effect becomes more pronounced after two days of announcement. The Cumulative Average Abnormal Returns (CAAR) remain negative and statistically and economically significant two days after the event and they remain significant for up to fifteen days. This might be due to the slow spread of information in the security prices. Another possible reason is the fact that legal authorities took action a considerable time after the event. Markets might have learned about the relationship between promoters and contracting firms during this period.

Smaller firms likely to fall into the trap

Looking now at the returns of firms that were being promoted by the same Investor-relations firms, but were not named in Securities and Exchange Commission complaints, it appears that these firms also suffered negative abnormal returns on the dates that the SEC took legal action. Although, these returns were economically significant, they were not statistically significant. The reason could have been the small number of events. Only 21 such firms with usable data were found.

Subsequently, firms in the sample are being matched with firms from Compustat database on the basis of fiscal year, industry (SIC code) and exchange listed. Using logistic regression is a convenient way to predict what characteristics distinguish the sample firms from the matched firms. Different accounting variables are used such as total assets, Research and Development, Capital expenditure, free cash flow and leverage as some of these characteristics.

Logistic regression analysis indicates that smaller firms are more likely to hire Investor Relations' specialists. These firms are also more likely to have free cash flow. This supports Jensen's Hypothesis about the severity of the agency problem. The severity of the agency problem might have induced these firms to hire IR specialists. These firms are also more likely to have higher capital expenditure. They might hire IR specialists to explain the investment opportunities they are facing and the increased capital they are investing.

The existing literature suggests that the motive behind the use of promoters by firms' managers might be to increase the liquidity of the firms' securities. This possibility was explored by looking at different measures of the liquidity of the shares of the firms both before and after the event. The daily average trading volume (measured in the number of shares traded) is compared over one year prior to and one year following the event. Paired sample comparison is a means of seeing if promotions increase the number of shares traded on a given day. It appears that there is a significant increase in the trading volume after the event and it lasts for one year. Looking next at the average number of trading days during one year prior to and one year following the event, there is a significant increase in the number of trading days for these firms after the event. This suggests that there is an increase in the liquidity of the stocks after the event, as suggested by existing literature.

Looking then at the change in ownership of insiders before and after the event, the average insider ownership decreases from 25.93% to 22.30% after the event. The change is statistically significant in paired sample mean comparison at a 5% level of significance. This indicates that increased liquidity might have been the motive behind hiring these promoters. The managers of the firms might then have been able to decrease their stakes in the firm. This might be an important consideration for the managers of young firms. Diversification might have been an important consideration for these managers. However, the sample size for insider ownership is limited to 33 firms.

Spreading true information with dubious means

The motive behind spreading information (true or false) might vary from one market participant to another. Rival firms might spread false information about competitors to damage their reputation. Short sellers might spread negative information to drive the stock price of a security down. A recent study by L. Frieder and J. Zittrain (2006) finds that spam works and it earns profits for touters. They suggest numerous regulatory actions to stop the exploitation of investors through this medium. Although studies looking at the impact of information being spread through Internet have enhanced our understanding of this new phenomenon, there has been no attempt to differentiate among those who spread information. Events in which investor relations targeted "buy-side investors" to promote the companies that had hired them were looked at. The medium used for promotion varied from Internet to television. However, different methods using Internet were the predominant way of spreading the information. The information being spread was not necessarily false. However, those who spread the information failed to disclose their relationship with the firm. This fact is important for the receiver to judge the credibility of the information and could have an impact on the credibility of the data released. In one of the earliest studies on the credibility of source and information content by C.. Hoveland and W. Weiss (1951), the authors find that subjects were more likely to change their opinion when the information appeared to emanate from a highly credible source as compared to a less credible one.

S.P. Kothari and J.E. Short (2003) look at the impact of disclosure by different sources on stock return volatility and the cost of capital of the firms. They find that positive disclosure by the firm's management does not impact either of these variables. However negative disclosure by management leads to increased stock return volatility and cost of capital. They do not find any impact on cost of capital or stock return volatility when the information emanates from analysts. However, when the positive or negative information comes from the press, it does affect the cost of capital. It increases the cost of capital when the information is negative and decreases it when the information is positive. They conjecture that it might be because of the higher credibility being attributed to financial press as compared to analysts. But in our opinion, the positive returns found in the study are due to the fact that information is apparently coming form a third source rather than from management.

Not always worth the fuss

The events in which investor-relations' firms receiving compensation try to hide their relationship from investors was studied in this paper. Firms hiring these promoters show an initial increase in the price of their stocks. There is, however, a negative reaction resulting in significantly negative returns when the legal authorities charge the promoters. Now, smaller firms who have more free cash, and who are investing heavily in capital expenditure are more likely to use these promoters. Their decision to hire IR firms might be an attempt to reduce the agency problem associated with having more free cash flow and a higher level of capital expenditure. Another possible motive might be to increase the liquidity of the stocks. There is support for the hypothesis that managers hire these promoters to create a more liquid market for their securities. Thus, average volume increases during the year following the promotion as compared to the average volume preceding it. The average number of trading days also increases following the promotion, in comparison with the average number of trading days prior the promotion.

As a result, there is increased liquidity resulting from higher trading volume in the underlying securities. There are positive abnormal returns around the event date. This might be considered a result of increased trading and incorporation of stale information in the security prices. It might also be due to the fact that investors really believed the promoters. Another important factor is the fact that these promoters targeted only buy-side investors, which might have led to higher stock prices.

Ethical issues concerning the hiring of investor-relations' firms by different firms were raised here. The fact that these investor-relations' firms were charged, and that the firms that employed them were rarely charged, shows the complexity of enforcement of laws. These firms clearly benefited from the illegal behaviour of the investor-relations' firms. However, the law enforcement agency did not/could not take any action against them. It might have been difficult to prove in court that the hiring firms knew about the activities of the promoters. But one can argue that these firms were agents of the hiring firms and consequently these firms should have known what their agents were doing, and should, in that capacity, have been prosecuted.

Bibliography

Antweiler, W./ Frank, M.Z., 2004. "Is all that talk just noise? The information content of Internet stock message boards", in: *The Journal of Finance 59 (3)*, 1259-1294.

Barber, B.M./ Odean, T., 2001. "The Internet and the investor", in: *Journal of Economic Perspectives 15 (1)*, 14-54.

Bushee, B. *et al*, 2005. *Investor Relations, Firm Visibility and Investor Following*, published in Knowledge@Wharton.

Deller, D. *et al*, 1999. "A survey on the use of the Internet for investor relations in the USA, the UK and Germany", *The European Accounting Review 8 (2)*, 351-364.

Frieder, L./ Zittrain, J., 2006. *Spam Works: Evidence from Stock Touts and Corresponding Market Activity*, Harvard: Berkman Center Research Publication, No. 2006-11.

Hong, H./ Huang, M., 2005. "Talking up liquidity: Insider trading and investor relations", in: *Journal of Financial Intermediation 14 (1)*, 1-31.

Hovland, C./ Weiss, W., 1951. "The Influences of Source Credibility on Communication Effectiveness", in: *Public Opinion Quarterly 52*, 635-650.

Kothari, S.P./ Short, J.E., 2003. *The Effect of Disclosure by Management, Analysts and Financial Press on the Equity Cost of Capital*, Paper 195, Cambridge, Sloan School of Management.
Wysocki, P., 1998. *Cheap Talk on the Web: Determinants of Postings on Stocks Message Boards*, Working Paper No. 98025, Cambridge, University of Michigan Business School.

PART III

SOLIDARITY AND SUSTAINABILITY

17

SOLIDARITY FINANCE AND THE DEMOCRATISATION OF MONEY

Nicolás Meyer

Solidarity finance is an ethical form of finance because it helps to re-forge the social and human links that are being damaged on a daily basis by an increasingly aggressive capitalism that puts forward the accumulation of goods and capital as a development model for communities, promoting concentration instead of fair distribution. Community banks create a space where entrepreneurial women from vulnerable communities manage their savings autonomously, in full security and transparency, helping to repair that shaken trust.

Community banks as an instrument of solidarity finance

Is it possible to create mechanisms that promote the democratisation of money? The mission to which the not-for-profit organisation *Nuestras Huellas* [Our Footprints] has decided to devote all its energies may be described as fostering the comprehensive development of people in their own communities. This is being done through solidarity finance programmes whose purpose is to promote participatory, self-managed and ethically responsible actions, all within a social economy structure.[1]

Solidarity finance implies "*a kind of democratisation of the financial system, whose objective is to match financial products with the basic needs of people and to underpin the social economy being developed in each region. Solidarity finance gives priority to those excluded from the traditional banking system, creating links that help to integrate people and maintain a sustainable relationship between economy and society. The goal of this relationship, which is built upon the foundations of ethics and social solidarity, is to create ideal conditions for human development, which must necessarily be an overall and sustainable development.*"[2]

In order to meet this challenge, we have worked to support the establishment of community banks in areas of high social vulnerability. Our community banks are one of the main instruments helping to consolidate the social economy structure. They provide a means for groups to save and pool funds, also providing loans and some financial training to help set up businesses or undertake infrastructure improvements. At the same time an effort is made to provide a comprehensive service to the partners in the community banks, including technical assistance in marketing and business training. *Nuestras Huellas* is currently working hand-in-hand with 120 community banks.

"Finance is the discipline which has to do with the use of money, its cost and yield, ways of producing and capturing economic surpluses in liquid form, its protection, transfer and control, the creation of services to assist those who hold money surpluses on the one hand and those who are seeking credit on the other. But this descriptive overview makes no mention of the kind of people involved, the specific aims being pursued,

---

[1] *Nuestras Huellas*, *www.nuestrashuellas.org.ar*

[2] Dias Coelho, Franklin, "Finanzas Solidarias", in: Cattani, D. (ed.), *A otra Economía*, Buenos Aires: UNGS-Altamira-OSDE, 2004.

the kinds of intermediation mechanisms and the whole question of what the existing structures aim to do and what the alternatives might be."[3]

A community bank is a neighbourhood self-managed organisation. Each group consists of at least seven people and sometimes as many as 20 or more members. The only condition for participating, besides the desire to work with team spirit that is required of the predominantly female participants,[4] is that the members must be on the point of setting up a business initiative or have done so recently. Thus each partner – the name given to social entrepreneurs who are members of the community banks – obtains a personal loan, with the possibility of a gradual increase, the guarantee being based on the trust that the borrower's own group have in her to meet her commitments. The loan might be used to boost a business initiative that she has started up or to make improvements to her accommodation.

In order to ensure that the alternative finance offered by the working groups at the community bank is likely to have a genuinely transformative effect and help build the social economy, savings mechanisms are promoted that also offer the possibility of enabling other neighbours in the community to obtain solidarity finance loans. The aim of this savings system, always structured and voluntary, is to help these groups to become independent of *Nuestras Huellas*, i.e. that they should build up their own capital with which to make loans among themselves, to their families and neighbours.

In its first year of operations, a community bank has an average of some 2,000 Argentine pesos ($US500) in savings on deposit and the average growth rate in savings is around 15%. The loans that a community bank grants from these reserves vary between 400 and 1,500 pesos. In March 2011, the total savings of the community banks amounted to 500,000 pesos ($US125,000), with 900 active loans under their own

---

[3] Sabaté, Alberto Federico *et al.* (eds.), *Finanzas y Economía Social*, Buenos Aires: UNGS-Altamira-OSDE, 2005.

[4] Currently 95% of all members are women.

management, granted within their own communities. At the same time, the active loan portfolio of *Nuestras Huellas* was 643,562 pesos, which means that the community banks had practically the same amount of capital with which to make loans as an officially-registered not-for-profit organisation. It should also be underlined that repayment defaults on loans granted by community banks amounted to less than 2% of the sums lent.

Each community bank elects from among its partners a board of directors, a chairman, treasurer and company secretary who are responsible for managing the bank. These roles are exercised in rotation and are taken on as a service to the general assembly of shareholders, which is deemed to be the highest decision-making body of a community bank. *Nuestras Huellas* appoints a coordinator to assist with the management process at each community bank, his task being to provide the methodology and the tools needed to ensure that each working group is able to move towards greater autonomy, by learning how to do things and gradually taking on all necessary tasks.

In parallel, the shareholders' assembly draws up its own rules and lays down its own lending policies, the rights and obligations to be assumed by each partner, plus meeting format. It decides on the bank's values and the means of unifying the various interests and goals of the bank's various partners. For these reasons, every community bank is self-managed from day one and grows gradually with full autonomy.

2. Solidarity finance and the democratisation of money

"Solidarity finance, like any other financial system, is an instrument of intermediation. In the capitalist economy, the financial system becomes a powerful tool for concentrating and centralising capital. The question that arises when we try to conceptualise the notion of solidarity finance is whether we have financial instruments capable of democratising economic relations. Such instruments must be able to create optimal conditions for human development and underpin the social economy in each region. These new relationships must also meet the basic needs of each community by giving priority to people who are excluded from the traditional banking system. Their actions must be guided by ethics and social solidarity".[5]

The community bank programme developed by *Nuestras Huellas* is mainly aimed at women who have decided to work for themselves. This experience leads us to reflect on the relationship women have with work. We have discussed with these women on many occasions their reasons for wanting to set up a business and the reasons vary: to generate some extra income; the fact that she has inherited a trade or would like to learn a trade; to have a pastime and something other than housework to do; to have her own money without having to ask her husband; to have the chance to meet with and relax with friends or neighbours; or simply because having her own job allows her to get out of the house and meet people. These are some of the infinite number of different reasons. What they all have in common is that starting your own money-making activity engenders a change deep down inside each of the partners of a community bank that touches on all aspects of their lives. Undoubtedly, in the course of this process, a feeling of self-esteem arises and produces new attitudes, such as the desire to take better care of their appearance, to improve their look and take more account of their femininity. And this makes the woman's family and immediate circle also recognise the value of starting an independent business. Creativity is reactivated and the fact of being linked with new groups of people and going to new places tends to awaken many new skills that rapidly engender positive effects.

In order to create a real solidarity finance proposal where the main aim is to democratise money, it is vital to start out from the concept of work. The savings generated by these social enterprises do not come

[5] Dias Coelho, Franklin.

from inherited capital or from income generated simply by putting capital to work by itself. An essential aspect of this whole process is that the savings obtained are the result of work, either the work of one person or the work of a whole family. By placing the entire family's surplus funds in a community bank, women are usually the ones who manage and channel savings generated through their own work and that of their partner, older children, a grandparent who lives in the same house, etc. Women consequently tend to become the main managers of the income of the whole family. They take charge of budgeting for food, clothes, education and coping with demands for expenditure on family celebrations or emergencies.

If in addition to the management of income and outlay, the woman takes on the management of the family's surplus funds, this tends to produce a powerful effect on women in terms of self-education and self-esteem. We should not forget that on top of this new responsibility comes the fact that the money saved is being harnessed to cover the financing needs of their families and neighbours. This little extra, combined with that of other neighbours, soon becomes a capital sum that, little by little, will be able to pay for things that would have seemed entirely unaffordable before. As far as commercial banks are concerned, these women who are setting up social enterprises fulfil hardly any of the requirements for obtaining a loan. Other types of finance providers, including illegal loan sharks, charge such high interest payments that it is simply not worth making the investment and women often do not have the necessary funds to repay loans from family or friends, often the main backers.

This scenario demonstrates that by setting up community banks, the partners can put an end to the "just can't do it" syndrome, to being shut out of the system, not having the means, and all sorts of fatalistic ideas that they have been hearing since birth in their traditionally poor communities. By dint of their own work, modest and simple though it may be, women can begin to generate wealth in order to meet the needs of their families and that of the other families in the community.

The priority goals set by the community banks for making loans are not only for basic needs. On a scale of priorities, social events such as birthdays, weddings and baptisms are placed fourth, while family holidays are listed in last place. At the top of the scale is obviously health care, accommodation, enterprise initiatives and business plans. This model strengthens our commitment to the social economy and demonstrates that the ultimate purpose of solidarity finance is not to help capital to grow but to help people to grow and broaden their lives. "Just as the capitalist company is the proper form of basic micro-economic organisation for capital, the household or the domestic unit is the proper form of basic micro-economic organisation for work. Capitalist companies are able to merge, form official or de facto networks and consolidate into groups with common interests, the better to accumulate capital. In the same way, domestic units can extend their raison d'être through partnerships, organised communities, various formal or informal networks, while at the same time building up socio-economic entities whose goal is to improve their members' living conditions."[6]

For the reasons mentioned above, one characteristic of solidarity finance is that everyone connected with the financial activity knows exactly what is happening to his or her money. The money produces a sort of whirlwind effect within the community, which in turn creates a leverage effect in terms of development whereby people begin to look at their own neighbourhood with fresh eyes. They start to identify their particular needs and are able to share the challenges facing them. Similarly, the inhabitants of the neighbourhood get together to celebrate when a neighbour has managed to overcome his difficulties or has achieved her dream. And it is at that moment that the positive spiral of solidarity fi-

---

[6] Coraggio, José Luis, "Economía del Trabajo", written for the review *A Outra Economia* (the other economy): *www.coraggioeconomia.org/jlc/archivos para descargar/ECONOMIA DEL TRABAJO3.pdf*

nance starts to achieve its full purpose and completes the circle of life's renewal.

Just as no member of the community is denied the opportunity to save, however small the amount may be, in order to capitalise a local organisation that devotes its resources to its own community, no-one should be denied a hand in the management of those resources. This principle might appear to be self-evident but putting it into practice might prove difficult. It would be naïve to imagine that the hitherto accepted way of doing things, at least in the eyes of a large part of society, can be overturned simply by saying so and repeating it. There exist a number of tools that help women to believe in their own abilities because they understand both how things work and also the logic behind the system.

It is perhaps useful to point out that those within the formal financial system are proud to use language, explanations and tools that are incomprehensible to the majority of ordinary people and therefore give those insiders a sense of superiority. Nor does the author think it too naïve to claim that if we could all grasp this financial logic, it would lose its power over us. On the other hand, it is essential that all the operations carried out by a community bank must be basically easy and transparent. Each and every partner must be able to understand what is going on so as to be able to analyse the pros and cons and spot the tendencies that take root over time. On many occasions we have thought about the possibility of computerising the community banks' systems to enable every individual to carry out the management of his or her assets from a computer terminal. That would make the system much more efficient and reduce the risk of human error. Nevertheless, we believe that the "digital divide" between the computer-savvy and the rest is still quite wide and there is still a long way to go to bridge the gap. While we do believe that information technology can make an enormous contribution to the management of an organisation, we are nonetheless well aware that people's time – especially when we are talking about collective time in a historical context marked by marginalisation – calls for a completely different logic. Given this situation, while we are designing and preparing for the shift to computerised management of the community banks, they are still for the moment carrying out all their operations on paper, using tables and noticeboards intended to provide simple visual checks on the state of savings and the loans granted to members.

The self-auditing and self-regulatory mechanisms at the community banks constitute a major challenge. The people are more used to being told what to do and how to do it than asking for details of how to correct errors or drawing attention to the mistakes made by a colleague. It is the job of the coordinator designated by *Nuestras Huellas* to work hand-in-hand with the group in this area. S/he is the first person the members call on to show them how to proceed or advise on the best decision to take. With this simple move, what the group is doing is delegating all responsibility for their own money and what happens to it to a third party who is not involved in the savings that are at stake or in the cultural reality of the neighbourhood or the links that have been forged. The solution the coordinator comes up with is merely a surface varnish on top of the really basic questions to be asked and answered to ensure that the financing is genuinely appropriate for the people concerned. From time to time we ask ourselves what would happen to the community banks should *Nuestras Huellas* cease to operate. Our conclusion is nearly always one of striking optimism: that the community banks would not hesitate to continue with their activities since self-management is fully rooted in the training they have received. And it is through this learning process based on asking questions, as Paulo Freire points out, that we are able to encourage these groups of women to take charge of their own money, their own organisation, their needs and their own destiny.

The fact that each cycle of a community bank begins with the drawing up of a set of internal rules, decisions on lending policy, cohabitation and other specific rules is not sufficient to attain autonomous self-management. It is interesting to note that it is only when the partners come to realise over time that they actually own the organisation that they for example become able to challenge one of the members who is requesting a loan that may exceed his or her repayment capacity. That does not mean that the person in question will not be able to repay the loan but that in order to do so s/he will have to give up some priority – or even indispensable – household items. The culture of individualism means not interfering in other people's business – the "every man for himself" attitude. Breaking through this individualism to offer good advice based on a link that has been forged is a great achievement and should be seen as one of the revolutionary changes the social economy can bring about.

As a sign of transparency we would first and foremost mention the link that is forged between people who organise themselves around a stock of capital that arises from the work of households and the management of their savings and whose purpose is to encourage people to broaden their lives. That is to say because people know where all the various partners got their savings from. No one would be able to build up large savings without having to account for their origins and prove that they didn't come from illegal business, arms trafficking or drug dealing. Of course we cannot claim that this kind of scenario could never come about, but if it should happen, the partners in a community bank would be able to decide whether they wanted this "dirty" money in their bank or not. This implies asking themselves whether, in order to improve the quality of life of those living in the neighbourhood, to use funds that have come from activities that do harm, destroy lives and break up families. It is necessary to mention this last point because it is of course not the same thing whether the consumers of the cheapest and most health-damaging drugs are children or teenagers from other communities or even other countries instead of your own children, grandchildren or nephews and nieces.

So anyone who goes to the community bank to apply for a loan generally knows where that money has come from, who is dealing with his loan application, what criteria will be applied, why the bank does not at a given moment have the necessary funds to grant a loan or why s/he will have to wait a week to obtain the loan. Every day we see cases where two people turn up asking for a loan at the same time but the bank does not at that precise moment have sufficient funds, and the one who is first in line gives way to the second-comer, whose need for the loan may be more urgent or vital than his or her own. Little stories like this have an enormous impact on communities because they help to create good relations, which are then frequently transposed to other similar situations that arise at school, at the supermarket or in a public place.

During these years, in which we have worked with and supported over a hundred community banks, we have on several occasions encountered two particular situations that tend to destabilise the organisation, jeopardising its meticulous and transparent functioning and even threatening its continued existence.

The first case arises when a person who has taken out a loan is unable to repay the full amount of the debt. The reasons are many and varied but nearly all have one common denominator: a complicated situation of social and economic vulnerability affecting the home. A second characteristic is that in general this is a temporary situation, i.e. the borrower has to delay payments for just a few days, which confirms that it is not intentional but a case of genuine inability to repay at that moment. For such cases we have set up a solidarity fund, fed by monies the community banks raise from neighbourhood gambling activities, such as bingo and tombola, or the sale of food. This provides the group with a fund to support people who find it impossible to make loan repayments to their community bank on time, even if it is only for a few days.

It is important to prevent reimbursement delays not only in order to keep the level of overdue debts down but also to avoid the borrower feeling that s/he has failed in her duty. When people feel supported at a difficult moment this creates a powerful force for changing the cold hard logic of finance and the general feeling of alienation that seems to characterise the world of finance. When the idea that a payment delay of less than thirty days is a frequent and perfectly normal occurrence is generally accepted, that will greatly change the way judgements are passed on people. Realising that each and every person might go through some difficult times – unexpected illness, inability to go to work because of flooding or severe damage at the house – encourages the whole group to commit to supporting the solidarity fund. Of course, this commitment comes with very clear rules regarding the return on the funds.

The second situation that we often encounter is that in many cases the partners take out a loan to cope with an emergency, most frequently due to ill health, a death or disaster. We have never thought it was fair to have to pay interest on the loan under this type of circumstance when a family finds itself in a very difficult situation that affects income and increases expenses. It is important to point out that in many cases a loan is paid out of the savings that the loan applicant has himself deposited. So when a person has to pay interest on an emergency loan s/he is paying out when in fact s/he needs to be saving as much as possible. Any member is entitled to withdraw his or her savings from the community bank at any time but is encouraged not to do so in order to avoid decapitalising the organisation. That is why we have inaugurated community funds. These are funds set up by each of the community banks by allocating a percentage of the interest taken in, and in some cases supplemented by a contribution from each partner or group of partners. The exclusive purpose of these funds is to provide interest-free loans to members facing emergency situations such as those listed above. The payment schedule is decided on a case-by-case basis and the mechanism also tries to create an order of priority for the various different needs a family might face and prioritise those emergencies that cause its members the most worry and pain.

Conclusion

We face numerous challenges each and every day in our attempts to improve solidarity finance and create a powerful tool for local development in impoverished communities. Experience has shown us that we can't just set off armed with a compass and hack a trail through the undergrowth from scratch with a machete. We are convinced that people possess an enormous wealth of mechanisms for organising themselves and managing their resources, including their own money. Our process of creation always requires us to arm ourselves with tools and strategies before we plunge among the masses of knowledge and practice that have been developed in the daily life of the home, the business, the neighbourhood club, the school and the many significant social happenings. We try to find out for example how people raise and manage the money needed to enlarge the football pitch for the local children, how an entire family plans and organises a fifteenth birthday party at which a girl becomes a woman and joins the adult world.

In this process, the middle and upper classes sit calmly on their thrones of wisdom and do not deign to come down except to take over their ancestral wealth, update it and then use it to make more. We cannot ignore the fact that at this moment in history there are forces opposed to the process. It is perfectly clear why some people would like to see these self-management mechanisms fail as they do not aid the concentration of economic power and by extension the domination and manipulation of people's lives. In this context, one of the biggest challenges we are facing is that a community bank needs time to accumulate the funds necessary to meet the demands of the community. It must not be forgotten that their ability to generate surpluses is rather weak due to the low personal incomes and the rising cost of living, which is weighing more and more heavily on household budgets. This is why we believe governments and authorities ought to live up to their responsibilities and commit to creating mechanisms to tip the balance a little more in favour of this type of experiment. *Nuestras Huellas* has decided to establish a line of credit to community banks so as to help them capitalise more rapidly and gather more funds in order to meet the requirements of communities. This credit line, which we decided to call a *complementary account*, charges a much lower interest rate than the loans granted to the partners, with special conditions for repayments and so on.

We would like to finish this article by looking at the question of dependency. When we begin to conceive of a methodology for solidarity finance we have to ask ourselves whether these individuals, communities and organisations will remain dependent on an entity that will finance and support them indefinitely. Our position is that it is vital to channel the maximum amount of energy into creating mechanisms that will lead to autonomy. And since that is our goal, we should not just be making use of economic and financial tools, we also have to be able to count on education and community organisation experts who can foster the process towards independence, autonomy and liberation. And at that point, finance needs some extra help and needs to dialogue with other disciplines set up to help people broaden their lives. So we can imagine a future where in all primary and secondary schools and universities, irrespective of the faculty and main subject of study, all young people would be encouraged to think about their relationship with money, how it circulates, its role as a means of payment, and the identity of the movers and shakers of the economy, which is an inescapably social phenomenon and so ought to be run in a spirit of solidarity. In the same order of thinking, we also believe that scientific and technological progress ought to be harnessed in order to help create a financial system that is ethical and transparent.

Throughout this article we have tried to highlight and explain the relationship between solidarity finance provided by community banks and a financial structure that can be supported by an ethic that promotes life, diversity and care for our fellow human beings. *"No society past or present has ever been able to live without a code of ethics. As social beings, we need to develop a consensus, to discourage certain kinds of actions and create community projects which give direction and align us with the march of history. Today, at a time of globalisation, we see lots of ethical projects begun but which are not all mutually compatible. In this new era of globalised humanity we feel the urgent need for an ethical base which can win the acceptance of all and thus make possible coexistence between peoples (...). A caring ethic provides, preserves, heals and protects. By its very nature, such an ethic is not aggressive and when it intervenes in the real world, it stops to think about whether the consequences of that intervention will be beneficial or malign. In other words, this kind of ethic takes responsibility for all human actions. Care and responsibility always go hand-in-hand."*[7]

Solidarity finance is an ethical form of finance because it helps to reforge the social and human links that are being damaged on a daily basis by an increasingly aggressive capitalism that puts forward the accumulation of assets as a development model for communities, promoting concentration instead of fair distribution of wealth.

Community banks create a space where entrepreneurial women from vulnerable communities manage their savings autonomously, in full security and transparency, helping to repair that shaken trust. In this way, a group of neighbours can give new sense to values and principles that are closely bound up with one another. Thus the ethic put forward by solidarity finance is an ethic based in experience that rejects cold, abstract precepts. The word "solidarity" ought never to be separated from con-

---

[7] Boff, Leonardo, "Ética para la Nueva Era" (ethics for the new era), *www.servicioskoinonia.org*, 3 July, 2009.

crete facts and day-to-day situations where you need to bring together the best of each individual in order to achieve the common good.

In conclusion, we believe that ethical finance and solidarity finance are synonymous when it comes to deciding which way to go in order to reconnect ourselves with the riches that each and every community has the ability to create, manage and share in order to propagate life, in all senses of the word.

18

ETHICS VS. FINANCE? AN ANALYSIS OF THE ORIGINS, PROBLEMS AND FUTURE PERSPECTIVES OF THIS RELATIONSHIP

Bruno Federico Fernández

The recent crises remind us of the serious consequences that financial ills can bring upon a society: recession, unemployment, bankruptcies, poverty, greater inequality, loss of trust, breakdown in social cohesion, etc. The disconnect between ethics and finance is mostly to blame for these ills. The purpose of this dissertation is to show that finance can contribute in a sustainable way to the common good as long as ethics can be permanently integrated into its theory and practice. This will require a profound paradigm shift, a humanisation of finances at both personal and institutional level. We will explore here the origin of the current disconnect between ethics and finance, analysing the theoretical foundations and how these impact on social trust and the common good. We will also look at the challenges faced by financial ethics in the context of globalisation, corporate social responsibility and education.

The financial system has helped the economy to reach levels of productivity and growth in terms of riches and consumption that could never before have been envisaged. However, the recent crises demonstrate once again the disastrous consequences that flawed finance can wreak on society: recession, unemployment, bankruptcy, poverty, greater inequality, loss of trust and a breakdown in social cohesion, to mention just a few. The disconnect between ethics and finance is to a large extent responsible for these ills.

In this paper, we will show that finance can contribute in a sustainable way to the common good (by which we mean the good of mankind and the objectives of all men) only if we succeed in introducing ethics into both theory and practice. This necessitates a profound paradigm shift, a humanisation of finance at the individual and institutional levels.

We will start by looking at the origins of the current disconnect between ethics and finance, starting with an analysis of their theoretical foundations and how these impact via the financial sector on social trust and the common good. We will then formulate some proposals to help meet the challenges of globalisation using ethical means and a more efficient approach to corporate social responsibility. Finally, we will touch on the importance of teaching financial ethics.

Ethics in modern economic thought

The problems of moral hazard in principal-agent relations, "free rider" behaviour, the increase in speculative finance (e.g. speculative funds, the Ponzi scheme conceived by Bernard Madoff and sub-prime loans) are examples of a real divorce of ethics from finance. However this divorce is not only confined to the financial sector, but involves the whole economic sphere. Finance, as a branch of the economy, has inherited its ethical stance.

In a context of total separation

We can cite three stages in the modern history of economic thought: first, where finance and ethics were united; second, where they were rubbing shoulders; and third, where the separation was complete (Ferullo, 2010).

Adam Smith is considered to be the father of modern economics. In his time – the late eighteenth century – this professor of moral philosophy at the University of Glasgow succeeded in conferring scientific status on knowledge of economics.

Today it is wrongly believed that Smith created an economic theory for business that was entirely removed from any ethic. But if you read his works in depth, as did the Nobel prize winner Amartya Sen, you can see that in his *Inquiry into the Nature and Causes of the Wealth of Nations* (1776) there is a practical application of ethics that follows on from his earlier book *The Theory of Moral Sentiments* (1759). Stemming from this overall moral view, it is no surprise that the Scottish professor saw moral values as being intimately bound up with human behaviour.

For Smith and his contemporaries it was superfluous to write about ethics in business because ethics were already implicit in business. Commerce based on self-interest was mutually advantageous as long as neither party tried to cheat the other.

The stage where finance and ethics were juxtaposed began towards the end of the nineteenth century when Alfred Marshall, a Professor at the University of Cambridge, succeeded in separating economics from the department of moral philosophy. Writers started to talk about "economics" rather than "political economy" to try to avoid the behavioural questions traditionally linked to political science.

But these economists continued to recognise that although the economy was an independent science, ethics still played an important role in practical questions on the economy.

We come to the third stage towards the middle of the twentieth century, when the "neo-classicists" brought a total separation between ethics and the economy into mainstream economic thinking. Economists such as Friedman and Stigler preached that all value judgements should be taken right out of economics if it aspired to being a predictive science. If there were any moral obligation, it would only be that of acting in accordance with the criteria of "rational choice", which would guarantee optimal results through efficient market forces. It made no sense to distance oneself from logical-mathematical rigour and discuss ethical values, they argued.

Basing itself on a superficial reading of Smith and influenced by liberalism and positivism, the mainstream of contemporary economic thought today runs counter to the deepest convictions of the first classical economists. The aim of creating a science that is ethically neutral and predictable has led to the use of models that, although elegant from a mathematical point of view, have deprived people of any motivation other than that of self-interest. By taking equivalent exchange as the only valid means of contributing to rationality and the common good, we seem to have adopted a system that has removed human beings from centre stage.

Theoretical foundations

The theory of modern economics is based on two pillars: *Homo economicus* as an anthropological view of the human being; and the mechanism of the free market as the regulator of relationships. While recognising the contributions of these two pillars to the development of the science of economics, we will see the ethical problems that arise when we try to exaggerate their virtues.

Self-centred anthropology

Homo economicus is the representation of Man that economics uses as a unit of analysis. This theoretical construction has two main characteristics:

- Rational instrumentalism: the individual uses available resources efficiently in order to achieve his objectives
- Self-interest: this is the driver of economic behaviour that contributes to social well-being, through the market mechanism.

Individual choices are exogenous and not to be questioned. The individual seeks to maximise his profit using the goods he consumes.

This view only takes account of the profit that the individual makes from his relationship with objects. Happiness in the sense of Aristotle's *eudaemonia* – self-fulfilment – is achieved through relationships between people. However, according to the "Robinson Crusoe" model, an individual can maximise his "utility" – a proxy for happiness – even when he completely alone.

If one believes that Man can be happy on his own, this implies that there is no incentive to act in the interests of another person or to feel part of society. The social benefit becomes the sum of individual utilities and is based on individual choices. According to this way of thinking, social well-being may increase even when, for example, inequality increases – which is of course socially unacceptable.

Some more recent models, such as game theory, recognise that the fulfilment of individual preferences depends on how others act. However, these views still continue to be biased towards merely selfish motivation whereby it is perfectly rational to take the other person into account and to cooperate, but solely in one's own interest. The other is seen as a *means* while in reality he is an *end* in terms of achieving happiness. The famous prisoner's dilemma reminds us that to behave selfishly is not always the most efficient way to behave.

A model is useful when it sacrifices some aspects of reality in order to isolate those that are key to the analysis. The problem with *Homo economicus* is not the theoretical abstraction in itself but the aspects of the human being that economists see as necessary to isolate.

Here we have a first ethical challenge regarding the choice of model. To postulate that an individual's sole motivation is his own self-interest, and that reason is only to be found in the means and not the ends, seems to be a very limited view that does not explain the mechanisms (such as donations and voluntary work) through which human beings build fraternal relations.

The free market

The state, the market and civil society bodies are the three elements that, in line with their relative sizes, can give rise to different types of socio-economic organisation.

In the orthodox model of the economy, what counts is the market, which uses the exchange of value – contract – to govern interpersonal relationships. The state should play the smallest role possible and should only concern itself with the defence of private property, the creation of the conditions for the market to function freely, and the fair distribution of the efficient production of the market. The economic organisations of civil society – also known as the "social economy", not-for-profit companies or the "third sector" – are outside the usual domain of economic study. They are an exception to the rule whereby companies maximise their profits, as they pursue different objectives.

The free market posited by this school of thought is always perfectly capable of channelling individual interests, quite free of the sheen of ethics or motives of social solidarity, towards the common good. The "invisible hand" described by Smith allows this as long as there is no interference hampering the market's functioning.

Neoclassical liberalism proclaims that the market is ethically and socially neutral. Its objective is efficiency in the sense of the Pareto principle, i.e. to increase the size of the pie as much as possible. Social solidarity begins only later when time comes to cut the pie up. As a result, any intervention in the competitive functioning of the markets, even with noble objectives – such as the Tobin tax – ends up being harmful.

We know that one of the great virtues of the market is its capacity to generate egalitarian and voluntary cooperation between individuals. This helps to eliminate conflicts, a "dependency" society, and oppressive relationships. However, believing that the market is an automatic mechanism that leads inevitably to the common good has generated excessive confidence in its workings. Thus economic agents thought that they were exempt from moral judgement of their actions and so exonerated from any responsibility for their actions on the markets.

By analogy with Gresham's law where "bad money drives out good", bad intentions, such as unconditionally seeking profit, end up by driving out good intentions, such as charity. If human exchanges are only motivated by price, other positive forms of human relationships are excluded. This will end up by shaking the very foundations of the market, such as trust and willingness to cooperate. (Zamagni-Bruni, 2007).

Is finance ethically neutral?

Ethics is linked to free human action from a moral point of view – good or evil – because such action is Man's ultimate objective. Action in the financial sector stems from a human activity so this action is therefore subject to moral judgement. And it follows that if this action is liable to moral judgement, then finance cannot be ethically neutral.

These days finance, and the dominant trend of economic thinking, act as though they were exempt from all moral interference. The neopositivism that prevails in the financial system sees observation (for example, has the value of the good X risen or fallen?) and prediction (e.g. what will its value be in the future?) as rational but steers clear of making judgements on these facts such as is it better for the real economy if the price of that good continues to rise? What about the common good?

Many dysfunctions that arise in the financial sector, and sometimes even lead to real crises, are first and foremost the result of a moral crisis. The 2008 sub-prime crisis showed that it is not enough to have confidence in the market because market action is not purely mechanical or technical. We need to adopt an overall, responsible view regarding the impact of our actions on the common good. All the phases of the financial process (savings, loans, investments, and reimbursement) must be guided by ethics and based on civic virtue.

Ethics must be the cornerstone of finance – not vice versa – and must be based on two pillars: respect for human dignity and the moral standards of the natural order. If one or the other is lacking, ethics loses its essential quality, leaving behind only the label. Nowadays we hear about training programmes in business ethics, certification of a company's social responsibility ethics, ethical investment funds, microfinance, etc. Though we should applaud all these initiatives, the challenge is still to create a truly moral framework for judging actions, because the adjective "ethical", used in a generic fashion, may in some cases mask pecuniary interest or injustices that go against the common good (Pope Benedict XVI, 2009).

The word "ethical" must not simply be a label distinguishing those who have a certificate from those who do not. In order to achieve a fraternal commitment that has been freely entered into, true ethics must be prevalent among all players in the financial sector, not just an isolated group among them.

The paradox of trust

Some empirical studies have shown the positive correlation between the degree of trust in a country and its private investment sector, and thus its growth rate (Zak-Knack, 1998).

Trust is very important in all financial transactions, but in the financial sector it becomes a *sine qua non* condition for it to function, essentially because financial activities are transacted over more than one period of time (Arrow, 1972), which tends to create uncertainty.

In order for the market to achieve mutually beneficial results, individuals must not only agree to the conditions of the contract, they must also trust each other. A frequent problem is that one of the parties breaks this trust, either by drawing up contracts based on asymmetrical information or by breaking a promise. These two forms of betrayal were both clearly illustrated in the 2008 crisis. First, customers were persuaded to accept loans without understanding the enormous risks they were incurring. Second, they then found themselves unable to repay the loan due to a lack of liquid funds.

A curious result is what Fred Hirsh has called the "paradox of affluence". This happens when, after a period of economic growth based on high levels of trust, excessive rational instrumentalism comes along and undermines it (Ferullo, 2010). Once the level of trust starts to diminish, not only the financial system is affected but also economic growth and social well-being are also affected.

The history of the last century was a clear example of this paradox. After the Second World War there was widespread economic growth thanks to the financial markets. During the 1980s, capitalism – focused only on profit – seemed triumphant in the old Western economies, Japan and South-East Asia. But in 2008, history suddenly changed. Hand in hand with a food crisis and an oil crisis, the financial crisis arising from the "sub-prime" loans in the United States ended up causing the collapse of the world economy.

What is the solution to this paradox from the financial industry's point of view? The proponents of the current model claim that the financial markets have worked quite well and that the economy has simply undergone a short-term shock. If we have to blame someone it should be the state, which did not do its job properly, or the selfishness of some isolated groups – as in the greed of Wall Street. Given the "rebound effect", the economy will get back on its growth track and trust will be reestablished. Consequently, there is no need for any substantial changes.

Even though this point of view may be valid, it is an extremely limited one. If we continue to support the current financial system on the basis of *Homo economicus* and the monopoly of the free market, we will end up triggering new crises in the future as stated in the "paradox of affluence".

The challenge is therefore to maintain trust in the long term, even when the market seems to be functioning perfectly and completely securely. I am convinced that in order to maintain sustainable progress there is only one solution: that the financial system and the economy in general, must act on an ethical basis. This implies taking on board means of action other than that of self interest and analysing the way what we do affects not only those who are close to us, but also society and the environment.

The deficiencies of the financial markets prevent us from foreseeing a crisis of confidence within that field of activity. The state can establish an appropriate legal and supervisory framework, but there will always be some "tricky" financier, such as Bernard Madoff, around to defraud others and destroy trust. Long term, acting in an ethical fashion is the most efficient way of not only maintaining trust but also propagating it throughout the whole economic system, while at the same time making an outstanding contribution to growth and the common good.

The challenge of globalisation

Globalisation has changed the rules of the game. Companies relocating their businesses and ever faster international capital flows have resulted in governments losing a certain amount of control over their respective markets.

From a financial point of view, this scenario raises new ethical challenges. As Pope Benedict XVI has said, globalisation brings us together, but does not cause us to act like brothers. Acting without ethical principles has already led to negative consequences, especially for the poorest countries, and for less well-off individuals. Here are several examples:

- Multinational companies that invest in or withdraw their capital from various countries due to the need to reduce production costs, often regardless of the impact that this action has on the local economy – unemployment, pollution, etc

- Countries that are overprotective of their advances in the fields of health and food technology, so that emerging countries are denied access to these products and incur unnecessary expenditure
- International financial institutions that recommend to – and impose on – weaker countries reductions in essential social spending so that they are able to meet their loan repayments
- Speculation among ill-informed investors, who follow the herd, and who sell shares, leading to the bankruptcy of companies that they do not even know

The globalised financial system may entail negative consequences on a grand scale if it is governed only by the logic of trade and pure profit-seeking, and ignores ethical principles such as social solidarity and charity. Finance governed by moral values is more than just an alternative, it becomes a must if we are to attain the common good.

Integrated goals

We have already seen that the current capitalist model confers an excessive role on the market in relation to that of the state and civil society bodies. History shows that when one of the three elements gets the upper hand this results in untenable models being set up, as happened with communism and the welfare-state.

A healthy socio-economic organisation demands a subtle balance between its component parts because each of them has its contribution to make to social well-being from its own vantage point. The market achieves efficiency by means of the contract, the state achieves fairness through its redistribution policies, and civil society bodies succeed in strengthening social bonds through charitable donations as an exercise in reciprocity.

Even if we suppose that the actions of the financial sector may be guided by ethical principles, globalisation still poses another challenge. The roles played by the state, the market and civil society bodies should not only be in equilibrium, they must also rethink their ways of working and the scope of their action in order to successfully promote the common good through values such as social solidarity and charity.

Nowadays, the two-step logic – the market produces, then the state distributes – no longer suffices in the pursuit of fairness. Even corporate philanthropy is insufficient since it feeds a syndrome of dependence that contributes very little either to the personal development of those in difficult circumstances or to fraternity in society.

The model we are proposing provides an integrated balance of the three components. The state, the market and civil society bodies must take on board all of society's objectives as if they were their own. Even though each one has a comparative advantage for attaining efficiency, fairness or fraternity respectively, incorporating the other objectives will help maximise the extent to which they are implemented overall.

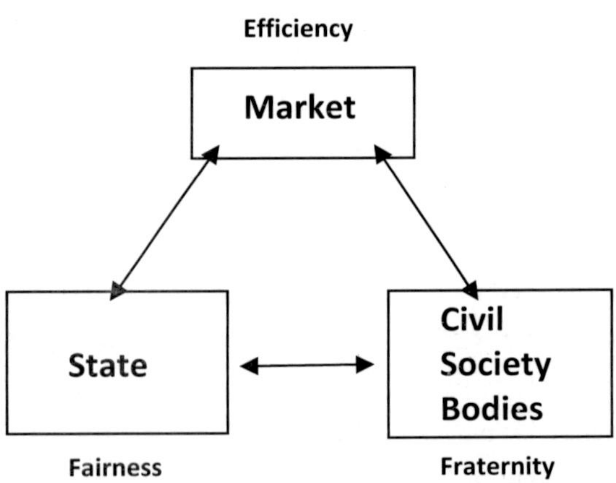

If they wish to contribute to the common good, companies that participate in the financial markets should start to distribute more fairly the fruits of their activities while still continuing to create economic value. Distributive justice is inherent in markets as well, in a fraternal society where people concern themselves not only with their own self interest but with that of their fellow-citizens and act in a spirit of social solidarity.

We are able to engage in commercial exchange first and foremost because we exist in a community and in certain cases – as with most disadvantaged people – that community requires us to give.

As the "civil" economy preaches, the fruits of the financial market must be everyone's gain. This is not a matter of giving handouts but of reintegrating into the market people who have fallen into poverty through no fault of their own, and as a result are not in a position to exchange goods or services. This is the concept proposed for example by the winner of the 2006 Nobel Peace Prize, Muhammad Yunus, whose Grameen Bank is the embodiment of this approach.

As well as the contract, financial companies ought therefore to be using the concept of reciprocity. Contracts and gifts both derive from a much older principle, that of reciprocal aid, or reciprocity. Reciprocity is all about "giving" and "taking" in equal measure. In a contract, this equivalence is manifested in the monetary value of the good. When it comes to a gift, the equivalence cannot be measured quantitatively as in the form of a price tag, but through the quality of the response, which may also be conferred on a third party outside the initial relationship.

When it comes to giving and the response to giving no direct comparison can be made. In a contract, agreement on price precedes the transfer of the object. With reciprocity, the transfer is free and precedes the *quid pro quo* or reciprocal value, which gives rise to an expectation, but does not confer a right. What differentiates giving from aid or philanthropy is that giving requires an equivalent response (Zamagni-Bruni, 2007). But the form of this response is not fixed in advance, which means that the exchange is made on a fragile basis that requires trust.

By turning to reciprocity, financial markets will not only be able to produce material goods; they will also be able to produce the kind of "relationship goods" that characterise the social economy. These goods produce utility, not only because of their objective characteristics, but through their capacity to give pleasure to others. Relationship goods have no price but since they satisfy human needs they still have economic value.

Financial markets should re-create themselves based on the principle of reciprocity, if they wish to strengthen social fraternity. This implies that Pareto optimality is not the only goal worth attaining. The fact that financial companies do pursue objectives other than those of pure profit – contrary to the preaching of economists such as Milton Friedman – means that today we see different types of organisation cohabiting in the financial sector – foundations, charities, community banks, non-governmental organisations, social enterprises like that of Muhammad Yunus – aimed at making profits, community investment entities, etc. This is not to suggest that incorporating fairness and fraternity into financial market objectives is a fast, trouble-free process. Nevertheless, it is the only means of making the best possible contribution to the common good.

More efficient CSR

As far as for-profit financial companies are concerned, corporate social responsibility (CSR) is one of the most sophisticated mechanisms accepted by the market as an instrument to serve the common good.

The International Labour Organisation (ILO) defines CSR as a set of actions agreed by companies so that their activities will have a positive impact on society. Through CSR these companies demonstrate the principles and values that govern them, both in their own internal methods and in their relations with other players. CSR is a voluntary initiative that implies commitment to all its stakeholders in the economic, social and environmental fields and demonstrates a respect for ethical values in building the common good.

Nowadays, hundreds of financial companies worldwide are seeking to achieve this triple goal – socio-economic and environmental. When companies start to envisage objectives other than that of pure profit maximisation this helps them to renounce the two-step logic and take on an approach to their activity that is more distributive and responsible.

Ethics is closely linked to the concept of CSR because CSR is of necessity based on moral values that bind the company to its environment. However, this necessity carries with it the danger we have described above. Ethics might become dependent on certification or could be used to varnish over nefarious intentions. These false ethics might then become a constant syndrome among all financial institutions, not just a handful, with consequences for society of which we are all well aware. This should not be regarded as an unduly pessimistic notion, given the excesses created by many companies that have, for example, acted in an ethical way towards the environment but not at all ethically towards their employees.

Another danger we see is that many financial institutions become inefficient when they try to attain the triple socio-economic and environmental objective. By inefficient we mean that financial institutions aiming to satisfy all three objectives are likely to spend enormous resources on positive social and environmental action. But if these same resources had been channelled into other activities, they might have achieved much greater overall socio-economic and environmental benefits.

We constantly observe examples of this inefficiency, such as banks that send their staff to collect rubbish from public parks, teach the rules of the road to drivers, repaint schools, etc. We would not wish to say that these activities are not socially and environmentally useful, merely that the effort made and the resources invested could be better focused on activities that increase the overall socio-environmental impact.

Our criticism is based on our observation of how some financial institutions seem, through their CSR policies, to demonstrate an erroneous vision of the all-powerful market. Even though the market needs to be able to achieve objectives such as socio-environmental goals, this does not mean that at any given moment it is the only or indeed the best mechanism for undertaking such activities.

We should remember that in an integrated socio-economic vision, apart from the market, the state and the civil society are pursuing the same objectives, and each has a comparative advantage due to its inherent characteristics. Of course it is laudable for a commercial bank to clean up a public park, but it would be better for the state to take charge of that – as it is one of its normal tasks – or, if it does not, civil society should demand that it does so. If stock exchange employees repaint a school, that is all well and good, but there must surely exist a foundation and voluntary workers who know how to make a good job of this kind of initiative.

We suggest that financial institutions running CSR activities channel their efforts into activities they are best at. Instead of teaching the rules of the road, they could be teaching basic financial concepts to young people in schools, or concentrating on developing new micro-finance products for the less well-off, thus strengthening social links.

Our proposal may well meet with criticism from those who say that it may allow these financial institutions to forget about the other CSR objectives, particularly those linked to the environment. However, taking care of the environment, for example, does not only depend on major investment in the world outside. If all institutions share the same vision, small internal actions may contribute significantly to achieving environmental objectives: better communication across IT networks in order to save paper, installing equipment to promote economic sustainability, giving up the use of aerosol cleaning products that damage the ozone layer, sorting rubbish, using low consumption light bulbs, and so on.

By following these recommendations, financial sector institutions can become an efficient and civilising means of fighting for greater fairness and will help create the reciprocal links society needs.

The importance of education

The ideas that financial theory tends to create about market players ends up by influencing their actual everyday behaviour. A study carried out among students from different faculties in a university in the United States showed that Finance and Economics students educated in the way rational agents should act are more likely to act in a selfish way than students from other disciplines. This happens because the individuals concerned perceive that if they act in a way that is contrary to what is considered rational the consequences would be a loss of time or money. Education is one of the most powerful drivers of cultural change. Creating a financial system that can make a contribution to the common good depends on education. It is therefore vital that universities and business schools include ethics as a basic element of their study programmes across the board, rather than as optional courses or one-off seminars.

Fortunately, after the latest crisis, more and more centres of financial studies have recognised the importance of teaching ethics to their students. If the majority of institutions were to follow suit, a good critical mass of ethical financiers of the next generation would already be in training.

Concluding remarks

According to George Orwell, "Sometimes the first duty of intelligent men is the restatement of the obvious." The latest financial market crisis gives us the opportunity to reintegrate ethical principles into the theory and practice of the sector, something "obvious" that seems to have been forgotten recently. There is a well-known saying to the effect that in business "there is no such thing as a free lunch". If the financial industry continues to function with a disregard for ethics, there will always be someone – whether it be financial players or society in general – who will end up paying dearly.

Bibliography

Benedict XVI, "*Caritas in veritate*" (charity in truth), Papal Encyclical, Rome, 2009.

Bruni, Luigino/ Zamagni, Stefano, "*Economia Civile*" (civil economy), Il Mulino, March 2004

Ferullo, Hugo Daniel, "*Luz y sombra del pensamiento economico moderno*" (light and shade in modern economic thought), Tucumán: UNT, May 2006.

Ferullo, Hugo Daniel, "*La complejidad social del pensamiento económico. Ensayos*" (the social complexity of economic thought. Essays), Tucumán: UNSTA, 2010.

Sen, Amartya, "The Role of the Ethical Company in the Modern World" – Speech on ethics in international business for a trainer-training session, 2009.

Stigler, George J., "Economics or Ethics?" in: McMurrin, Sterling M., *The Tanner Lectures in Human Values II,* Cambridge: Cambridge University Press, 2011, 143-192.

Zak, Paul/ Knack, Stephen, *Trust and Growth*, Claremont Graduate University – Centre for Neuroeconomics Studies and the World Bank – Development Research Group (DECRG), 1998.

19

IN SEARCH OF HONESTY AND ALTRUISM

Raina Abdul Rahim Mousa

Ethics in general is concerned with human behaviour, which is the acceptance or "right", or non-acceptance or "wrong", based on conventional morality. General ethical norms encompass truthfulness, honesty, integrity, respect for others, fairness and justice. They relate to all aspects of life, including business and finance. Financial ethics is therefore a subset of general ethics.

Ethical norms are essential for maintaining stability and harmony in social life, where people interact with one another. Recognition of others' needs and aspirations, fairness, and co-operative efforts to deal with common issues are examples of aspects of social behaviour that contribute to social stability. In the process of social evolution, we, as human beings, have developed not only an instinct to care for ourselves but also a conscience to care for others. Situations may however arise, in which the need to care for ourselves runs into conflict with the need to care for others. In such situations, ethical norms are needed to guide our behaviour. As M. Dempsey (1999) puts it: "ethics represent the attempt to resolve the conflict between selfishness and selflessness; between our material needs and our conscience."

Ethical dilemmas and ethical violations in finance can be attributed to an inconsistency in the conceptual framework of modern financial-economic theory and the widespread use of a principal-agent model of relationship in financial transactions. The financial-economic theory that underlies the modern capitalist system is based on the rationale of profit maximisation, whereby individuals become self-centred, and aim to maximise their own profits and serve their own interests. The principal-agent model of relationships refers to an arrangement whereby one party, acting as an agent for another, carries functions on behalf of that other. Such arrangements are an integral part of the modern financial system, and it is difficult to imagine it functioning without them.

When moral behaviour is foolish

The behavioural assumption of the modern financial-economic theory runs counter to the ideas of trustworthiness, loyalty, fidelity, stewardship, and concern for others that underlie the traditional principal-agent relationship. The traditional concept of agency is based on moral values. As R. Duska (1992) explains it: "To do something for another in a system geared toward maximising self-interest is foolish. Such an answer, though, points out an inconsistency at the heart of the system, for a system that has rules requiring agents to look out for others while encouraging individuals to look out only for themselves, destroys the practice of looking out for others."

The ethical dilemma presented by the problem of conflicting interest has been addressed in some areas of finance, such as corporate governance, by converting the agency relationship into a purely contractual relationship that uses a carrot-and-stick approach to ensure ethical behaviour by agents. In corporate governance, the problem of conflict between management (agent) and stockholders (principal) is described as an agency problem. This theory is value-free because it does not pass judgment on whether the maximisation behaviour is good or bad and is not concerned with what might constitute just pay for the manager. It removes the ideas of honesty and loyalty from the agency relationship because of their incompatibility with the fundamental assumption of rational profit maximisation.

Most of our needs for financial services – management of retirement savings, money market and fixed income investment tools, and protection against unforeseen events, to name a few – are such that they are better entrusted to others, as we have neither the ability nor the time to effectively manage them on our own. The corporate device of contractualisation of the agency relationship is, however, too difficult to apply to the multitude of financial dealings between individuals and institutions that take place in the everyday financial market. Individuals are not as well organised as stockholders, and they are often unaware of the agency dilemma. Lack of information also limits their ability to monitor an agent's behaviour. Therefore, what we have in our complex modern financial system is a paradoxical situation: on the one hand, the ever-increasing need for getting things done by others, and on the other, the dimension of human nature that tends towards selfish behaviour. This paradoxical situation, or the inconsistency in the foundation of the modern capitalist system, can explain most of the ethical problems and declining morality in the area of modern finance.

Four categories of ethical questions

In general, the kinds of ethical questions that emerge in finance fall into four general categories; particular problems may relate to more than one specific level. A. Wicks (2003) defines those levels from the broadest to the most specific as follows: society, corporations and corporate policies, stakeholders (with focus on employees) and personal.

The societal level focuses on the basic institutions of society and the arrangements created to make them work. The focus here is on the conduct of financial affairs: what are the larger goals for financial welfare, and how should the economy be structured to best realise such goals? Is capitalisation the preferred method of structuring an economy? Is the American version preferable to alternative models, such as those found in Japan, Germany, or Canada? What sort of role should government play with respect to business and functions of financial institutions?

At corporate level, the emphasis is more specific, relating to the operation of a particular company and the groups that affect or may be affected by its operations (for example: suppliers, customers, stockholders, local communities, employees). Pertinent questions include: the relative importance of these groups to the firm, what are the mutual obligations and duties owed to and by each of these groups, and how the firm can develop strategies and forms of interaction among stakeholders to realise its primary goals.

At stakeholder level, the focus is on the approaches a firm takes in its relationships with its various stakeholders, including employees. What sorts of contracts are equitable? What employee rights (over and above those dictated by law) is it appropriate for the firm to acknowledge and observe (for example: is e-mail confidential)? What are the reciprocal responsibilities between workers and the firm? Issues of leadership, motivation, rewards and incentives, and layoffs are all part of this field.

Finally, the personal level is related to how people should treat each other in their roles within the firm. To what extent do I have duties to respect others: to be honest and open with them, to value their contributions, to empower them? How are roles defined, and do they create reasonable expectations of employees both as persons and as individuals who fill work roles? An underlying concern here is the issue of the extent to which the firm treats people strictly as a means to achieving its ends, rather than as an end to be respected regardless of the financial status of the firm.

Violations of trust and loyalty

The most frequently occurring ethical violations in finance relate to insider trading, stakeholder interest versus stockholder interest and investment management. Businesses in general and financial markets in particular are rife with examples of violations of trust and loyalty in both public and private dealings. Fraudulent financial dealings, influence peddling and corruption in governments, brokers not maintaining proper records of customer trading transactions, cheating customers of their trading profits, unauthorised transactions, insider trading, misuse of customer funds for personal gain, incorrect pricing of customer trades, and corruption and larceny in banking have all become common occurrences.

Insider trading is perhaps one of the most publicised unethical financial behaviours of traders. Insider trading refers to trading in the securities of a company to take advantage of material "inside" information about the company that is not readily available to the public. Such a trade is motivated by the possibility of generating extraordinary gains with the help of non-public information (information not yet made public). It gives the trader an unfair advantage over other traders in the same security.

Arguments for ethical management

Managing in ethical ways is not merely about avoiding bad outcomes. According to R. Bruner (2006), there are positive arguments for bringing pressure to bear on financial decision-making.

The first argument is concerned with the notion of sustainability. Unethical financial practices are not a foundation for enduring, sustainable enterprise. According to R. Bruner, this first consideration focuses on the legacy one creates through one's financial transactions. What legacy do you want to leave? To incorporate ethics into our financial mindset is to think about the kind of world that we would like to live in and that our children will inherit.

The second argument calls for ethical behaviour that is capable of building trust. The branding of products seeks to create a bond between producer and consumer: a signal of purity, performance, or other attributes of quality. As markets reveal, successfully branded products command a premium price. Bonds of trust tend to pay. If the field of finance was purely a world of one-off transactions, it would seem ripe for opportunistic behaviour. But in the case of repeated entry to financial markets and transactions by, for example, active buyers, intermediaries, and advisers, reputation can be of great importance in the shaping of expectations. This implicit bond, trust, or reputation can translate into more effective and economically attractive financial transactions and policies.

Finally, ethical behaviour builds teams and leaders, which underpin process excellence. Standards of global best-practice emphasise that good business process drives good outcomes. Stronger teams and leaders result in more agile and creative responses to problems. Ethical behaviour contributes to the strength of teams and leadership by uniting employees around shared values and by building confidence and loyalty. An objection to this argument is that, in some settings, promoting ethical behaviour is no guarantee of team building. Indeed, teams might even fall apart over disagreements on what is ethical, or what action it is appropriate to take. But typically, this is not a failing of ethics *per se*, but rather of the teams' process management for handling disagreements.

Ethical codes beyond laws and regulations

Ethics sets higher standards than laws and regulations. To a large extent, the law is a crude instrument. It tends to result from unacceptable behaviour rather than to anticipate potential behavioural patterns. It contains gaps that can become recreational exploitation for the aggressive businessperson. Justice may be neither swift nor proportional to the crime. To use only the law as a basis for ethical thinking, is to settle for the lowest common denominator of social norms.

Motivating ethical behaviour only by trumpeting its financial benefits without discussing its costs is inappropriate. According to some estimates, the average annual income from a lifetime of crime (even counting years spent in prison) is high – it seems that crime does pay. If income were all that mattered, most of us would switch to this lucrative field. The business world features enough cheats and scoundrels who illustrate that a myriad opportunities exist for any professional to break promises – or worse – for money. Ethical professionals turn down such opportunities for reasons related to the kind of people they aspire to be.

Case study in regulatory jurisdictions

One of the most important and powerful official regulatory agencies for the securities' industry is the United States Securities and Exchange Commission (SEC). It is responsible for implementing federal securities laws, and, as such, it establishes rules and regulations for the proper conduct of professionals operating within its regulatory jurisdiction. Many professionals play a role within the financial services industry; the most important include accountants, broker-dealers, investment advisers, and investment companies. Any improper or unethical conduct on the part of these professionals is of great concern to the SEC, whose primary responsibility is to protect investors' interests and maintain the integrity of the securities market. The SEC can censure, suspend, or bar professionals who practice within its regulatory domain on the basis of lack of requisite qualifications or unethical and improper conduct. The SEC also oversees self-regulatory organisations, which include the stock exchange, the National Association of Security Dealers, the Municipal Securities Rule-making Board, clearing houses, transfer agents, and securities information processors.

In the United Kingdom, the Financial Services Authority (FSA) is a statutory body set up under the Financial Services and Markets Act 2000. It is accountable to Treasury Ministers and through them to the Parliament. It is operationally independent of the UK government and is funded entirely by the firms it regulates through fines, fees and compulsory levies. The FSA aims to promote market confidence through maintaining confidence in the financial system; promote public understanding of the financial system; secure the appropriate degree of protection for consumers; and reduce the extent to which it is possible for a business carried on by a regulated person to be used for a purpose connected with financial crime.

Approaches to dealing with ethical problems in finance range from establishing ethical codes for financial professionals, to efforts to replace the rational profit-maximisation paradigm that underlies the modern capitalist system by one in which individuals are assumed to be altruistic, honest, and basically virtuous. It is not uncommon to find established ethical codes in many countries all over the world that provide sound directions on the conducting of financial markets. Ethical codes for financial markets are established by the official regulatory agencies and self-regulating organisations to ensure ethically responsible behaviour on the part of the operatives in the financial markets.

In search of honesty and altruism

There has been an effort to address the ethical problems in finance by re-examining the conceptual foundation of the modern capitalist system and changing it to one that is consistent with the traditional model of agency relationship. The proponents of a paradigm shift question the rational profit-maximisation assumption that underlies the modern financial-economic theory, and reject the idea that all human actions are motivated by self-interest. They embrace an alternative assumption – that human beings are to some degree ethical and altruistic – and emphasise the role of the traditional principal-agent relationship that is based on honesty, loyalty, and trust. R. Duska (1992) argues: "Clearly, there is an extent to which [Adam] Smith and the economists are right. Human beings are self-interested and will not always look out for the interest of others. But there are times when they will set aside their interests to act on behalf of others. Agency situations were presumably set up to guarantee those times."

The idea that human beings can be honest and altruistic is an empirically valid assumption; it is not hard to find examples of honesty and altruism in both private and public dealings. There is no reason why this idea should not be embraced and nurtured. As N. Bowie (1991) points out: "Looking out for oneself is a natural, powerful motive that needs little, if any, social reinforcement... Altruistic motives, even if they too are natural, are not as powerful: they need to be socially reinforced and nurtured." If the financial-economic theory accepts that behavioural motivations other than that of wealth maximisation are both realistic and desirable, then the agency problem that economists try to deal with will become a non-problem. For J. Dobson (1993), the true role of ethics in finance is to be found in the acceptance of internal good ("good" in the sense of "right" rather than in the sense of "physical product"), which, he adds, is what classical philosophers describe as "virtue" – that is, the internal good toward which all human endeavour should strive. He contends: "If the attainment of internal good was to become generally accepted as the ultimate objective of all human endeavours, both personal and professional, then financial markets would become truly ethical."

The Grameen Bank and financial ethics

The experience of the Grameen Bank serves to highlight the straight-jacket on ethical issues that most of us must accept as we seek to serve our institutions. Nevertheless, exceptions remain possible – those who remain within the financial world and yet attempt to impose their own ethics of belief – to the extent that the institutionalised system is in fact forced to concede. The experience of the Grameen Bank serves to highlight this possibility. In the wake of the 1974 flooding in Bangladesh that had led to widespread crop failures and hunger, Professor Muhammad Yunus at Chittagong University in the southern part of the country, was conscious that his abstract economic theories were far removed from the reality of local village populations. Even in more fortunate times, these people had been obliged to remain poor, because the greater part of the value added by their endeavours was exploited by those who financed their activities. For example, the rickshaw pullers who after twenty years still could not become the owners of their rickshaws.

Money was required to make money, so that is seemed that the purpose of the poor was to make the wealthy rather wealthier. Yunus began with a list compiled by his students containing the names of forty-two local people, whose initial capital requirements, in order to purchase materials to work freely, added up 856 takas, about US$26. The villagers accepted the money as a loan and Yunus arranged for its repayment in small daily instalments.

When Yunus attempted to persuade a bank to provide a loan to the villagers on the same principle, he was informed, notwithstanding the evidence of his own experiment, that the bank could not lend money to the poor because they had no collateral and would therefore not repay. For this reason, governments, not banks, existed to help the poor. The bank would lend to Yunus but not to the people. That was the rule of the bank.

A socially conscious capitalist enterprise

For Yunus, the principle was that the bank should be prepared to fund the entrepreneurship of the poor, not his own collateral. In the end, Yunus achieved his first loan of 10,000 takas (US$ 300) with the compromise of being the guarantor himself, while simultaneously actually promising the bank that should the villagers fail to repay their loan, he would be under no obligation to repay the bank. When the experiment turned out to be a success, Yunus approached the bank to continue the experiment in its own name. He was told that he must submit a proposal for a project with a budget, which the manager could send to his boss, who in turn might decide to send it to his managing director; but he was warned: "Even the managing director cannot give his authority just like that. He has to take it to the board and the board has to decide. And there are things that the board cannot change, because they have to do with fundamental principles of the bank. So you have to go to Parliament or whoever made the laws for that. And your suggestion involves that kind of change" (Bornstein, 1996).

In the end, with a loan from the bank, Yunus opened the first branch of his Grameen (the word gram means village) Bank in the village. True to its name, the Grameen Bank works only in villages, which is one of the ways it has redefined the idea of a bank. Another is that it lends mainly to women in small amounts and for short periods of time. Yet another is its method of screening borrowers. To qualify for a loan, a villager must show that her family's assets fall below the bank's threshold. She will not be required to furnish collateral, demonstrate a credit history, or produce a guarantor. Instead, she must join a five-member group and a forty-member centre, and must assume responsibility for the loans of her group's members.

Grameen Bank and the United Nations

Yunus has campaigned for the United Nations to amend its 1948 Universal Declaration of Human Rights to incorporate credit for self-employment. This is not only a fundamental human right, it is recognised as a human right that plays a critical role in attaining all other human rights. Article 25 reads: "Everyone has the right to a standard of living adequate for the health and well-being of himself and his family, including food, clothing, housing and medical care, and necessary social services, and the right to security in the event of unemployment"; and continues, "there is nothing inherent in the nature of credit that keeps it away from the poor. Nevertheless, the poor have no access to credit institutions. Since the poor cannot provide collateral, the argument goes; there is no basis for lending to them. If collateral alone can provide the basis for the banking business, then society should mark out the banks as harmful engines that create economic, social and political inequality by making the rich richer and the poor poorer" (Bornstein, 1996).

Two decades later, the bank has extended an equivalent of US$ 3 billion in tiny loans for self-employment purposes to 2 million of some of the poorest people in the world, mainly women. It has lent half that amount in just two years. With loan repayment exceeding 98%, it has outperformed all other banks in Bangladesh and most banks around the world. Nevertheless, the Grameen Bank is not a charity. Interest rates are commercial, and have been as high as 16%. It is a business that scrupulously controls costs and aims at profitability while adhering to a social programme whose mandate is to end poverty and hunger, not just in Bangladesh but from the face of the earth. Yunus maintains that the bank represents a socially conscious capitalist enterprise.

Grameen Bank vs. world financial systems

The Grameen Bank crosses the gap between an entrepreneurial institution that has actually made the case for less "charitable" government, and an enlightened social welfare institution that argues in favour of the value of government involvement that is able to conceptualise in terms of the potential of people to add to their own lives. For Yunus, the problem is that the financial systems through which governments of developing countries attempt to operate do not inherently believe in people, whose poverty alleviation has been largely forgotten, but in wealth-generating projects understood in terms of "income" and "GNP". Nonetheless, if increases in the villagers' incomes are to be achieved by movements of the population from the village to the vastly overpopulated city – where expenses are also many times increased – it is by no means clear that increases in income – and GNP, which measures such increases – are the good thing they are made out to be. Added to which, GNP does not recognise half the population's (women's) work, while the concept of income appears to be understood in terms of statements such as "Bangladesh has a per-capita annual income roughly equal to US$ 200". If this indicates that people in Bangladesh live for an entire year on the quantity equivalent to what a New Yorker can receive for US$ 200, is nonsensical, since they would have all died; and if it does not mean this, it is unclear what it does mean. To date, the government of Bangladesh has acquired more then US$ 25 billion in institutional aid for infrastructure projects such as roads, bridges, and power stations. Notwithstanding that Bangladesh needs these kinds of things to attract investments; Yunus believes that many of the ideas have been so ill-conceived by the World Bank experts, that the country has been turned into a graveyard of ideas and projects, with little or no impact on the poorest 50% of the country. And the debt constraints remain. For Yunus, the system is financially flawed because the concept of linking income and GNP – rather than real concerns for people and an appreciation of their potential to engage productively as individuals in their own right – are responsible for the accounting systems that produce the figures, that in turn determine public policy. In effect, Yunus holds out the possibility that society's profit-maximisation objective at the macro level is ultimately compatible with assisting the poorer members of society to help themselves.

The Grameen Bank remains committed to a clientele that is inherently expensive to serve – a clientele that in the absence of an ethical imperative would have remained outside of the big capital markets. The example is perhaps daunting, emphasising the compromised position that we may feel with regard to the ethical codes of our financial institutions today. On the other hand, the example is perhaps uplifting, demonstrating that a single individual, who remains committed to its beliefs, can have the potential to initiate a significant paradigm shift in the ethical functioning of financial institutions, within which most of us seek to leave a mark of our creative energies.

Bibliography

Bornstein, D., 1996. *Price of a Dream: The Story of the Grameen Bank.* Chicago: University of Chicago Press.

Bowie, N., 1991. "Challenging the Egoistic Paradigm", in: *Business Ethics Quarterly 1 (1)*, 1-21.

Bruner, R., 2006. *Ethics in Finance*, Working Paper, Charlottesville, University of Virginia.

Dempsey, M., 1999. *An Agenda for Window-Dressing or for Radical Change?* Working Paper, Nathan, Griffith University.

Dobson, J., 1993. "The Role of Ethics in Finance", in: *Financial Analysts Journal 49 (6)*, 57-61.

Duska, R., 1992. "Why Be a Loyal Agent? A Systematic Ethical Analysis", in: Bowie, N./ Freeman, E. (eds.), *Ethics and Agency Theory: An Introduction*, New York, Oxford University Press.

Wicks, A., 2003. *A Note on Ethical Decision Making*, Working Paper, Charlottesville, University of Virginia.

20

MICROFINANCE: GETTING MONEY TO THE POOR OR MAKING MONEY OUT OF THE POOR?

Joy Mueni Maina Kiiru

Microfinance institutions are currently experiencing very high repayment rates of between 95-99%. Coupled with growing loan sizes by clients, these institutions are even making profits. No wonder there seems to be a good reason for the world to celebrate the microfinance revolution. It is not necessarily wrong to reduce poverty and make some money on the side. The question however arises as to whether that is indeed what is happening with microfinance.

R.P. Christen (1997) defines microfinance as the means of providing a variety of financial services to the poor, based on market-driven and commercial approaches. These services may include savings, insurance, money transfers and credit. However the microfinance movement to date has generally favoured microcredit, which is the provision of small loans to households who are perceived to be too poor to qualify for loans from formal financial institutions. This essay mainly discusses microfinance to these very poor clients who cannot even borrow as individuals, but must borrow through a joint liability group.

Poor households are caught up in a vicious cycle of poverty, where labour, their best resource, is locked up due to different constraints including a lack of liquidity. The household's productivity as such is limited to a level whereby the available household income is insufficient to sustain good standards of living. For example a poor household may have family members who are willing to work in the family garden to grow sufficient food crops. However if they cannot afford improved crop varieties and farm inputs then it will not be possible for the family to grow enough food. The household's labour is therefore said to be locked up due to a liquidity constraint among other constrains. Many governments and donor communities believe that the liquidity constraint is the most important constraint impeding poor households and that if it is addressed it will be possible for households to escape poverty. Economists argue that to break the vicious cycle of poverty, there needs to be an outside force that will break the vicious chain by injecting some liquidity, thereby unlocking the household labour. Microfinance promises not only to break the vicious chain of poverty but also to initiate a whole new cycle of virtuous spirals of self-enforcing economic empowerment that leads to increased household well-being.

Misleading assumptions

Such is the model that has promoted the microfinance institution and given it the polite and respectable image it currently enjoys. With all due respect, it is worth raising some questions regarding the underlying assumptions of such a popular model.

In the first place, proponents of the model assume that many poor people can become micro-entrepreneurs. Entrepreneurship skills and managerial capability are assumed as given, thus the ability for microfinance to create employment even if self-employment. Secondly, even if the first assumption were correct, the model continues to assume that there is going to be a vibrant market for goods and services and that it will be possible for all micro-entrepreneurs to gain access to markets for their products; otherwise how else can incomes be improved from entrepreneurship if there were no markets? Thirdly, the supporters of this model also assume that as long as the poor can repay at market rates, or slightly above market rates, it is a good indication that they are doing well financially. Ironically, one of the major reasons why it was felt so justified to bring more formal financial services to the poor was because it was assumed that the local money lenders were exploiting the poor by charging extortionate interest rates. Yet the poor were paying even then!

The point is that microfinance should be understood as a resource reallocation policy tool and, just like any other such policy, it is important to keep close watch of the underlying assumptions, for if they are not valid, the policy objectives may not be realised.

The main objective of this essay is not to challenge, prove or disapprove anything, but rather to bring to light the realities of what the poor people have to cope with in order to repay their loans promptly. The goal is to bring the social and financial costs associated with microfinance instalments to the awareness of the policy maker.

Keeping loan repayments high

Over 120 million people currently benefit from the services of over 10,000 microfinance institutions paying interest rates of between 15 and 35%. In November 2006 the official Microfinance Information Exchange, Inc. released some thought-provoking statistics from the leading microfinance institutions. The most profitable microfinance institution in 2006 was in Africa, with an average of 30.90% return on assets, followed by another in Asia with an average of 30.2% return on assets. On average the top 100 most profitable microfinance institutions worldwide have an average of 10.44% return on assets. The second largest microfinance institution after Grameen (in terms of client outreach) is ASA, with over 4 million clients. ASA has a 14.53% return on assets and it is among the top 15 global microfinance institutions in terms of profitability. The top 5 Microfinance institutions in terms of outreach are all in Asia where high population density is the norm, coupled with a high level of poverty and lack of alternative finance. These unfortunate social characteristics make Asia a prime market for microfinance. D. Roodman and U. Qureshi (2006) argue that the real genius in microfinance is not because they firmly believe that the poor can pay, but rather it is because they have been able to come up with clever solutions to the problems of building volume, keeping loan repayment rates high, retaining customers, and minimising scope for fraud, and being able to deliver cost-effective microfinance to thousands and millions of poor clients.

Microfinance institutions have innovatively shifted two classic banking obligations to the borrowers. Firstly, it is the poor who decide the credit worthiness of borrowers through peer selection into the borrowing groups. Secondly, it is the poor who impose debt collection from peers while being governed by innovative contracts that are too costly to breach.

Four principles for repayment

The popular explanation of how the poor repay their loans is based on four principles. The first is the principle of dynamic incentive to loan repayment. This means that the lending institution will offer the prospect of a larger loan once an individual borrower has been able to repay the current loan. This alone is supposed to be an incentive to the clients to finish repaying their current loan and qualify for a larger one. Proponents of joint responsibility borrowing argue that dynamic incentives make microfinance for the poor operate in a similar fashion to the credit card in developed countries, whereby clients repay because they want to access more credit in the future. Other writers have argued that the same dynamic incentive is a great incentive for providing bridging loans to poorer households in order to clear their earlier debts. Poor microfinance clients are therefore likely to get locked up in a vicious debt cycle, contracting more debts to repay microfinance debts in order to get more funds and hopefully offset the debts so far incurred. The clients keep borrowing to repay, until the ultimate face to face with excess debt. Excess debt can deplete household capital assets and other basic livelihood assets, thereby leaving the household exposed and vulnerable. The second is the principle of joint responsibility borrowing. This means that a group of borrowers rather than the individual is responsible for repaying microfinance loans. If the individual borrower defaults, the whole group is held responsible.

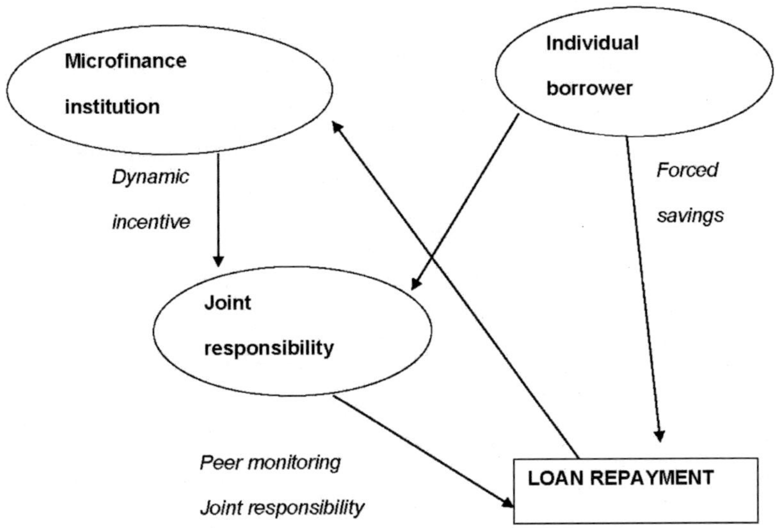

Figure 1: Loan repayment by the poor

The third is the principle of peer monitoring and peer pressure. The individuals within a group monitor and bring pressure to bear on each other to ensure that all loans are repaid on time. In case the individual is not able to repay due to having made wrong investment decisions or for some other reason, then all the members of the group have a moral obligation to help in the repayment. Finally, joint liability borrowing is purported to thrive due to the principle of forced savings. Individual borrowers are forced to save a fixed regulated amount of money every month. Neither the group nor the individual can access the forced savings at will, but they can be used as security for future loans and can only be paid back if the individual borrower is dropping out of the project and has been cleared by all members of the group. The forced saving is not only a partial security for loans borrowed by an individual, but can also be seized by the microfinance institution if any other member(s) of the group defaults on their loan repayment.

A success story…

The best-known story in microfinance is that of Muhammad Yunus, the founder of the Grameen Bank who has inspired many other microfinance institutions worldwide. The Grameen Bank started in the aftermath of the country's war of independence. At this time Bangladesh was plagued by desperate poverty aggravated by very high birth rates. The economy was still very rural, coupled with a government that was perceived to be weak and corrupt. In order to deal with the poverty situation, there was a strong preference for non-bureaucratic grass-roots and other collective approaches. This prompted the formation of self help groups for equally disadvantaged groups in order to pool resources for the mutual benefit of the group members. It was in this environment that Muhammad Yunus, an Economics professor at the University of Chittagong, began an experimental research project, providing credit to the rural poor of Bangladesh. He began by lending people a little money out of his own pocket and soon realised that it was enough for villagers to run simple business activities like rice husking and bamboo weaving. He later found that borrowers were not only benefiting greatly by accessing the loans but they were also repaying reliably even though they could offer no collateral. Later, with the support of the central bank of Bangladesh and donor support, that humble experiment developed into the world's most famous microfinance institution, the Grameen Bank, and institutions that replicate its pioneering methodology worldwide. The Grameen Bank today boasts a Nobel Prize, 1.700 branches, 16, 000 employees, and 6 million customers of which 96% are women.

... Not always that good

However, the microfinance story does not always have such a good track record. A study by the International Food Policy Research Institute (IFRI) that focused on the Malawi Rural Finance Corporation came up with rather "unconventional" results (Diagne, 2000). The results were in sharp contrast to conventional wisdom and assumptions regarding the informal advantage of the joint liability and its implications of incentives for peer selection, peer monitoring and peer pressure with respect to loan repayment. The findings did not support the widely held assumption that joint liability is responsible for the high repayment rates of the successful group lending programmes. In particular the study found that no effective peer monitoring was taking place in the credit groups because of the associated social costs.

Another important finding of the same study is that peer pressure took place less frequently than implied by the joint liability, and when it did in most cases it failed to induce defaulters to repay their loans. M. Schrieder (2003) argues that joint liability borrowing may lead to domino effects, in which borrowers who would have repaid, choose to default because they would lose access to future loans in any case, due to the default of others. In reality joint liability may not cut the cost of lending but rather shift it from lenders to borrowers.

A study by J. Kiiru and J. Mburu (2007) found that joint responsibility borrowing in Kenya today does not necessarily mean zero collateral loans. Peers no longer agree to guarantee each other's loans based on sociological ties and trust alone; rather they demand a tangible guarantee that the loans shall be repaid. Unlike in Asia where shame, honour and reputation are important incentives to loan repayments by poor clients in the groups, those are of no great importance in Kenya, where it is possible for a client to get a loan and move to another village or city, without being much concerned about social stigma. On the contrary D. Roodman and U. Qureshi (2006) write: "Even MFIs (in Asia) that do not employ either joint liability or regular group meetings for transaction purposes tap into this sensitivity to reputation for delinquency control: XacBank in Mongolia posts names of clients and their instalment repayment reports on the walls of its branches. Peer pressure, […] is pressure arising from public transactions in communities where individuals worry about reputations. And the discovery is not really new to micro credit; money lenders too have used public honor to motivate repayments. When interviewed, a woman street vendor who was a client of a group of moneylenders called the Bombays in the Philippines noted that the Bombays always picked the busiest hour of the day to collect so that there would always be witnesses to her embarrassment."

Trust is not enough

Faced with the fact that trust does not provide systematic solutions, joint liability borrowing groups have invented drastic measures to deal with un-cooperating peers. In the study by J. Kiiru and J. Mburu (2007), the joint liability groups studied had included two preconditions for prospective new members that had to be met before being admitted as members of the group. The first precondition is that a prospective member will have to formally sign a contract with her peers, guaranteeing her future loans with collaterals; the assets used for this kind of transaction are basic livelihood assets such as livestock, household furniture and cutlery; also accepted are capital assets such as sewing machines, and electronic equipment and the suchlike. Secondly, the prospective member must also provide an acceptable guarantor for her loans. The guarantor's acceptability is based on his or her ability to repay. This person is obliged to sign documents accepting responsibility for defaulted loans by the borrower.

The same study revealed the existence amongst all solidarity groups of a rigorous administrative structure to ensure that every loan is repaid on time. For example, in order to minimise the risk of non-repayment by some poorer borrowers, solidarity groups advise their weaker members to start submitting their loan instalments to the group's treasurer on a weekly basis. There is need for research to help understand the extent to which forced savings and weekly loan repayments lead to undercapitalisation of small enterprises and to what extent this undercapitalisation compromises returns and therefore incomes.

Microfinance lending institutions impose financial penalties on groups that delay the remittance of a loan instalment. These penalties are borne equally by all group members. This gives an incentive for group members to exclude very poor households or colleagues who have a bad debt repayment record, in order to minimise the risk of penalties in case of default. The financial penalties also have the effect of making peers extremely aggressive when dealing with a colleague who is not in a position to meet her immediate financial obligations. In many cases such instances lead to strained relations in social networks. Again there is a need to understand the extent to which strained social relations lead to a depletion of the social capital in poor communities.

From harassment to loss of property

Group meetings are held on a weekly basis, and are usually attended by a loan officer to ensure that all due instalments are collected. In some cases the loan officer will not agree to end a meeting until all the instalments have been repaid. It frequently means the groups' officials (chairperson, treasurer and secretary) are obliged to use the groups' pooled fund. These funds are raised through group registration fees, and regular contributions to a pool. Usually this money is not banked, but held by the treasurer of the group. In the event of there not being enough money in the pool, the officials may resort to borrowing from friends; and if this is still not adequate, they may even choose to borrow from the local money lenders to avoid the consequences imposed by the microfinance institution, and to keep their records clean with the institution. Once the group has cleaned its records with the microfinance institution, they may take possession of the assets of the defaulted borrower until every cent of the debt has been repaid.

Currently the only way to avoid repaying a loan and get away with it (at the risk of the forced savings only) is if all members of the group decide to do the same. However microfinance institutions already have taken measures to minimise these kinds of eventualities. They do not grant loans simultaneously to every member of the group, but rather do so on a rota basis. In this way, at any given time, there are those members who have already begun repaying and have almost finished their repayments. This group will rationally exert pressure on the others to repay. In this case it is almost impossible for the entire group to default, and leads to the likelihood of all loans being repaid. D. Roodman and U. Qureshi (2006) observe that through an interaction of human ingenuity and evolutionary dynamics, microfinance leaders have found a set of techniques in their product design and management, that solve the fundamental problems of microfinance of cost control, building volume, keeping repayment high, and preventing internal fraud, while operating in a poor country.

A study by J. Kiiru and J. Mburu (2007) revealed that at least 60% of microfinance clients had experienced some form of harassment by fellow group members in an attempt to convince them to repay loans on which they would otherwise have defaulted, given their current financial capability: 4% had some of their property confiscated by group members to settle loans on their behalf, while another 17% sold some of their pre-existing assets in order to meet their repayment obligations, and a further 2% had to borrow from friends and relatives to meet their repayment obligations. Domestic animals, furniture, and electronic goods and sometimes clothing were some of the major assets sold or confiscated from the poor to repay the loans.

There is a greater-than-ever need to set up a regulatory framework for microfinance that would protect existing property of the borrowers. As expected, such a regulatory policy is likely to change the operations of microfinance institutions in an attempt to reduce the risk to their clients. However this should not be viewed negatively, as microfinance is a policy tool for resource reallocation. And like any other such policy, subsequent adjustments are inevitable, to ensure that the policy intervention tool continues to be relevant to the objectives for which it was devised.

A call for regulatory policy

Just as personal bankruptcy should not be a reason for banning access to credit cards or mortgages in richer countries, it is also not rational to denigrate the whole idea of loaning to the poor. It is nevertheless important to realise that in the quest to alleviate poverty, it is possible to capitalise on the benefits of microfinance, while minimising vulnerability to crisis, by improving debt management capacities of the poor and by setting up clear regulations in the microfinance sector. There is therefore a need to create policies that increase the demand for goods and services in rural areas; otherwise the benefits of entrepreneurship to peoples' livelihood cannot be achieved.

It is not necessarily wrong for the poor to borrow to meet basic food needs. However savings rather than microfinance would offer a better alternative. This is because it is unsustainable to depend on excess debt for consumption purposes. This calls for innovative yet cheaper technologies to meet the very basic needs of food, health and education. All this should be neatly wrapped together with responsible governance, in terms of resource mobilisation and reallocation. This should be developed to ensure that households would need credit for reasons other than for meeting basic consumption needs, but rather to use for income-generating activities that bring about real increases in income. This would provide an efficient way of lending money to the poor, since only those who can make best use of it in terms of entrepreneurship will require access to credit.

Finally there is currently a receptive attitude within the national and international community to microfinance instruments and, by and large the microfinance institutions still have a respectable image among many donors and governments. It is also true that there is no major apparent crisis or emergency in the microfinance institutions. But there are signs of cracks in the overall impact that microfinance has had among poor borrowers. These borrowers continue to operate under such tight debt schedules that it is a real struggle for them to build business volume and therefore growth for the enterprises, let alone escape poverty. This calls for regulatory policy, and it is important to note that policies implemented in tranquil times can help prevent major problems in the future.

Bibliography

Christen, R.P., 1997. *Banking services for the poor: Managing for financial success*, Washington, DC: ACCION International.

Diagne, A., 2000. *Design and Sustainability Issues of Rural Credit and Savings Programmes: Findings from Malawi*, Washington, DC, IFRI Policy Brief No. 12.

Kiiru, J./ Mburu, J., 2007. "User Costs of Joint Liability Borrowing and their Effect on Livelihood Assets for Rural Poor Households", in: *International Journal for Gender Women and Social Justice*, July-December.

Roodman, D. and Qureshi, U., 2006. *Microfinance as Business*, Working paper No. 101, Washington DC, Centre for Global Development.

Schreiner, M., 2003. "A Cost-Effectiveness Analysis of the Grameen Bank of Bangladesh", in: *Development Policy Review 21 (3)*, 357-382.

21

THE SOUTH AND CARBON DIOXIDE EVERY CLOUD HAS A SILVER LINING

Jem Bendell and Inderpreet Chawla

Money makes the world go round. The growth of the now 370 trillion dollar derivatives market, according to a Bank of International Settlements estimate for the first half of 2006, serves to remind us that the financial sector is the compass from which both companies and countries take their direction. Yet as news about climate chaos, persistent poverty and intensifying inequality continues to percolate our pleasant lives in the West, we have to ask whether money is now causing the downfall of the world. In recent years more people have been choosing to engage in global finance to solve problems of the environment and international development. Their efforts herald a new paradigm for ethical finance, which no longer focuses on personal ethical dilemmas within existing professional frameworks but on how to use opportunities as a financial services professional to transform those frameworks so the world's most powerful motor – money – makes the world work around barriers to a more sustainable, just and healthy future.

Our paper outlines how this is happening both in professions and in academia. It identifies urgent interconnected challenges of climate change, unemployment, local enterprise and poverty reduction, and suggests that a new approach to socially responsible investing is required to create new frameworks for the innovative financing of sustainable enterprise in the global South. Investors can make money while contributing to low-carbon high-employment societies, if they help support the development of appropriate risk adjusting mechanisms. This focus on creating new financial frameworks is one of the highest embodiments of a commitment to our common humanity and ecology, which is the ground of all subsequent ethical discourse and philosophy.

Emerging trends in business ethics

To a large extent the question and practice of ethics in finance is influenced by the broader category of ethics in business. Both because financial firms are companies and because questions of ethics cut across various types of business, and also as business ethics is an established discipline within management schools around the world. Therefore reflecting on the situation in business ethics academe can help us to see emerging trends of interest, hence what the future of ethics in finance might entail, both practically and intellectually.

The traditional academic approach to business ethics has been largely focused on esteemed philosophers, such as Aristotle, Kant, and Mill, and typically engages in an unending debate about whether certain business practices are either right or wrong. However, since 2003 there has been evidence of a changing paradigm. That year saw the main association for business ethics scholars in Europe, the European Business Ethics Network (EBEN), hold its conference titled "Building Ethical Institutions for Business" and allowed "the participants to reflect and debate on the role of institutions in the transformation of business toward a more human and ethical form". This was not the focus on the individual manager's ethical dilemmas and problems that has characterised much business ethics work in the past, but rather a discussion of "stakeholder activism, global governance structures, corporate social responsibility, corporate governance, corporate citizenship, ethical investment, stakeholder society, Internet-enabled corporations, environmental regimes, human rights, future generations, and ethical institutions for corporate accountability".

Another illustration of this trend is the best-selling textbook, *Business Ethics: A European Perspective* (Crane and Matten, 2003). The subtitle "Managing Corporate Citizenship and Sustainability in the Age of Globalisation" indicates that this is not a traditional business ethics tome. The book still discusses ethical theories and ethical dilemmas, but it frames these within the broader debates conjured up by the subtitle.

The problem with business ethics has been that ethics is a post-business creation, both literally and conceptually. The context was nearly always assumed and managers asked to respond to a consequent dilemma. Today many managers and students of business are asking for something different – for ethics to be the starting point for their work.

This is partially due to a growing awareness of the power of business and finance, and the responsibility this brings. Of the world's 100 largest economic entities, according to an Institute for Policy Studies report, 51 are now corporations and 49 are countries. With daily stories of private equity and hedge funds demanding dramatic changes in corporate structure, and ratings agencies able to influence the value of a national currency with their assessments of credit risk, no one can ignore the financial sector's cumulative effect as a compass steering both companies and countries.

The pressure of civil society

Consequently, people who are concerned about social and environmental issues have been turning to the financial sector. This is highlighted by the growing interest and activity of non-governmental organisations (NGOs). In the UK a variety of campaigning organisations including Amnesty International, Greenpeace, People & Planet, and WWF joined together to launch FairPensions, a campaign to mobilise UK pension fund owners to put pressure on their trustees, fund managers and ultimately the companies they invest in, to behave in a responsible and sustainable manner. An international coalition of NGOs also formed Banktrack, and agreed a common declaration of what they want to see from responsible banks. Many people with an NGO background have gone into the City, in order to effect change from there, including people like Rob Lake (formerly at Traidcraft now Head of Governance at Hendersons Global Investors), Nick Robins (formerly of International Institute for Environment and Development now Head of SRI at Hendersons) and Steve Waygood (formerly of WWF-UK now Chair of UK Social Investment Forum).

This indicates an approach to finance whereby a person's ethical interests are the starting point for engaging in a career in finance. Consequently ethical issues are not seen so much as questions of how one should behave within a given office context, but rather how one wishes to contribute to the wider world by choosing a career within the financial sector. The new trend in the business ethics academe reflects this, no longer just treating managers as victims of circumstance but helping them become masters of destiny, to change the circumstances for the better. If this is our starting point and if we consider finance to be, collectively, the most powerful driving force in the world, then we must be clear about the greatest challenges of our time, and the areas where finance could do a lot more to help.

Key challenges of our time

With global consumption levels five times what they were just 50 years ago, the natural world is buckling under the weight of demand. The impact tolls of all this are clear: climate instability, ecosystem pressures (already leading to complete collapse in some instances), soil loss and degradation, ground water depletion, loss of productive land, and toxic accumulation are some of the key issues. The global scientific consensus on climate change, as exemplified in the 2007 Report of the UN Intergovernmental Panel on Climate Change, proves beyond doubt that there are limits to what our atmosphere can take, and what changes in our atmosphere our nature, agriculture, water supplies and cities can cope with. The UK Stern Review on the Economics of Climate Change 2007 predicts a 20% reduction in Global GDP, which is equivalent to two world wars combined. Already, people are losing their lives and livelihoods due to climate change. The scientific imperative is to control greenhouse gas emissions so that climate change can be kept within two degrees of pre-industrial levels. This implies a global halving of such emissions by 2050 at the very least.

Pollution and inefficient consumption is everyone's problem and responsibility. The over half a billion middle-class Asians are consuming significant and growing amounts of resources with negative impacts on their own rural and urban environments as well as abroad. For example, the Indian middle class have higher carbon lifestyles than the UK average. We urgently need to focus on how to help the global South to develop, using low-carbon technologies and business activities.

In such countries there are very real concerns about poverty. The current boom in investment, which we discuss below, is mainly focused on large companies and urban centres. Yet the world's top 200 corporations account for over a quarter of global economic activity, while employing less than 1% of its workforce. There is a need to stimulate small and medium sized enterprises (SMEs) that employ more people. In addition, it is these SMEs that need to be targeted if we are to meet the challenge of climate change. Promoting low-carbon high-employment societies is possible. The European Trade Union Confederation recently concluded that "less dependence on natural resources can be coupled with more intensive use of labour" and predicted that "by 2010, it is estimated that the global market for environmentally friendly products and services will be worth around €700 billion".

Thus we believe that the dual climate-employment challenge, particularly in emerging markets, is crucial, and one with which financial services need to engage. It is essential if we are to promote the sustainable economic development in the global South that can raise people out of poverty without destroying the basis for human life on Earth. Consequently, within a new paradigm of ethical finance, we turn to the question of how to facilitate investments in sustainable SMEs in emerging markets.

Only backing the big guns?

With the liberalisation of financial markets in Asia, Africa, and Latin America, *emerging markets* have emerged as an important asset class for investors in developed countries. Further, recent macro-economic trends such as strengthened banking sectors, increased use of Generally Accepted Accounting Principles, increased focus on Return on Investment (ROI), and decreasing information inefficiencies have made this asset class an increasingly popular one with the investment community in Europe, North America and Japan. The prevailing argument in the international investment arena suggests that although emerging markets are more volatile than their developed market counterparts, the inclusion of an emerging market asset in a balanced investment portfolio can actually reduce volatility of the entire portfolio, while simultaneously increasing the global return. Needless to say, the fundamental principle of profit maximisation underpins most of the investment activity in relation emerging markets. Profit maximisation, in itself, could be a fair goal to pursue, and it could be said that most investment activity relative to Emerging Markets Enterprises (EMEs) takes place within ethical norms or *book-balancing ethics*; but given the complexity and interconnected nature of the present-day world, such a judgment would be partial at best.

For a meaningful discussion on the role of ethics within the world of finance and its interaction with the EMEs, it is crucial to look at the broader sociological, economic and cultural contexts within which these new market economies are *emerging*. It is also important to acknowledge that such economies exist within countries, mostly low to middle income and developing, that are characterised by numerous development challenges including endemic corruption, ineffective public institutions weak regulatory systems, and wide-spread environmental degradation. Seemingly benign investment decisions that are made in London, New York, and Tokyo with the simple intention of maximising profits could have far-reaching implications on the development of countries with emerging economies. Particularly, when such investing decisions embed a bias towards large firms that are subject to the short-term expectations of the stock markets, they could have serious negative impacts on the development and growth of such economies.

Socially Responsible Investing and emerging markets

Social investors have been using three basic strategies to protect financial returns while pursuing a social agenda. Screening (and divesting) excludes certain securities from investment consideration based on social and/or environmental criteria. For example, many investors screen out arms company investments, or divest when they make a decision no longer to hold such assets. Shareholder activism and engagement involve efforts to positively influence corporate behaviour by initiating conversations with corporate management or submitting and voting proxy resolutions.

Positive investing involves investment in activities and companies believed to have a positive contribution to society. Positive investing activities can target underserved communities, or clean technologies.

Socially Responsible Investing (SRI) is not a new phenomenon. Over the past thirty years, it has evolved from what was initially a limited movement advocating morally informed investment decisions, to become an international industry worth over $2.7 trillion in assets. The current approach to SRI, while having clearly delivered tremendous benefits, creates a traditional dichotomy of the good versus the bad in the investment community at large. This not only limits the growth of SRI to a mainstream investment trend, but also hinders its application in emerging markets. As a result, it remains largely a developed-country phenomenon. Only an estimated $2.7 billion, or 0.1% of all SRI fund assets worldwide, are currently held in emerging market securities. Complexity of the application of ethics in investing in general, and in emerging markets in particular, needs to be acknowledged. While it is the socially responsible investment community and the development community at large that is interested in the sustainable development of EME countries, it is the mainstream investment community that is primarily concerned with maximisation of ROI.

Guiding money to where it is needed

What is required, therefore, is for financial professionals to embark on an innovative approach to SRI, and focus on creating new frameworks and incentives to guiding money to where it is most needed. Two examples of this transforming framework approach have taken place in London. The first is the Enhanced Analytics Initiative (EAI), where asset managers and asset owners with over €380 billion assets under management are actively supporting better sell-side research on extra-financial issues concerning society, the environment and corporate governance. They are committed to the individual allocation of a minimum of 5% of their respective brokerage commission to sell-side researchers who are effective at analyzing material extra-financial issues and intangibles. The second example is the Institutional Investors Group on Climate Change (IIGCC) who are helping investors to promote appropriate change in public policy to help address the climate challenge. This resonates with the new paradigm of ethical finance as described above: the domain of business and finance ethics has shifted from legal concerns, to exploring what can be done over and above the law, to shape legal frameworks and incentives.

This new paradigm and new framework-changing approach to SRI needs to be applied to the challenge of increasing investments in sustainable SMEs in emerging markets to create more low-carbon high-employment societies around the world. And this ethics-first approach to deciding which ethical-financial issues to address is both the approach of the future and the most laudable one, because it truly embraces the responsibility that comes with the power of finance.

Size matters: the role of emerging market SMEs

The role of small and medium enterprises in emerging economies is now widely recognised. For instance in Africa, SMEs form the backbone of the private sector at all levels of development, and make a significant contribution to economic development in general and industrial development in particular. SMEs and the informal sector represent over 90% of businesses in Africa, contribute to over 50% of GDP, and account for about 63% of employment. Being labour intensive, SMEs absorb labour and other productive resources at all levels of the economy and flourish in villages, towns, and cities helping to develop technical and business skills while reducing the rural-urban income gap. In addition, the following characteristics of SMEs make them particularly valuable for development goals (Luetkenhorst, 2004):

- *SMEs are more labour-intensive.* SMEs play an important role in generating employment and thus alleviating poverty, often providing employment opportunities at reasonable rates of remuneration to workers from poor households, and to women;
- *SMEs contribute to a more efficient allocation of resources in developing countries.* SMEs tend to adopt labour-intensive production

methods and thus more accurately reflect the resource endowment in many countries where labour is plentiful and capital is scarce;

- *SMEs support the building of systemic productive capacities.* They help to absorb productive resources at all levels of the economy and contribute to the establishment of dynamic and resilient economic systems in which small and large firms are interlinked;
- *SMEs tend to lead to a more equitable distribution of income than larger enterprises.* There is evidence that countries with a high share of small industrial enterprises have succeeded in making the income distribution more equitable. This, in turn, is a key contribution to ensuring long-term social stability by alleviation of economic disparities between urban and rural areas;
- *SMEs are a seedbed for entrepreneurship development, innovation, and risk-taking* behaviour and provide the foundation for long-term growth dynamics and a transition to larger enterprises. With the advent of globalisation, such linkages are of increasing importance whereby trans-national corporations (TNCs) seek reliable domestic suppliers for their supply chains.

The above-mentioned non-exhaustive list emphasises not only the importance of SMEs to emerging economies but also their tremendous relevance to the socio-economic and cultural context of many developing countries. Many researchers conclude that SMEs, more locally anchored than large corporations, are more likely to have ties of dependence and familiarity to their communities, which will ensure they protect their reputation and relationships among neighbours and customers. It is essentially through the promotion of SMEs that individual developing countries and the international community at large can make progress towards reaching the Millennium Development Goals of halving poverty levels by 2015.

The trouble with being small

Despite the widely acknowledged importance of the SME sector, SMEs in emerging market economies face many obstacles, including corrupt governance structures, an unfavourable macro-economic environment, poor physical infrastructure, and a multitude of administrative challenges. However, inadequate access to financing continues to be one of the most significant impediments to creation, survival, and growth of SMEs. The most important factor here is risk: credit risk, currency risk and country risk. These are all higher for SMEs in developing countries and thus make the risk profile of emerging market SME funds too high for most ordinary investors.

As a result, private sector activity in many emerging market countries is hindered by a missing middle. While investors primarily focus on large firms (with over 500 employees), the development and microfinance communities are largely focused on very small businesses or micro-enterprises (5 or less employees). Furthermore, large enterprises and multinational corporations can exercise their influence in emerging markets to gain easy access to financing, whereas development and aid agencies primarily concentrate on the promotion of micro-enterprises. SMEs (employing 10 to 100 people) find themselves caught between these two extremes. In many African countries, banks remain highly liquid and are reluctant to extend credit to other than the most creditworthy borrowers. While microfinance institutions have expanded vigorously, their limited scale remains largely insufficient for meeting the needs of many SMEs seeking start-up or growth capital. This leaves SMEs with little choice other than to seek the long-term risk capital that is crucial for starting-up or scaling-up their businesses. Moreover, SMEs also suffer from an image problem, particularly in the eyes of foreign investors. SMEs are often seen as being too small to serve as significant drivers of economic growth.

The difficulties confronting SMEs to finance their development mean that they do not have the required support to plan for the future. Consequently investments in cleaner technologies and production processes, which only pay off after a period of use, are not affordable to many SMEs. This results in the SME sector in many countries not being as environmentally appropriate as it could be. With the anticipated growth in global carbon markets, with heavy polluters being paid to reduce their carbon emissions by using new technologies, SMEs could miss out, due to the very high transaction costs involved in administering the carbon credit process. This presents an opportunity to address the SME financing issue linked to an effort to green the sector, and thereby support more low-carbon jobs in emerging markets.

Meeting the challenge

Recognising the relevance of the SME sector to the growth of emerging market economies, a few innovative mechanisms have emerged that target the financial needs of SMEs. Initiatives include the East Africa Fund by the Shell Foundation and the Africa Enterprise Challenge Fund by the UK Department for International Development (DFID). While these initiatives are steps in the right direction, their focus is on a handful of African countries. Success of such initiatives is yet to be critically reviewed. Furthermore, no matter how successful such initiatives are, if the SME sectors in emerging economies are to be given a true boost, ways will have to be found for scaling up existing successful models. New mechanisms will have to be developed to either provide direct finance or to create conditions that enable SMEs to gain more ready access to finance.

Charity won't work. A systemic approach is required that changes the balance or risks and incentives for ordinary investors, not socially responsible ones, so that more money flows towards sustainable SMEs. The most important factor here is finding new ways of reducing credit, currency and country risk at the same time as both screening and engaging SMEs to ensure that their activities are contributing to a low-carbon development pathway. Exploring the potential for what we call Risk Adjusting Philanthropy could solve this problem.

The potential of Risk Adjusting Philanthropy

In the light of recent donations to charities by large banks dedicated to more traditional charitable activities, e.g. HSBC's US$ 18.4 million funding of the WWF, large banks with strategic interests in growing the SME economy could make million-dollar philanthropic donations to a charitable organisation. The objective could be to set up a new foundation aimed at establishing criteria for sustainable enterprise, and certifying emerging market sustainable SME funds that meet specific criteria (there would be cascading criteria for the funds, the banks, and the SMEs themselves). This would drive improvements in SME practice as well as encourage entrepreneurship in areas such as clean technology and agro-ecology.

This new foundation would also:

- underwrite partial credit guarantees, in the form of a letter of credit, essentially guaranteeing reimbursement to investors of a certain percentage of any losses on the certified funds. This would reduce the risk profile of the funds and their ability to raise funds at a lower cost of capital i.e. attracting normal capital rather than socially responsible capital. If the funds were carefully identified then this foundation would not incur high losses, and could maintain or grow its assets over time;
- spend some of the interest earned from investments on reducing the insurance premium payments for the certified funds. The premium cost of political risk insurance can often make SME investment targets funds untenable (if you're expecting a 5% Return on Investment (ROI), you can't afford risk coverage costing 4% of the investment).

By reducing the cost of insurance this would make the funds more attractive to traditional investors;

- spend some of the interest earned from investments on supporting capacity-building in countries, through NGOs and local Chambers of Commerce, to promote the viability of sustainable SMEs. A key focus could be on helping to create credible carbon offset markets, so that SMEs could gain financially from investing in less carbon-intensive energy production processes.

A new initiative with resources and experts is needed to explore this hypothesis, and other relevant ideas for the innovative financing of sustainable SMEs, and the public policy innovations that may be required for implementation. This would apply the new domain of ethics in finance, and the newest approach of SRI, to a key interconnected challenge of our time – promoting low-carbon high-employment economies in the global South. It would be satisfying for more of the world's investors to care about the future of our planet and our children, but we believe it would not be ethical to rely on this in order to deliver the urgent changes required. Instead, if we create frameworks that enable investors to do the right thing, whatever their motivations, we are using our influence in the most conscientious possible way.

Bibliography

Crane, A,/ Matten, D., 2003. *Business Ethics: A European Perspective – Managing Corporate Citizenship and Sustainability in the Age of Globalisation*, Oxford: Oxford University Press.

Luetkenhorst, W., 2004. *Corporate Social Responsibility and the Development Agenda: Should SMEs Care?* UNIDO, Small and Medium Enterprise Branch.

22

INVESTING AS IF PEOPLE AND PLANET MATTERED

Pernille Jessen

If we examine the lessons of the financial crisis, we can see that a system built on both trust and the rational value-maximising paradigm is fostering conflicts. The current situation therefore provides us with a unique opportunity to study the role of ethics in the financial system and to make concrete suggestions as to how to implement improved business codes of conduct. This article touches on two key areas in this development: the general public's investments and the education of actors in financial markets.

After the storm

In the developed Western world, the preservation of fundamental aspects of human well-being sometimes seems to rank as peculiarly low priority. The effects of non-monetary value are frequently disregarded: success and prestige are typically associated with wealth. Environmental concerns are often ignored in favour of GDP And third world humanitarian catastrophes are likely to receive only the amount of attention from the global community equivalent to their influence on the global economy.

The overlooked rationale is the fact that the values we feed into our systems, be they financial, social or environmental, are inevitably going to be reflected back at us with considerable accuracy. When we ignore the fragility of many of the ecological systems of our planet, the climate may change. When we neglect moral code and ethics in finance, the system may crash. The financial crisis did not happened *to* us as individuals much as it was created *by* us, if not by our direct actions then by our acceptance of the underlying set of values.

A major obstacle in quantitative finance theory is the theoretical simplification of the belief that more monetary wealth is always better. This is the essence of the rational value-maximising paradigm. Qualities such as fresh air and human well-being are soft intangibles with no role in a quantitative financial model. At least that is the broad massage that come across in almost 50 years' worth of modern finance literature. Unless of course, some economical association can be made, such as risk management, public relations or avoidance of health-care expenses.

An emerging shift in social norms

An encouraging empirical finding is the growing market share and awareness of Socially Responsible Investment (SRI). This approach pays much attention to Principles for Responsible Investment (PRI), the UNEP Finance Initiative collaboration with the UN Global Compact (www.unpri.org). An ever-increasing list of major institutional market participants have signed up to the voluntary codes of conduct of this programme. It can be seen as a clear indication of an emerging shift in our social norms; a larger degree of corporate social responsibility is required. The are some signs that ethics are starting to be integrated into finance.

An important observation in the SRI market is that small retail investors still hesitate to participate in responsible investment. North America has a slightly better record than continental Europe, where many countries seem completely disinterested in retail SRI (www.eurosif.org). This is quite strange, as the retail sector in particular is made up of the general public, and can therefore be the very source of emerging moral values. Additionally, this segment is the key stakeholder in the act of protecting the environment and acting as watchdog for social concerns. The immaturity of retail SRI seems puzzling yet it has previously been observed that small retail investors occasionally show perplexing behaviour. The usual suspect is their potential lack of understanding of investment characteristics, and of risk in particular. Now the somewhat inaccessible concept of a social impact factor has been added, and the intricate combination may lead us towards an explanation.

The forthcoming analysis emphasises two frontiers in implementing ethics in finance. The first rationalises retail investor's awareness of the potential ethical implications of their investment decisions. This is an attempt to increase the level of deliberate choice in retail investment decisions, irrespective of their nature, and whether they are responsible or neutral. If a moral code of conduct of a society is rooted in the general public's behaviour, the most direct way of affecting the system is by a bottom-up change in behavior. Strengthening conscious, deliberate consumer choices in the financial market by mainstreaming responsible investment by the retail sector may accelerate a positive progression. The second frontier recognises the culture among participants in the financial market as being a major facilitator of integrity and a fixation on the rational value-maximising paradigm. It argues how crucial a factor education is in developing a sound relationship between these conflicting concepts. Implementing ethics in finance thus requires an investment in the skills of future market participants.

A new portfolio allocation

The SRI mutual fund industry is keen to announce the performance of their activities compared with conventional counterparts. Over the last ten years, researchers have been eager to investigate whether environmental, social and governmental (ESG) factors hold additional financial information, that has not yet been recognised by the general market (Renneboog *et al.*, 2007). Findings are not strictly homogeneous but the general conclusion appears to be that the SRI mutual fund industry is not outperformed by their value-neutral competitors. It leads to the convenient but perhaps hasty conclusion that portfolio responsibility can be provided as a free add-on to an investment. Still, it is definitely a positive dimension to add to the promotion of SRI

From a theoretical point of view it is also a very motivating result. Classical portfolio mean-variance analysis suggests that any limitation to the investment universe will naturally cause diminishing opportunities for diversification and imply higher risk taking or lower expected returns on portfolios. Likewise, it means that social ratings should include extra financial information that has hitherto not been used in the market, and that the advantage is sufficient to cover the costs of diversification.

Alternatively, it may be interesting to take a closer look at exactly how different the holdings of SRI mutual funds really are compared with value-neutral funds (Hawken, 2004). The fact that a lax definition of sustainable, green and responsible investment is leading actors in the financial market to focus mainly on financial performance might be an emerging concern. Portfolio responsibility analysis might be limited to a bare minimum and only considered applicable to the extent that it does not interfere with the risk-return profile of the investment. Wisebrod (2007) suggests a technique for choosing a portfolio, where responsibility is preferred to the extent that it is possible to do so without worsening the financial risk-return profile.

The turning point is reached, however, when the subset of funds aim to have a significantly positive impact on social or environmental concerns. They are also confronted by the market sentiment that responsibility should come as a free add-on. But does our environmental situation allow us to only consider climate change to the extent that it does not affect our financial performance? Any sincere stakeholder in the environment would probably say no. Exercising this view in the investment decision requires a new type of portfolio allocation that is equipped to allow for personal values.

Quantification of values

Within portfolio theory the utility function is a tool that is often applied in order to express a potential preference for certainty. It is generally accepted that small retail investors are somewhat or even very risk-averse, and the utility function can easily capture this feature in the allocation of assets. Questionnaires on gambling preferences are often applied in order to perform the actual quantification. A logical way of incorporating preferences for responsibility could therefore be to enhance this utility function with another dimension (Hallerbach *et al.*, 2002).

Wisebrod (2007) suggests that the habitual mean-variance analysis can be applied to an investment universe such as that situated in the group of investments that have the highest Sharpe's ratios, i.e. the optimal portfolios, the socially dominant portfolio is chosen. The Sharpe's ratio is conventionally calculated as the expected portfolio excess return per unit of risk inherent in the portfolio. If the investor is not willing to compromise on the risk-return profile of the investment, then this approach is quite sufficient. If, on the other hand, the investor has a strong preference for responsibility and for certainty, then this method does not necessarily provide the best solution. The rational, responsible investor will consider the broader set of portfolio attributes: risk, expected return and responsibility.

It is therefore necessarily to quantify the preferences for certainty and responsibility in an integrated manner (see Figure 1). It means that two out of the three relationships need to be determined, since the third relationship will be implicitly given.

Extended evaluation of investment outcome

A very simple way of extending the usual evaluation of investment outcome is to consider the affine combination

$U(x,s)=(1-\alpha)\, u_1(x) + \alpha\, u_2(s)$

where x describes the payoff of the investment while s denotes the weighted portfolio responsibility level. The parameter α can be used to weigh the preference for non-financial outcome against financial outcome appropriately.

The affine combination in Box 1 suggests that the responsible investor also considers how the corresponding value-neutral optimal investment would be constructed and which risk-return profile it would have. Thereby the investor is always well informed of the cost of responsibility.

The shape of utility function

It can be a challenging task for the provider of responsible retail investments to assist in the quantification of U as well as the parameter α. Empirical estimations of these have so far not been possible, due to the lack of data on retail responsible investor behaviour but it will constitute an interesting future investigation. It is indeed a new type of preference but it is important to stress that fundamentally it is no different from the preference for certainty.

Figure 1: Preference for certainty and responsibility

Creating the right incentive

One way to establish the responsibility trade-off is to confront the investor with two opportunities as follows:

- A portfolio with a high and transparent social or environmental impact and with a given Sharpe's ratio.
- A neutral investment constructed using the market portfolio, i.e. the tangency portfolio of the capital market line in the mean variance-analysis.

The latter is the optimal portfolio when considering only financial aspects. By construction it has a higher Sharpe's ratio than the prior opportunity since the market portfolio is defined by the highest possible Sharpe's ratio that can be obtained in a given investment universe.

The question is therefore: what social rating creates the right incentive for the responsible investor to choose one investment over another? The investor can decide to be neutral, or only want to make a responsible investment if it does not largely affect the risk-return profile. Yet, the investor should also have the opportunity to prefer a certain responsibility profile on the grounds of either a lower expected payoff or a higher acceptable risk.

This is the essence of the determination of preferences for responsibility. Note that the general concept of socially aware consumption already takes the quantification of non-materialistic personal values into account. Consider the example of goods sold under the *Fair Trade* label or something as common as organic produce. Both embody the quantification of a price premium based on a personal belief or benefit to the consumer.

The example of organic produce is, however, only valid in this setting when considering the positive environmental impact of the sector, i.e. not considering the health implications of not consuming dangerous chemicals.

The problem of the responsible investor is how to choose a weighted investment portfolio, *w*. It summarises the common maximisation of expected utility, both financial and non-financial, at maturity of the investment (see Box 1).

$$Max_w\, E[U(x,s)] \text{ s.t. } W_0$$

where W_0 loosely describes a budget constraint or initial investment.

Box 1: Common maximisation of expected utility

The setup is technically simplified yet should be conceptually clear: the investment universe is evaluated with integrated preferences for certainty and responsibility.

The right investment

The investor is now equipped to choose an investment that fits with his or her personal values. Some indexes, as the Dow Jones Sustainability Index (DJSI), have established themselves on the best-of-industry method. DJSI World includes the 10% highest socially rated companies in a number of different sub-sectors guaranteeing a reasonable diversification profile (*www.sustainability-index.com*). This type of approach is meaningful, well explained and well founded.

Many SRI mutual funds also establish themselves with similar strategies. For the small retail investor choosing a responsible investment according to the previous section, however, it may not provide the best type of investment. Firstly, the improvement on the common industry average that the index or fund embody in their holdings may not be information that is readily available to the retail investor. Secondly, most of a given industry may not have a major impact on a given social or environmental factor, as even the top 10% can havevery variable attitudes to sustainability. Thus, if an investor is particularly interested in social welfare and global issues, it might be worth selecting a smaller basket of stocks with very high social ratings in the particular area of interest. This would imply that the investor could obtain a large utility premium on the social side in the equation defining the utility function U.

An investor who is willing to compromise the risk-return profile in order to obtain a highly rated investment will thereby be better off and essentially more satisfied with an investment chosen in the socially integrated optimal portfolio model than with the value-neutral conventional counterpart. The suggested meta-model is indented as an encouragement for investors to also consider their personal values in investment activities and to evaluate whether a responsible investment will provide them with an improved investment holding.

Any individual has the right to choose his or her values; religiously, environmentally, socially – or even contra-responsibly, if preferred. What all small retail investors could benefit from, however, is simply to become aware of their personal values: they might be positioned to benefit from a non-financial gain of a responsible investment, which in turn may significantly affect the ultimate level of satisfaction with their investment activities.

The road ahead: the role of education

Altering the norms of an entire industry is by no means simple. An essential key to implementing ethical considerations in the financial market is the education of financial professionals, regulators and teachers at the very beginning of the careers. The priority of what is taught in business schools worldwide plays a major role. Sadly, finance related courses with focus on sustainability concerns, moral conflicts or the human perspective are often simply not offered in a masters programmes in finance. The technical level of the education and a tight time schedule may be the cause, but the fact remains that many financial engineers will eventually have to cope with working on potentially complex underlying human perspectives, even in asset valuation. It is fundamental to understand such questions as: what is fairness in the financial market? How does market regulation seek to balance efficiency and sufficiently equal opportunities without compromising competition and the free market? And what are fair and unfair advantages in terms of access to information?

It is likely to benefit the financial system as such to have both the industry as well as regulators equipped with an early understanding of the necessary conditions for an efficient capital market, the often considered theoretical ideal. The theory of financial contracting includes the question of agency theory that concerns conflict of interest and the respect of confidentiality. As the financial market grows more complex, it is of ever increasing importance that this particular area be properly understood. Consumers often have no choice but to rely on official bodies that oversee competition in order to ensure that they are treated fairly by the various financial institutions. Stakeholders in the industry will all stand to gain from the inclusion of a basic moral code of conduct in the intricate contracting that exists. How else can we expect fund managers *not* to take advantage of the lax definitions of responsible investment, making it a value-generating advantage, when they have been taught in university that rational value-maximisation is the only virtue?

If we consider the financial crisis, ethical aspects of selling practice and financial advice also play a key part in the future development of a healthy financial service sector. The integrity of complex financial products is extremely difficult to guarantee by regulation alone, simply because of their perplexing nature. It is necessary for financial institutions themselves to have a solid understanding of the potential moral conflicts that exist in their line of business. Along with the suggested educational input, morer research on ethical issues in neoclassical finance theory is also essential.

Twenty years ago, Horrigan (1987) already gave a clear Kantian analysis of the most frequent assumptions that exist in many areas of finance. He found clear scenarii of system break-down in several cases. He proved the need for ethics not only within the subjects of qualitative corporate finance but also for the quantitative scene. Since that analysis was made, the complexity of the financial market and pricing models has increased exponentially. Yet they still build on the same underlying norms and values; an observation that only enhances the relevance of Horrigan's study.

People and planet matter

This article aimed to demonstrate two important ways of implementing ethics in finance; portfolio allocation of the small retail investor with preferences for responsibility, and the education of future finance industry stakeholders. We put forward the idea that the financial crisis provides a unique opportunity to engage the general public in an informed, value-based choice of investments as well as to promote awareness of the implications of their investment activities. We also demonstrated that potential personal benefits from a responsible portfolio allocation can exist, and we can conclude that for the SRI industry to thrive, it is vitally important that responsibility is not reduced to a green stamp confered by a loose definition of SRI.

The second lineof implementation looked at the necessary investment in education: business schools worldwide are centrally positioned in developing the integrity and efficient use of ethics in finance. The major theme is the comprehension of underlying, complex non-financial values in finance theory as well as in business practice. So should we invest as if people and planet mattered? Well, it all depends. It depends on what we consider as really important to us, on our values as professionals, individuals and society. If we make sure to feed these values into our financial system, it will produce the right answer.

Bibliography

Hallerbach, W. *et al.*, 2002. *A Framework for Managing a Portfolio of Socially Responsible Investments*, Erasmus Research Institute of Management report, May.

Horrigan, J., 1987. "The Ethics of New Finance", in: *Journal of Business Ethics 6*, 97-110.

Hawken, P., 2004. *Socially Responsible Investing. How the SRI industry has failed to respond to people who want to invest with conscience, and what can be done to change it*, Natural Capital Institute, *www.responsibleinvesting.org*.

Renneboog, L. *et al.*, 2007. *Socially Responsible Investments: Methodology, Risk Exposure and Performance*, ECGI working paper, June.

Wisebrod, J, 2007. "Social Impact Ratings: How to Make Responsible Investment Appealing", in: *Finance & the Common Good/Bien Commun 27*: Chapter 10 in this volume.

23

VIRTUOUS ENTERPRISES: THE PLACE OF CHRISTIAN ETHICS

Jan Thomas Otte

There are certainly many ways of writing a paper about the intersection of business and theology. On the one hand, simply describing the different models of corporate social responsibility (CSR) in the business world and, on the other, summarising those Bible passages that mention business in some way, which certainly would be an interesting if rather unfocused method. Given these various methodological approaches methodology, I have decided to focus on the normative question of Christian ethics. Initially, with a less than theological approach, I shall ask if companies should have a moral obligation to implement CSR; and if so, how this could look in practice without taking an excessively naïve approach.

Christian, corporate and collective responsibility

The term "responsibility" is derived from the Latin "responsabilis", which means able to respond to the obligations and expectations of others. To recognise these responsibilities, managers tend to use a mixture of intuition and rationality. But is it true that only individual persons can be responsible, as they have a conscience? In this context, it is certainly much easier for medium-sized and small companies to live virtuously according to the principles of CSR then it is for bigger companies.

Do companies really have a character and, therefore, can they be made responsible for things? Peter French (1984) initiated this debate twenty years ago: "Certainly a corporation doing something [...] usually can be described as having reasons for *[its]* behaviour. In fact, by virtue of those descriptions they [companies] may be properly held responsible for their behaviour, *ceteris paribus.*" In his argumentation, saying that companies, as well as employees and managers, have a character that includes responsibility, French also uses the terms "reasons", "desires", "intentions", and "decision-making", which support the focus on the character of individuals in CSR. In jurisprudence, companies usually are considered as legal persons.

The church in economic life

With the influence of the Enlightenment and industrialisation in the late eighteenth century, Europe changed politics to provide more economic freedom for business. This was partly a reaction by trade union movements to industrialisation. Individual labour rights were reinforced. At this time, economics as an academic discipline became separated from theology, as the market became a separate dimension from religion and politics.

However today in Germany, one of the most secular countries in modern Europe, the Roman-Catholic and Lutheran-Protestant traditions remain the second biggest employers in the public realm. The church in Germany owns and manages highly regarded companies, especially in three different branches of public life: firstly, as one of the market leaders in healthcare including hospitals and homes for the elderly; secondly, in education, such as universities, schools, and kindergartens; and finally, in the media, including magazines, bookstores, and radio.

While taking the separation between church and state into consideration, the established churches still have close ties to politics in ways that differ from the Evangelical movement in the USA. They even provide more jobs than the two biggest privatised companies, the postal services and the telecom industry in Germany (Schwarz, 2005). Globally, many NGOs such as the YMCA, World Vision, and the Salvation Army are also linked to politics and use their Christian background as a guideline for their work on CSR.

Are companies responsible?

John Ruggies, who works for the UN and is a member of the faculty of the Harvard Kennedy School, wrote in a special report in the Economist in 2008, that the *theological* question of the obligations for CSR would be irrelevant today, as most companies would already implement them. According to this special report, "some of the big banks, including Goldman Sachs and UBS, have started to integrate environmental, social and governance issues in some of their equity research" (Special issue on corporate social responsibility, *The Economist*, 29.01.2008). In this regard, most scholars and practitioners today focus more on the how and less on the whether of doing CSR.

The conclusions of the Economist, bearing in mind an enlightened form of self interest, were that failing to take CSR into account would be risky: "Ignoring something that makes business sense" would constitute a certain recipe for failure in the management of the company.

In this context, Peter Pruzan (2008) raises three challenging questions: can a company be responsible? Why should it be responsible? And what role does the Christian faith play in this business case?

In times of financial crisis, managers tend to speak on the basis of their own visions, moral virtues, and financial values, but also increasingly on that of their company. But do companies also possess intuition, empathy, and reflection? Pruzan argues two possible affirmations concerning this idea: 1) companies are judicial entities with legal responsibilities; and 2) companies are involved in the social system of relationships with share- and stakeholders. Similar to the phenomenon at a football match, in which fans tend to say that "we" (they) have shot the golden goal, even employees tend to speak and think in the first-person plural, that "we" have lost our jobs at General Motors in Detroit, for example. In such a participative and self-referential corporate culture, people tend to feel that way because these interpersonal actions are important in the development of the individual's identity.

Values and virtues

Christian faith was founded on unique virtues, that can be considered to have derived from Jesus' greatest commandment to love thy neighbour as thyself (Matthew 22:37-40). From Adam as the first worker in Biblical times who experienced the sweaty nature of work, via the Scriptures of sin and the fall (Genesis) to the end of a greedy and worried world (Revelation), finance has not been intrinsically connotated at all pessimistically in theological thought. The Old Testament in particular speaks quite deferentially about money issues, although this exegesis is not the focus of this paper. In modern times however, some discrepancies between faith and finance on Wall Street are frequently discussed in a controversial and sometimes even hostile manner.

In the current financial crisis, public theology has gained new relevance as it focuses on the intersection of Christian ethics and capital-oriented finance. How do Christian ethics look in business? What are the challenges a Christian manager faces in the neo-liberal economy?

Many managers have started to reflect on their values (finance), virtues (faith), and on Christian ethics in between. Especially in the current crisis, managers with strong leadership skills and education feel able to integrate both CSR and the Christian faith in the workplace. To some extent, one cannot overlook the fact that pastors, churches, and theology are distinct from managers, companies, and economics. However, many of the theological-minded have still missed an important issue: how to integrate the workplace Monday to Friday in a Sunday-centered church that also endorses CSR

I do not want to say that business is all good, since the current crisis shows how immediately Wall Street needs more moral virtues in addition to the financially-driven values. Secular companies need managers and pastors who encourage those who are in despair, but try to live according to Christian virtues rather than merely the values of stocks. As a field of theological research in Christian ethics, it can be assessed that in practice, CSR has received more attention from Christian managers than in the general teaching of business schools.

Certainly diverse strategies and political views exist on transforming CSR and Christian ethics in companies. Having evaluated both useful and counterproductive strategies, the paramount conditions of CSR are "to demonstrate that spirituality brings new dimensions that are otherwise inaccessible by an approach that is only humanistic" (Pauchant, 2002).

CSR and Christian ethics in companies

In this paper, it is argued that CSR stands at the intersection of Christian ethics (faith) and business management (finance). For clarity and control of arguments in the areas of conflict, the terms "virtues" and "principles" will refer to the faith aspects; and the terms "values" and "preferences" will refer to the financial ones.

Prayers, teachings, and sermons preached in the realm of the church are neither able nor bound to make concrete decisions on CSR in the economic sphere, but they do evoke more important issues than the clergy might imagine: convincing managers again that the church does not remain stuck in a counterproductive, biased, or one-way defence of Christian traditions.

Christian communities can also invite managers to their meetings, or visit them in their workplaces. This can offer unique opportunities for developing Christian faith, and for building constructive relationships through mature identities, as well as obeying virtues that help business to become more thoughtful in the light of CSR. In this ethical framework, even mergers and acquisitions, which usually tend to cause reductions in labour, although they are aimed at ensuring the continued existence of the company in a competitive market of global capitalism, are merely business cases that require strong quantitative skills, and where "the fundamental principle, 'do good and avoid evil', cannot become the basis on which to decide whether to go through" (Pauchant, 2002).

A nominative approach

Probably, the answer to the research question of whether or not companies have a moral obligation to implement CSR is not a satisfactory one, but it does aim to build greater clarity: it depends on the individual cases in the grey areas. Yet, in a black-and-white scheme, no clear answer can be given, because the effectiveness of CSR depends on the knowledge of the grey areas. Instead of describing the faith at work movement, which would tend too much towards sociology or edifying literature, especially that written by Christian-evangelical scholars in the last two years, I prefer to take the nominative approach. This is not problem-free as to how economists qualify and quantify things, even though these value judgments are necessary in everyday business practice. Christian ethics has criticised these values in light of the eminent virtues that define the difference between mere business goals and the ultimate good (Fischer, 2002).

3C model: character, company, Christ

With regard to the three major models of CSR presented in Figure 1, I would like to examine the normative ways in which managers make their individual moral decisions: on the one hand based on economy, they make the more "rational" decisions; on the other hand, from a theological point of view, the more "intuitive" decisions.

CSR is based on the relationships of the *character* of both managers and their employees, the corporate *culture*, and *Christ* as the ultimate transcendental purpose. Considering the micro, mezzo, and macro level of the moral obligations for CSR, all these fields are linked to each other. But there is much evidence to be found in the interdisciplinary literature of psychology and management that it is more efficient for CSR to use *identity* as a starting point, be it that of individual managers or their employees. Their personal interests, conflicts, and broader education through role-models are important – especially in the high-pressure business environment of Wall Street.

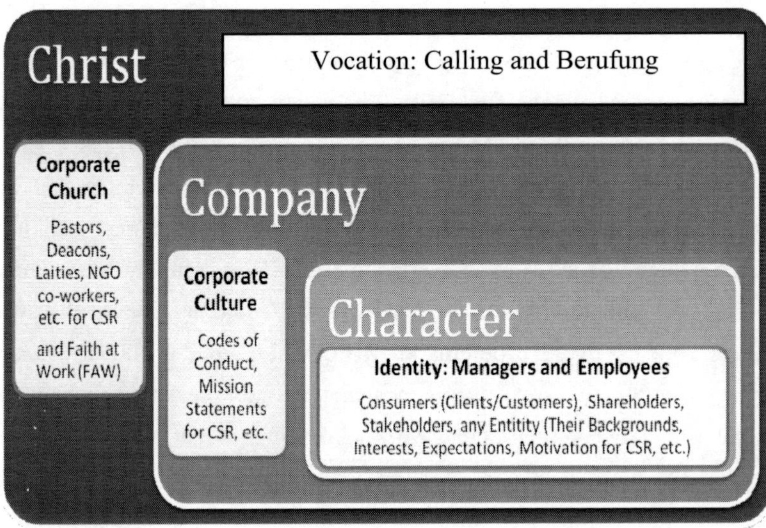

Figure 1: Integrative 3C-model of CSR

There should always be congruence on all three levels, harmonising the character of the individual, the culture of the company, and faith in Christ beyond the rationality of economics.

Managers should intrinsically encourage CSR through a less objective, and living attitude to corporate culture. CSR should also be instrumentalised, as this can be a support for virtuous behaviour, rather than considering individuals as a means to an end. In order to uphold CSR in an open and encouraging way to employees, all moral agents (including consumers) should behave in a less biased and more considered way, rather than pointing the finger at managers.

I suppose that CSR is really more than just legal compliance. CSR cannot be just a commitment to meet the legal standards through avoiding harm, as most people with no particular religious affiliation tend to do this anyway.

Individual character

CSR focuses firstly on the development of *individual* character. When individuals go too far in their imitation of role models, this may partially explain a lack of morality in the individual manager's. Managers behave differently in dealing with the interests of employees, clients, shareholders, and stakeholders, as was shown during the events of the current Wall Street financial crisis. Particularly in investment banking, which sometimes tends to reduce people in global companies to human capital, the alienation from higher virtues created by financial-driven values appears to be problematic. Recognising that these virtues are linked to a person's identity, many managers complain that there is no connection between their actual work and their personal identity.

Perhaps these managers feel this way because they never received any deep moral education during their time in business school. Achieving an MBA degree is still commonly understood as a stepping stone in one's career.

Moral education through role models is one of the key factors in implementing CSR in the corporate culture. Certainly, there appear to be quite a few discrepancies between what happens on a day-to-day basis and the desired behaviour expressed in the mission statement on the company's website. Some managers probably try to justify their behaviour because they never had any role models in their youth. In a survey of Harvard University MBA graduates, however, many young managers admitted "that they had received explicit instructions from their middle-manager bosses or felt strong organisational pressures to do things that they believed were sleazy, unethical, or sometimes illegal" (Boatright, 1999). Opposing a widespread opinion of virtue-neutral education, Harvard psychiatrists have found that both students and executives expect both virtue and even silence in teaching matters, which emphasises the responsibilities of role models (Piper, 1993).

Certainly, exemplary behaviour of the CEO and a more CSR-oriented human resource department are keys to a virtuous company. Despite the fact that most business schools paid little attention to this in the period between the fall of stock markets after 9/11 and the speculative climb before Black Friday on 2 October 2008, "management education can and should be more than the transfer of skills and knowledge; it should be a moral endeavour" (Piper, 1993). Students should focus particularly on a more participative, joined-up attitude towards CSR.

Can business ethics be taught?

In a triangle of virtue, knowledge, and skills, Thomas Piper (1993) has developed questions according to implicit models of CSR and the development of corporate culture: "How should an individual decision-maker, confronted with an ethical dilemma, reach a decision that is competitively, organisationally, economically, and ethically sound?"

According to Piper, CSR should be included in the mission of a business school as "a story of hope and concern, of progress and yet unfinished initiatives", trying to rebalance the educational dilemmas of ethics in management. In the system of moral obligations for CSR, business relationships should be "based on respect, honesty, fairness, and trust as fundamental to the effective and ethical functioning of organisations".

The question of how, the connecting factor, the methodology and the hermeneutics of CSR remain controversial. Piper writes that it would be relevant for CSR-oriented companies to exhibit through "rigorous reasoning, not indoctrination – that an active, enlightened concern for ethics and corporate responsibility often is the right path for a firm and for the individual in the long run, economically, organisationally, and competitively".

Assuming that business ethics can be taught, norms can be ambivalent, as some managers may say that rules are meant to be broken for the sake of maintaining a competitive edge. Certainly, norms can also be reactive, as they are usually based on past experience and their application to the *individual* character is not yet sufficiently precise.

It is no surprise, then, that even CSR-oriented or theologically minded individuals often tend to say "it wasn't me" or "everyone is doing it". Most managers obviously do not wish to instigate wrong or evil actions, but neither do they want to expose themselves too far by preaching to others in matters of law, ethical understanding, or social acceptance. Many prospective employees, both consciously or unintentionally decide to go with the flow. Managers in the course of their careers have to face many ethical challenges in different corporate cultures that all are subject to various expectations and pressures from their consumers, employees, and even society. However, decisions in business do have to be made, and temptation is rife.

But there are also dynamics that may inspire more CSR-oriented behaviour in *individual* managers. In the secular model of CSR as well as in Christian ethics, individuals trust in the idea of a better future, believing that their investments will change the quality of life. Interpersonal relationships in business require confidence in *identity*, maintaining moral principles and virtues in the widest sense.

The ethos of the company

CSR is also established within corporate culture and shaped by the individual identities of managers and employees. Every company has a culture, whether or not it is intentionally managed. Left to themselves, employees usually remain hesitant about implementing CSR in their business decisions. CSR-oriented actions may create jealousy among colleagues, or even isolate them from an existing culture of gossip, unfair pay scales, investment fraud, or exposure to job insecurity in times of financial crisis. This may be true of a person who has just been hired, or applied to an existing employee who needs more ethical guidance, personal support, and CSR education. All people bring their own virtues to the corporate culture, but many still leave them at the door. Individual ethics are therefore reshaped by the existing *ethos* of the company. However, if managers find an already existing, working model of CSR, it is also much easier for employees to respect these rules.

Many prospective employees search the web looking for a company's formal mission statement and aspects of its corporate culture before applying for a job. During the hiring process, applicants usually hesitate to challenge the interviewer with questions on the company's mission statement, code of conduct, and other statements that are posted on the website. New employees later discover any discrepancy between the stated intentions of management and the real goings on in the company. CSR has valuable side effects on the enhanced management of human resources, public relations, and financial risk. CSR not only serves to emphasise the motivation in human resources, it also contributes to the reputation of the company in public relations.

The purpose of CSR is not to make huge short-term profits, but to *transform* the character and culture of business in the long term. As a result, managers may tend to think of CSR as something it is nice to have. CSR should therefore be presented on the basis of its moral ability to transform and improve business. In accordance with the principles of the Christian faith, CSR should always be implemented freely and responsibly, but not as a tool to implement an excessively financially-driven business that might result in frustration at all levels within the company.

CSR and religion

Finally, CSR is derived from the Christian faith. Discussions on CSR are all about human actions, which have always been shaped by religion in the history of humanity.

Obviously, the first problem when theorising and discussing CSR in the context of religion is: which religious language or tradition we are talking about? Which specific faith, if any, has shaped the business practice of the company? Although there are sensitivities and complexities contained in these questions, we have to be aware of the dangers of slipping into Biblicism or eclecticism. Nevertheless, I believe that the Scriptures have been written with authority and can be understood through the Holy Spirit. We may become eclectic if we become excessively selective in the interpretation of CSR models or if we communicate them too one-dimensionally or to excess in public. We believe that an obvious link remains that underpins both faith and work in the basic concept of CSR. This can be found politically between left and right; socially between business and society; and ideologically between Christian ethics and capitalism.

The third dimension has taken on new relevance because of the financial crisis in capitalism, the decline of the established church in Christianity, and also the breakdown of traditional family structures at home, which is where strong foundations for ethical education were previously provided. On the other hand, longer work weekends, more intense social networking on the Internet, and the globalisation of companies encourage anonymity.

The Christian faith reconciles any existing gaps in ambiguous relationships through Jesus Christ, the scriptures of the Bible, and the fellowship of the Christian community. An example of this are the terms "corporation" (breaking bread at the Eucharist), "company" (having Christian fellowship), and even "economy" (salvation through the Holy Spirit within the Trinity), which have roots in Christian theological vocabulary. Becoming aware which public language is used in church history, it becomes possible to find patchworks of marketplace issues such as the Benedictine *ora et labora*.

In modern times, the Christian Evangelical movement in the Southern states of the USA, as well as other faith traditions like the Islamic-Gulen movement in Turkey, show the validity as well as the independence of academic public theology in the corporate world.

The church and economic issues

This suggests that the practice and development of CSR can be examined in light of the church's interest in dealing with economic and social issues. The church was not only created out of idealistic, altruistic, or selfless interests; giving makes people feel good because they have the resources to do so, and have gained the ability, discerned a certain vocation, or meaning in their own lives through God. As a strategic moment, the theological doctrine of vocation could be linked to human resources, both inside and outside the company. Martin Luther has provided meaning and vocation to profession, in the German term *Berufung*, which means both worship and work, and is similar to the Hebrew word *Avodah*.

In the church, leaders have started to ask how they might re-involve the missing majority of members who are involved in the secular marketplace; in companies, managers have again started to reflect on their business ethics, seeking a higher purpose, a meaning in ordinary work, and enhanced relationships through these and other virtues: trust, honesty, reliability, and credibility, all of which the Christian faith considers as challenges in the secular business world.

CSR is not a mere marketing tools kit aimed only at increasing company profits, or used to avoid grey areas in the law, circumventing the checks and balances of the federal government. Many companies certainly continue to interpret CSR that way, lowering their external costs by improved public relations and less costly lawsuits.

Some steps forward

When faced by the difficulties of moral education in management, Joseph Wharton founded the Wharton Business School (University of Pennsylvania) as the first business school in the USA. He did not do this in order to make a lot of money, but rather to proclaim the importance of CSR "as a vehicle for social enterprises" in the poorer suburbs of Southern Philadelphia. The European Business Ethics Network (EBEN), has helped many scholars to engage in discussions on CSR between members of academia, the churches, and the business world. This is illustrated in the academic sphere, with Archie Carroll as the right-wing "Godfather of CSR" and Peter Ulrich as the left-wing first chair for business ethics in the German-speaking area. Another example is the churches with the latest declaration by the German Protestant Church (EKD) on CSR and the role of the Christian faith as well as the business world with Klaus Leisinger from the Swiss Novartis foundation, one of the biggest global pharmaceutical companies, who was one of the first to sign the United Nations Global Compact. Unquestionably, the entire debate on CSR in the last 30 years is not trouble-free, in terms of how to manage the role of managers and employees, of stakeholders and shareholders (Crane, 2001).

To take this moral behaviour to an extreme, for the sake of clarity, the cases of fraud by Enron, as seen in the interview with Sherron Watkins and WorldCom, show the riskiness of those business operations that are the closest to the ethical margins. So from the very legal minimum and worst case scenario, there are quite a few incentives for any company to behave ethically.

Do absolute ethical standards exist?

CSR itself still needs more congruence, integrity, and adapting to the individual business than what offered by the Christian faith. In fact, any law, scripture passage, or conception of CSR require a degree of interpretation and depend on the given situation, and individual moral discernment. It would seem too rigid to state that there is any absolute moral standard beyond the Ten Commandments and Jesus' summary of the Law. So, is there any absolute moral rule businessmen should obey? Does morality change if businessmen engage in different roles? What would ethical training in the human resources department look like?

Individuals make very different moral judgments. Even if CSR were merely understood as a legal issue, contracts would require deeper agreement as far as keeping promises that have been made. Doug Lennick and Fred Kiel (2005) write on the importance of purpose and meaning in business: "Scientists who study behaviour tell us that humans have an innate need to make sense out of our lives". A businessman, who has discovered his vocation due to God's hearing him, as well as his own God-given talents and passions, is likely to be more successful holistically speaking, in achieving a sustainable balance. Leaders as role models need to be better understood, rather than giving way to their emotions, because if they "lack emotional control or insight into the moral needs of their followers, the work environment suffers". Lennick emphasises the moral lessons directly and indirectly communicated by the business leader as "giving back is more than a public-relations tool". This is in accordance with the Bible, as the more one gives, striving for the well-being of surrounding communities, the more one ultimately gets back.

In the rationality of economics it might not be initially clear that stewardship means more to some extent than mere ethical good.

As a critical tool, business ethics actually enable relationships, trust, and the redistribution of wealth needed in a global business community to simultaneously increase the markets for economic goods and services. Lennick embraces a universal list of virtues that appear in the Bible in a different language. Without any particular evaluation as to the order of presentation, they are integrity, responsibility, compassion, forgiveness, generosity, commitment to a transcending power, justice, temperance/self-discipline, humility, wisdom, courage, and care for living things and the environment.

The author also recommends that people identify core values such as affiliation and thriftiness, comfort and safety, wisdom and gratitude, community and friendship, loyalty and altruism, inner peace and open-mindedness, and last but not least, perseverance and meaningful work. *De facto*, managers are seen by their employees as role models in a way that could be even "more powerful and more persuasive than that of churches, schools, and families". Instead of blaming both companies and churches, theology and the behavioural sciences should work more collaboratively on CSR.

Bibliography

Boatright, J., 1999. *Ethics in Finance,* Oxford: Blackwell Publishing.

Crane, A. (ed.), 2008. *The Oxford Handbook of Corporate Social Responsibility*, New York: Oxford University Press.

Fischer, J., 2002. *Theologische Ethik: Grundwissen und Orientierung,* Stuttgart:, Kohlhammer.

French, P., 1984. *Collective and Corporate Responsibility,* New York: Columbia University Press.

Lennick, D. and Kiel, F., 2005. *Moral Intelligence: Enhancing Business Performance and Leadership*, Upper Saddle River, NJ: Wharton School Publishing.

Pauchant, T. (ed.), 2002. *Ethics and Spirituality at Work: Hopes and Pitfalls of the Search for Meaning in Organisations,* Westport, CT: Quorum Books.

Piper, T., 1993. *Can ethics be taught?: perspectives, challenges, and approaches,* Cambridge, MA: Harvard Business School.

Pruzan, P., 2008. "Spirituality as a Firm Basis for Corporate Social Responsibility", in: Crane, A. (ed.), *The Oxford Handbook of Corporate Social Responsibility*, New York: Oxford University Press.

Schwarz, F., 2005. *Wirtschaftsimperium Kirche: Der mächtigste Konzern Deutschlands,* Frankfurt: Campus Verlag.

Stackhouse, M. *et al.*, 1995. *On Moral Business*, Grand Rapids, MI: Eerdmans.

APPENDICES

THE GLOBAL PRIZE JURY

Prof Marc Chesney

Professor of Finance at the University of Zurich. Previously in Paris, he was Professor and Associate Dean at HEC, President of the CEBC (*Centre d'Etudes sur le Blanchiment et la Corruption*) and an external expert with the World Bank. He has published articles and books in the areas of quantitative Finance and also of financial crime mechanisms. In addition, he focuses on the subject of Ethics and Finance. At the University of Zurich, he is member of the Board of the Graduate Programme for interdisciplinary Research in Ethics and co-organiser of the Ethical Finance Research Series. He is also member of the advisory Board of *Finance & Common Good/Bien Commun*. Marc Chesney holds a PhD in Finance from the University of Geneva and obtained his Habilitation from the Sorbonne University.

Dr Carol Cosgrove-Sacks

Robin's mother. Lives and works in Geneva. She was formerly Director of Trade in the United Nations in Geneva (1994-2005); since 2006 she is a Professor at the College of Europe, Bruges; a Professor at the Europa Institute, University of Basel; and the Senior Advisor on International Standards Policy to OASIS, the global eBusiness standards organisation. She also maintains interest in some British academic centres, including the Institute of Development Studies (IDS), University of Sussex, and the Centre for Euro-Asian Studies (CEAS), University of Reading.

Prof Henri-Claude de Bettignies

Holds the AVIVA Chair in Leadership and Responsibility and is Emeritus Professor of Asian Business and Comparative Management at INSEAD He is also Distinguished Professor of Global Responsible Leadership at the China Europe International Business School (CEIBS), in Shanghai. He had been teaching ethics at Stanford Business School (for the last 16 years), and he started and led the development of the ethics initiative at INSEAD before moving to China where currently he is creating, with CEIBS, the Euro-China Centre for Leadership and Responsibility. Professor de Bettignies is director of AVIRA, an INSEAD programme pioneering a new approach to enlighten CEOs. Henri-Claude was the founder of the Euro-Asia Centre at INSEAD, seeds of INSEAD successful development in Asia. He is the Founder and Director of CEDRE (Centre for the Study of Development and Responsibility), Chairman of the LVMH Asia Scholarships, member of the Editorial Board of five academic journals and he is a member of the Board of Jones Lang LaSalle.

François Debiesse

After graduating from the HEC, François Debiesse joined the Bank of Paris and the Netherlands in 1971, holding various management positions. In 1999 he became Director of the Private Bank BNP Paribas, and in 2008 he was appointed Director of BNP Paribas Wealth Management. From 1995 to 2008 he also serves as Chairman of BNP Paribas. François Debiesse is now President of the Fondation de l'Orangerie for individual philanthropy since 2009 and Advisor for Philanthropy and Microfinance for BNP Paribas Wealth Management since 2011.

Christopher de Mattos

A director of London-based investment manager RAB Capital plc and sits on the boards of a number of regulated and unregulated investment funds. He has spent over 20 years in the financial services industry, working as a financial analyst and investment banker in Europe and Latin America. Christopher joined the founding team at RAB in 1999 and, as Finance Director, was instrumental in taking the company to flotation on London's AIM market in 2004. He holds a degree in Mechanical Engineering from Imperial College, London and gained SERC and Kitchener scholarships to study for his MBA at INSEAD Having reduced his involvement in the day-to-day management of RAB, he has taken a particular interest in the role of the board in promoting corporate governance in financial services businesses.

Prof Paul H. Dembinski

The initiator and Director of the Foundation of the Observatoire de la Finance. The mission of the Observatoire de la Finance is to promote awareness of ethical concerns in financial activities and the financial sector. Paul H. Dembinski is the founder and editor of the quarterly bilingual journal entitled *Finance & the Common Good/Bien Commun*. In parallel, he is partner and co-founder (with Alain Schoenenberger) of Eco'Diagnostic, an independent economic research institute working for both government and private clients in Switzerland and elsewhere. Paul H Dembinski is also Professor at University of Fribourg where he teaches "International Competition and Strategy".

Dr Robert Alan Feldman

Chief Economist and Co-Director of Japan Research at Morgan Stanley Japan Securities Co., Ltd. As part of Morgan Stanley's global economics team, he is responsible for forecasting the Japanese economy and interest rates. He is a regular commentator on *World Business Satellite*, the nightly business programme of TV Tokyo. Prior to joining Morgan Stanley in 1998, Robert was from 1990-97 the chief economist for Japan for Salomon Brothers. He worked for the International Monetary Fund from 1983-89, in the Asian, European, and Research Departments. Robert has a PhD in Economics from the Massachusetts Institute of Technology, where he concentrated on international finance and development. He did his undergraduate work at Yale University, where he took BAs in both Economics and Japanese Studies, graduating phi beta kappa, summa cum laude. Before he entered graduate school, he worked at both the Federal Reserve Bank of New York and at the Chase Manhattan Bank.

Dr Philippa Foster Back

Has over 25 years of business experience. She began her career at Citibank NA before joining Bowater in their Corporate Treasury Department in 1979, leaving in 1988 as Group Treasurer. She was Group Finance Director at DG Gardner Group, a training organisation, prior to joining Thorn EMI in 1993 as Group Treasurer. She was appointed Institute of Business Ethics' Director in August 2001. Philippa Foster Back has a number of external appointments, including at the Ministry of Defence, The Institute of Directors and the Association of Corporate Treasurers, where she was President from 1999 to 2000. In 2006 she was appointed Chairman of the UK Antarctic Heritage Trust.

Dr Andrew Hilton

Director of the Centre for the Study of Financial Innovation, a non-profit think-tank, supported by 65 City institutions, that looks at the future of the global financial system. The CSFI was set up 13 years ago, and has since published three books and around 80 reports. More significantly, it has organised well over 750 round-tables on issues of pressing interest in the financial services sector including EMU, the single market, the Internet, small business finance, high-tech start-ups, microfinance and regulation. Andrew Hilton also runs a small economic and financial consultancy. He has worked for the World Bank in Washington and has run a financial advisory service for the *Financial Times* in New York. He is a board member of the Observatoire de la finance in Geneva. Andrew Hilton has a PhD from the University of Pennsylvania, an MBA from Wharton and an MA from New College, Oxford. He was appointed OBE in 2005.

Peter Gakunu

Until 2010, an Alternate Executive Director at the International Monetary Fund in charge of Africa Group One constituency. Before joining the Fund, he served as Special Advisor to the Kenya Cabinet in charge of economic reforms from February 2003 to October 2004. In September 2000, he joined the "Dream Team", a team of high level personalities put together by the World Bank and UNDP to advise the Kenya Government on reforms. He worked as Economic Secretary and Director of Planning in the Ministry of Finance and Planning until December 2002. He coordinated the first Poverty Reduction Strategy Paper for Kenya. In 2003 he was appointed Permanent Secretary in the Ministry of Environment. Prior to returning to Kenya, he worked with the African Carribean and Pacific Group in Brussels from 1986 to 2000 as Director of Trade, and from 1977 to 1986 as Trade Expert in the ACP Secretariat. Dominique Jacquet is Visiting Scholar at Insead Social Innovation Center and Professor of Corporate Finance at Cedep, University of Paris Ouest and Ecole des Ponts ParisTech. He is a civil engineer (Ecole des Ponts), holds an MBA from Insead and a PhD from the University of Bordeaux. Before starting an academic career, he has been a finance executive in American and French corporations, holding controller, treasurer and CFO positions. His main areas of interests are the relationship with business and finance, the role of incentives in sustainable value creation and the link between uncertainty and financial strategy.

Peter O'Connor

An experienced global and regional asset allocation and manager selection adviser for financial institutions, family offices and charities. He is Chairman/Lead Director of a number of publicly quoted investment/production companies with particular personal experience in Asia for the past 30 years. After boarding school in Ireland, Peter O'Connor read Economics and Law at Trinity College Dublin and King's Inns Dublin respectively. He has lived and worked in London and Hong Kong, and he travelled frequently to most Asian countries, Canada and emerging economies in Europe.

Jean-Christophe Pernollet

Is a graduate from IEP and EDHEC and has completed the Columbia Business School Senior Executive Programme. As a lead bank auditor recognised by the Federal Banking Commission, he is a financial services industry specialist and benefits from more than fifteen years of working experience, three of which in Paris and two in New York. He is currently a member of the board at EFG Private Bank UK and Chief Financial Officer at EFG International.

John Plender

After taking his degree at Oxford University, joined Deloitte, Plender, Griffiths & Co in the City of London in 1967, qualifying as a chartered accountant in 1970. He then moved into journalism and became financial editor of *The Economist* in 1974, where he remained until joining the UK Foreign Office policy planning staff in 1980. On leaving the Foreign Office, he became a senior editorial writer and columnist at the *Financial Times*, an assignment he combined until recently with current affairs broadcasting for the BBC and Channel 4. A past chairman of Pensions and Investment Research Consultants (PIRC), John Plender has served on the London Stock Exchange's quality of markets advisory committee and the UK government's Company Law Review steering group. He is a non-executive director of Quintain PLC, a FTSE 250 company. His book, *All You Need To Know About Ethics And Finance*, is published by Longtail Publishing.

Domingo Sugranyes

Graduated from the University of Fribourg, Switzerland, in 1969. He was General Secretary of the International Christian Union of Business Executives (UNIAPAC), between 1973 and 1981. He joined MAPFRE, Spain's leading insurance group in 1981. He was active in the international development of the group in Latin America and in Reinsurance worldwide. From 1989 to 2007 he was in charge of the group's listed holding company and member of the group's executive. As complementary activities, Domingo Sugranyes was President of UNIAPAC from 1997/2000 and is currently Chairman of the Board of *Centesimus Annus Pro Pontifice Foundation*, a Vatican Center for Christian Social Teaching.

The Right Reverend Justin Welby

A senior executive in a UK oil company before ordination in the Church of England, Justin Welby has written extensively on ethics and finance. Previously the Dean of Liverpool Cathedral, he became the Bishop of Durham in September 2011. He is a member of the House of Lords.

THE IBERO-AMERICAN JURY

Juan José Almagro

Has a doctorate *cum laude* in Labour Sciences, as well as a degree in law. He specialised in public law, and is a qualified lawyer. He also studied economy. He is honorary professor of the University of Madrid, and lecturer in the Masters of Social Responsibility if the University of Alcala de Henares. Juan José Almagro was visiting lecturer at the Institute for Executive Development (IEDE) of the University of San Pablo CEU, at the *Instituto de Empresa* and various other business schools. Juan José Almagro works for MAPFRE, where he has held various management positions. He is a past president of the Human Resources Department, and General Director of Communication and Social Responsibility of the Group as well as General Director of the MAPFRE Institute of Social Affairs. He has given over one hundred lectures at universities, fora and institutions in both Spain and other countries, particularly in Latin America, on themes linked to the insurance sector and business, communication, leadership, the management of human resources and Social Responsibility. He is currently Member of different boards of directors of MAPFRE group.

Roberto Delgado Gallart

For the last 26 years has carried out dedicated social work with some of the most vulnerable social groups in Mexico and has trained many generations of new social workers on Mexico. This work won him the National Altruism Prize in 2004, bestowed by the Mexican Association of Private Welfare Institutions (l'*Asociación Mexicana de Instituciones de Asistencia Privada*). He also developed the first postgraduate programme in Social Responsibility in Latin America. He is the founder of Latin American Centre for Social Responsibility of the University of Anáhuac where he created the Diploma in Administration of Institutions and Social Welfare (*Diplomado de Administración de Instituciones de Asistencia Social*). This diploma course is also available in the groups in Cancún, Cozumel, León, Oaxaca, Puebla, Xalapa, Quintana Roo, and Torreón. This course has now been run for Twenty-three successive years. Roberto Delgado Gallart has also received recognition such as the Latin American Prize for Educational Excellence (*Premio Iberoamericano a la Excelencia Educativa*) in Peru in 2004 as well as many other awards and over 200 different diplomas and degrees.

Prof Paul H Dembinski

See Appendix 1.

Eduard Dommen

A specialist in economic ethics. He is past President of the Scientific Committee of the Swiss Network of International Studies (*www.ruig-gian.org*) and is currently a member of the Scientific Committee of the Swiss Network of International Studies (*www.snis.ch*). He is a member of the Actares association Shareholders for a sustainable economy (*www.actares.ch*), and member of the editorial board of the review *Finance and the Common Good/Bien Commun*. He was a founder member of the Ethics Committee of the Swiss Alternative Bank (*Banque Alternative Suisse*) and a member of the Council of the Caisse Publique des Prêts Contre Garantie as well as a member of the Council of the RAFAD Foundation, an institution that guarantees micro-credit. Eduard Dommen has been a university lecturer, but has spent most of his career before he retired as UNCTAD investigator. He written and compiled several books on the subject of economic ethics.

Fernando Flores Maio

Sociologist and journalist, contributor and columnist for several Argentine newspapers, was since 1990 director of the "Business Challenge" symposia, in Argentina, in France at the Institut des Hautes Etudes de l'Amérique latine and in Coface. Since 2001, he is the founder and director of the Ecumenical Social Forum, which disseminates the concept of social responsibility, realises ethical campaigns, and rescues core values with symposia in Latin America. Fernando Flores Maio is the director of the Open Chair of Social Responsibility and Citizenship, which began in 2002 in Argentina with the help of Georgetown University, and later from other universities including the University of Salamanca and the Rey Juan Carlos de Madrid. He organised presentations at the Instituto Italo Latinoamericano in Rome and at the Gregorian University and he is the author of several essays, including "Los hippies-Introducción", "Rebelión Juvenil y Cambio Social" y "Comunismo o Reino de Dios".

Following a short career in as a civil engineer, Filomeno Mira Candel joined the MAFRE group at the end of the 1970s as an industrial risk-prevention engineer. Since then he has held various management positions within the Group. He is now Vice-President of the Board of the MAPFRE Foundation, a priority shareholder of MAPFRE SA and President of the Executive Committee. After retiring from management positions, he remained a member of the Board of MAPFRE SA and other companies in the MAPFRE groups. He is also a member of the assembly of the Geneva Association and member of the Board of the Foundation of the Pontifical University of Salamanca. Filomeno Mira Candal was President of the Insurance Commission of the International Chamber of Commerce of Paris from 1994-1997, as well as president of AISAM, the International Association of Mutual Insurance Companies (*Asociación Internacional de Compañías de Seguros Mutual*) from 2002-2004.

Pal-André Sanglard

After working as Assistant in the Department of Political Economy of the University of Geneva, he was an economist in the Federal Department of foreign economic affairs. From 1978-1979 he was a research fellow at Stanford University and MIT. In 1979 he was nominated as head of Public Finance of the Canton of Jura, and since 1982 he has been a lecturer in public finance in Geneva University. From 1984-1989 he was a member of the executive committee of the World Economic Forum. Since 1989, Paul-André Sanglard has been an independent economist. He is currently President of the Board of the Banque Cantonale du Jura in Porrentruy as well as member of several other Boards. Paul-André Sanglard is also a member of the Board of the Foundation of the *Observatoire de la Finance.*

Leire San Jose

Professor of Finance at the University of the Basque Country, Bilbao (*www.ehu.es*) and visiting scholar at the University of Huddersfield (*www.hud.ac.uk*) where she is a member of the Financial Ethics and Governance Research Group (FEGReG). Her doctoral thesis examining the development of new technologies in the cash management gained the distinction of Summa Cum Laude unanimously and received a special prize. Leire San Jose is also specialised in social economy. She was president of the Scientific Committee of the XVII Congress of the European Business Ethics Network Spain in 2010. Currently, she combines her academic interests and research in the field of corporate finance, cash flow management in the short term, with themes of ethics and corporate social responsibility. Leire San Jose has also received the first Robin Cosgrove Prize for Ethics in Finance in the first Ibero-American competition sponsored by MAPFRE.

Simão Davi Silber

Professor in the Faculty of Economy, Business and Accounting of the University of Sao Paulo. For the last 18 years Simão Davi Silber has successively held the post of Research Coordinator (1991-1994), then Head of Research (1995-1999), followed by that of President Director of FIPE, the Foundation for Economic Research (*Fundação Instituto de Pesquisas Econômicas*) from1999-2003. He is currently member of the Board of FIPE. Since 2007 he has also been a member of the Conseil Supérieur d'Etudes Avancées – FIESP. His most recent publication (together with Marcos S. Jank) is *Comparative Trade Practice: Performance and Organisational Models* (*Políticas Comerciais Comparadas: Desempenho e Modelos Organizacionais*, Editora Saraiva, 2007).

Domingo Sugranyes

Graduated from the University of Fribourg, Switzerland, in 1969. He was General Secretary of the International Christian Union of Business Executives (UNIAPAC), between 1973 and 1981. He joined MAPFRE, Spain's leading insurance group in 1981. He was active in the international development of the group in Latin America and in Reinsurance worldwide. From 1989 to 2007 he was in charge of the group's listed holding company and member of the group's executive. As complementary activities, Domingo Sugranyes was President of UNIAPAC from 1997/2000 and is currently Chairman of the Board of *Centesimus Annus Pro Pontifice Foundation*, a Vatican Center for Christian Social Teaching.

THE AUTHORS

Preface and Introduction

John Plender
Senior editorial writer and columnist at the Financial Times, London, and current affairs broadcasting for BBC, specialised on financial markets. Author of books on the financial crisis such as *Going off the Rails: Global Capital and the Crisis of Legitimacy.*

Carol Cosgrove-Sacks
See Appendix 1.

Paul H. Dembinski
See Appendix 1.

Christoph Stückelberger
Executive Director and Founder of Globethics.net, Professor of Ethics at the Theological Faculty of the University of Basel, specialized in Economic Ethics, Environmental Ethics and Political Ethics. Author of many books in seven languages and hundreds of articles.

Authors/Prize Winners

(In the order of the book articles and with data at the year of the prize)

1 Jakub Kuriata, Winner 2011 of the global Ethics in Finance Robin Cosgrove Prize, (Polish), a Credit Risk Analyst at BNP Paribas, London.

2 Leire San-Jose, Winner 2009 of the regional Ibero-American Robin Cosgrove Prize, (Spanish), Assistant-Professor & Research Fellow in Ethics in Finance, University of the Basque Country, Bilbao, Spain.

3 Elise Pellerin & Marie Casimiro, Joint Winners of the 2009 global Ethics in Finance Robin Cosgrove Prize, (French), Elise Pellerein: Ethical Analyst, Paris, France. Marie Casimiro: Compliance Officer, BGL BNP Paribas, Luxembourg.

4 Clare Payne, Winner 2007 of the global Ethics in Finance Robin Cosgrove Prize, (Australian), Assistant Director of the Integrity Office of Macquarie Bank, Australia & Consulting Fellow on Ethics in Banking & Finance, St James Ethics Centre, Sydney, Australia.

5 Felippe Araujo, Winner of the 2nd Prize2009 of the regional Ibero-American Robin Cosgrove Prize, (Brazilian), finance professional working in Tokyo and currently (2012) in Brasilia, Brazil.

6 Meredith Benton, Winner of the 2nd Prize of the 2009 global Ethics in Finance Robin Cosgrove Prize, (American), currently Senior Director of Partnerships, AMTRACK, USA.

7 Carlos Eduardo Estapé Viana Winner of the 2nd Prize of the 2011 regional Ibero-American Robin Cosgrove Prize, (Uruguayan), a Public Accountant in Montevideo, Uruguay.

8 Carmen Lucia Carmona Paredes, ex aequo Winner of the 2nd Prize of the 2011 Regional Ibero-American Robin Cosgrove Prize, (Mexican), working as a consultant in London, UK.

9 David Sifah, Specially Commended for the 2009 global Ethics in Finance Robin Cosgrove Prize, (Ghanaian), a Retail Banker, Barclays Bank, Accra, Ghana.

10 Jonathan M. Wisebrod, ex aequo Winner 2007 of the global Ethics in Finance Robin Cosgrove Prize, (Canadian), Attorney at Skadden, Arps, Slate, Meagher & Flom, Singapore.

11 Faly Ranaivoson, Winner of the 2nd Prize of the 2011 global Ethics in Finance Robin Cosgrove Prize , (Madagascan), a Research Consultant in Geneva, Switzerland.

12 Simone Heinemann, Winner of the 3rd Prize of the 2011 global Ethics in Finance Robin Cosgrove Prize,(German), PhD student, Germany.

13 Geoffrey See, ex aequo Winner 2009 of the global Ethics in Finance Robin Cosgrove Prize, (Singaporean), University Fellow at Yale University, USA, and Executive Director, Choson Exchange, China.

14 Immacualte Dadiso Motsi-Omoijiada, well-evaluated for the 2011 global Ethics in Finance Robin Coscrove Prize, Zimbabwean), PhD student at HEI, Geneva.

15 Jaime Pozuelo-Monfort, well-evaluated for the 2007 global Ethics in Finance Robin Cosgrove Prize, (Spanish), currently studying for a Masters in Law at Georgetown University, Washington, USA.

16 Saif Ullah, well-evaluated for the 2007 global Ethics in Finance Robin Cosgrove Prize, (Pakistani), Ph. D. student, Canada.

17 Nicolás Meyer, Winner of the 2011 regional Ibero-American Robin Cosgrove Prize, (Argentinian), Director of "Nuestras Huellas" a not-for-profit organization in Argentina.

18 Bruno Federico Fernández, ex aequo Winner of the 3rd Prize of the 2011 global Ethics in Finance Robin Cosgrove Prize and ex aequo Winner of the 2nd Prize of the 2011 regional Ibero-American Robin Cosgrove Prize, (Argentinian), Economist, Central Office of Public Funds in the Ministry of Economy of Tucumán, Argentina.

19 Raina Abdul Rahim Mousa, Specially Commended for the 2007 global Ethics in Finance Robin Cosgrove Prize and awarded a special prize from Raiffeisen Bank, Geneva, (Egyptian), Ph D student at Birmingham Business School, Birmingham University, UK.

20 Joy Mueni Maina Kiiru, well-evaluated for the 2007 global Ethics in Finance Robin Cosgrove Prize, (Kenyan), Assistant lecturer at the School of Economics, Nairobi University, Kenya.

21 Jem Bendell & Inderpreet Chawla, well-evaluated for the 2007 global Ethics in Finance Robin Cosgrove Prize, Jem (British) is Director of Lifeworth Consulting, Geneva, Switzerland, and Inderpreet (Indian) is a Project Manager with the United Nations Environment Programme Finance Initiative in India.

22 Pernille Jessen, well-evaluated for the 2009 global Ethics in Finance Robin Cosgrove Prize, (Danish), post-doctoral Researcher, Institute of Economy, Arhus University, Denmark.

23 Jan Thomas Otte, well-evaluated for the 2009 global Ethics in Finance Robin Cosgrove Prize, (German), Financial journalist, Germany.

THE ROBIN COSGROVE PRIZE

The Ethics in Finance Robin Cosgrove Prize promotes greater awareness of ethics, trust and integrity among young finance professionals and advanced students of finance. The Prize aims to:

- advance the vision of ethics in finance
- stimulate a global debate among young people regarding ethical standards in finance
- encourage young people to be agents for change, going beyond compliance to promoting core values in their professional behaviour

Candidates less than 35 years old are invited to submit written papers (not previously published) on the theme "Innovative Ideas for Ethics in Finance".

There are two parallel competitions: a global prize where papers may be submitted in English or French, and a regional Ibero-American prize, for papers in Spanish or Portuguese. Independent juries comprised of distinguished finance professionals and respected academics evaluate the papers submitted.

The 2012-2013 prize competition will be launched in June 2012, with a final date for submission of papers on 31 March 2013. The prizes will be awarded at a special ceremony in the third quarter of 2013.

The prize is an ideal tool for staff development and training. Many major commercial banks and the IMF promote awareness of the Robin Cosgrove Prize through their internal communications networks. The prize encourages young professionals to be more aware of the important role of integrity and ethical behaviour in the finance sector in the private and the public sector, as well as not-for-profit organisations across the world.

The prize honours the vision of Robin, a young investment banker, who sadly died aged 31. He believed that high standards of integrity and good ethical practice were essential for sustainable finance and for the common good.

The rules of the prize and an official entry form will be sent when you complete the expression of interest, which is mandatory. For further information and the conditions for participation see *www.robincosgroveprize.org*

Globethics.net is a worldwide ethics network based in Geneva, with an international Board of Foundation of eminent persons. It provides an electronic platform for dialogue, reflection and action on ethics. Its central instrument is the internet site *www.globethics.net*. Globethics.net has three objectives:

Access to ethics resources: to ensure that people in all regions of the world are empowered to reflect and act on ethical issues. In order to ensure access to knowledge resources in applied ethics, Globethics.net has developed its *Globethics.net Library,* the leading global digital library on ethics. Globethics.net took this initiative to ensure that persons – especially in Africa, Asia and Latin-America – have access to good quality and up to date knowledge resources on ethics. The founding conviction of Globethics.net was that more equal access to knowledge resources in the field of applied ethics will enable persons and institutions from developing and transition economies to become more visible and audible in the global discourse on ethics. There is no cost involved in using the library. Individuals only need to register (free of charge) as participants on the Globethics.net website to get access to all the full text journals, encyclopedias, e-books and other resources in the library.

Networking: The registered participants form a global community of people interested in or specialists in ethics. It offers participants on its website the opportunity to join or form electronic working groups for purposes of networking or collaborative research.

Research: The international secretariat, based in Geneva, currently concentrates on three topics of research: *Business and Economic Ethics, Interreligious Ethics* and *Responsible Leadership*. The knowledge produced through the working groups and research finds their way *into collections* and *publications* in the two series *Globethics.net Series* and *Globethics.net Focus* that are also made available online for free in the Globethics.net Library.

www.globethics.net ■

Globethics.net Global

Globethics.net Global is a book series on ethical issues with global relevance and contextual perspectives. Each volume includes contributions from at least two continents.

The series editor is Prof. Dr. Christoph Stückelberger, Founder and Executive Director of Globethics.net, Professor of Ethics at the Theological Faculty of the University of Basel. Contact: *stueckelberger@globethics.net*.

1 Christoph Stückelberger / Jesse N.K. Mugambi (eds.), *Responsible Leadership. Global and Contextual Perspectives*, 2007

2 Heidi Hadsell / Christoph Stückelberger (eds.), *Overcoming Fundamentalism. Ethical Responses from Five Continents*, 2009

3 Christoph Stückelberger / Reinhold Bernhardt (eds.): *Calvin Global. How Faith Influences Societies*, 2009

4 Ariane Hentsch Cisneros / Shanta Premawardhana (eds.), *Sharing Values. A Hermeneutics for Global Ethics*, 2010

5 Deon Rossouw / Christoph Stückelberger (eds.), *Global Survey of Business Ethics in Training, Teaching and Research*, 2012

Globethics.net Focus

Globethics.net Focus is a second series of publications of Globethics.net. Each issue is focused on one actual ethical issue with global relevance, normally from one author.

1 Christoph Stückelberger, *Das Menschenrecht auf Nahrung und Wasser. Eine ethische Priorität*, 2009

2 Christoph Stückelberger, *Corruption-Free Churches are Possible. Experiences, Values, Solutions*, 2010

3 Vincent Mbavu Muhindo, *La République Démocratique du Congo en panne. Un bilan 50 ans après l'indépendance*, 2011

4 *The Value of Values in Business. Global Ethics Forum 2011 Report and Recommendations,* 2011

5 Benoît Girardin, *Ethics in Politics: Why it matters more than ever and how it can make a difference*, 2012

Print copies can be ordered at *infoweb@globethics.net*. All volumes can be downloaded for free as pdfs from the Globethics.net library *www.globethics.net*.